Assassination of a Saint

Assassination of a Saint

THE PLOT TO MURDER ÓSCAR ROMERO
AND THE QUEST TO BRING
HIS KILLERS TO JUSTICE

Matt Eisenbrandt

UNIVERSITY OF CALIFORNIA PRESS

University of California Press, one of the most distinguished university presses in the United States, enriches lives around the world by advancing scholarship in the humanities, social sciences, and natural sciences. Its activities are supported by the UC Press Foundation and by philanthropic contributions from individuals and institutions. For more information, visit www.ucpress.edu.

University of California Press
Oakland, California

Library of Congress Cataloging-in-Publication Data

Names: Eisenbrandt, Matt, 1975– author.
Title: Assassination of a Saint : the plot to murder Óscar Romero and the quest to bring his killers to justice / Matt Eisenbrandt.
Description: Oakland, California : University of California Press, [2017] | Includes bibliographical references and index.
Identifiers: LCCN 2016034797 (print) | LCCN 2016038417 (ebook) | ISBN 9780520286795 (cloth : alk. paper) | ISBN 9780520286801 (pbk. : alk. paper) | ISBN 9780520961890 (ebook)
Subjects: LCSH: Romero, Óscar A. (Óscar Arnulfo), 1917–1980— Assassination. | Violence—El Salvador. | El Salvador—Politics and government—1979–1992. | El Salvador—Foreign relations— United States. | United States—Foreign relations—El Salvador.
Classification: LCC BX4705.R669 E38 2017 (print) | LCC BX4705.R669 (ebook) | DDC 364.152/4097284—dc23
LC record available at http://lccn.loc.gov/2016034797

Manufactured in the United States of America

25 24 23 22 21 20 19 18 17
10 9 8 7 6 5 4 3 2 1

*For the voiceless of El Salvador, for whom
Monseñor Romero gave his life*

*For my parents, whose unwavering love and support
allowed me to follow my passion*

CONTENTS

On the surface, the advertisement buried in the middle pages of El Salvador's largest dailies was no more than a notice about a Catholic mass. A service that Monday night, the announcement said, would commemorate the first anniversary of the death of Sara Meardi de Pinto, the mother of Jorge Pinto, an outspoken publisher of a small Salvadoran newspaper. The ad began with a quote from Doña Sarita, as she was affectionately known, saying that her greatest hope in life had been to foster unity, love, and understanding. Farther down the page, a list of families sponsoring the mass comprised the elite sector of society from which Doña Sarita came. The names were instantly recognizable to any Salvadoran as a roster of the rich and famous who controlled the nation's economy. Doña Sarita, though, had led a charitable life.

The announcement included an invitation to the mass, to be officiated by the archbishop of San Salvador, the country's capital and largest city, in the chapel of the Divina Providencia hospital at 6:00 P.M. Óscar Romero, the ad's unnamed archbishop who would lead the mass, was troubled by the announcement. He was well aware that paid advertisements—*campos pagados*—were a common mode of political speech in El Salvador, and in those bloody days they carried grave significance. "Terrorists" were often unmasked in bold typeface and "fascists" were denounced in block letters. Even though El Salvador was overwhelmingly Catholic, Romero himself was a frequent target of print attacks because he dared to denounce the rampant injustices in the country. His detractors regularly called Romero a Marxist, and one publication ludicrously claimed that he ran his own terrorist cell. Now the newspaper ad broadcast to the entire country—and, more importantly, to the extremists who wanted him dead—Romero's precise location at 6:00 P.M. that night.

Romero learned about the announcement early in the day through a call from an alarmed supporter. As he hung up the phone, Romero tried to hide his concern, but the Carmelite nuns who worked with him at Divina Providencia, the tiny hospital for cancer patients where he lived, urged the archbishop to cancel the mass that night. The risk was too great, they said. The nuns knew Romero had spent the last three years in constant peril for refusing to stay quiet in the face of persecution by El Salvador's military. Even the murders of fellow priests did not keep Romero from denouncing the widespread repression. In spite of his fear, Romero's response to the nuns' caution was, as always, "We're in God's hands."[1]

Around six that evening, the doors of the chapel's north entrance were open to worshippers as well as a cooling breeze. With the sun setting behind Divina Providencia's lush tropical grounds, Archbishop Romero walked the short distance from his humble living quarters to the church. Draped in purple Lenten vestments, with short hair and outdated brow-line glasses, Romero began the liturgy while a few latecomers took seats in the back. Despite the ad in the newspapers, no more than two dozen people were there, a contrast to the hundreds who had attended Romero's Sunday mass the day before and the hundreds of thousands who listened to him on the radio. Romero led the small congregation through biblical readings and a recital of the 23rd Psalm before reaching the homily, the part of the service that allowed Romero to preach about the deplorable conditions in El Salvador by tying the people's misery to lessons from the Bible. Romero's Sunday sermons were legendary for their candor about the murders and torture committed throughout the country, but in the Monday memorial service, Romero gave a more measured homily. He spoke intimately about Doña Sarita and told the audience, "We know that every effort to improve a society, especially when injustice and sin are so present, is an effort that God blesses, that God wants, that God demands from us."[2] These were words that guided Romero's life.

As Romero preached, a freelance photographer, Eulalio Pérez, arrived at the chapel in a taxi. He entered through the main door, sat in the second-to-last row, and prepared his camera, completely unaware that the next photos he would take would soon appear around the world. At the same time, a car turned onto the long, tree-lined driveway leading into the Divina Providencia complex. The Volkswagen circled around the parking lot and came to an idle in front of the chapel, its red roof visible to a student looking out the window of a nearby building but not to the congregants inside the church. Their attention was on Romero as he finished the homily and turned to the communion hosts and wine on the altar, saying, "May this body immolated and this blood sacrificed for humanity nourish us also, so that we may give our body and blood to suffering and pain like Christ, who did so not for himself but to give justice and peace to his people." The words were prophetic. "Let us unite closely in faith and hope in this moment of prayer for Doña Sarita and ourselves—"

A deafening explosion crackled through the chapel. The worshippers threw themselves to the ground, all intimately familiar with the sound of gunfire. Several covered Jorge Pinto, assuming the bullet was intended for him. Some thought they heard a second shot. Within seconds, Eulalio Pérez jumped up, snapping photos. Pérez was so quick and so bold, in fact, that the congregants would later suspect him of being the assassin, a gun perhaps hidden inside his camera. The other churchgoers slowly raised their heads, not sure they wanted to see what horror awaited them. A woman ran to a window wondering if the shooter was still outside, while others looked toward the open door of the main entrance. A nun in another building heard the shooting and raced in terror to the chapel.

Archbishop Romero, the actual target, slumped to the floor behind the altar. A splintered bullet had already severed his aorta. A group rushed to the altar and, finding Romero on his side, tried to roll him onto his back. The blood gushed from Romero's mouth and nose, streaming down his face and pooling on the floor. A crucifix hanging on the wall above, showing the suffering Jesus nailed to the cross, provided a disturbing parallel to the tragedy unfolding below. A nun put her ear to Romero's chest and another knelt in desperate prayer while Pérez captured it all on film. Outside, the assassin's car drove quickly away.

A man offered his truck to take Romero to the hospital. The shocked congregants hurried his limp frame outside, lowered the tailgate on the yellow pickup, and pushed the dying archbishop into the camper. A nun and a few Divina Providencia employees jumped in. As they drove away, though, it was already too late. Romero was dead before they reached the hospital. A guiding light in El Salvador's growing darkness was extinguished. The nun would later say that Romero uttered his last words in the back of the truck, "May God have mercy on the assassins."[3]

INTRODUCTION

Óscar Romero is one of the towering heroes in El Salvador's history whose influence transcends the borders of that small country. Romero's impact can be measured quantitatively, by the 100,000 mourners who risked their lives to attend his funeral, or by the disturbing truth that his assassination accelerated El Salvador's descent into civil war. That conflict ended over two decades ago, but it still permeates every aspect of Salvadoran life, and Romero is honored in every corner of the country. Schools, highways, and the international airport carry his name. Romero's legacy spans the globe, with dignitaries like Barack Obama paying homage at his tomb. A statue of Romero now stands next to Martin Luther King's in Westminster Abbey, and his bust joins those of Mother Teresa and Rosa Parks in Washington, D.C.'s National Cathedral. Even after two decades of withering on the vine of Vatican politics, a campaign to name Romero a saint in the Catholic Church is succeeding. Pope Francis, the first Latin American pontiff, shepherded Romero's cause and declared him a martyr of the church. In May 2015, 300,000 followers stood in the San Salvador sun to witness Romero's beatification. His canonization, the final step to sainthood, is imminent.

For all his notoriety, Romero's time in the spotlight lasted only three years, from 1977 to 1980, when he served as archbishop of San Salvador, but they were years of tremendous upheaval. In 1977, a military dictatorship ruled the country and would soon hand over the government to another military leader under the guise of an election that was rigged from the start. The Salvadoran armed forces maintained power in this way for decades and justified their brute force and perpetual rule with the never-ending need to stamp out Communism. The specter of Marxism dated back to the 1930s, when the military massacred tens of thousands of Salvadoran peasants (campesinos) while putting down an uprising engineered in part by the Communist Party of El Salvador. But the ideology's appeal to certain Salvadorans in 1932, just as in 1977, had little to do with Soviet global hegemony and instead emanated from a hope to alleviate the dire socioeconomic inequalities in El Salvador. Throughout the twentieth century, a small, intermarried clique of moneyed elite, known as the oligarchs, dominated the Salvadoran economy, particularly the critical coffee sector, and benefitted from a system that denied *campesinos* their basic rights and the possibility of overcoming subjugation and poverty. The Salvadoran military, through an implicit agreement, defended the oligarchs' economic interests and used violence to maintain the status quo.

By 1977, however, the military's ability to suppress dissent was weakening. Social movements of all kinds—labor unions, *campesino* groups, teachers' federations, church organizations—more openly defied the threat of violence or imprisonment and called for change. Strikes, marches, and occupations of buildings increasingly paralyzed the country. At the same time that these groups advocated change, bands of armed guerrillas carried out a small-scale insurgency through bombings, kidnappings, and assassinations. These tactics were successful enough to convince some oligarchs that the armed forces could no longer protect them. Hard-line military officers, many of them trained by the United States, agreed and stepped up clandestine operations to murder and torture people they deemed "Communists."

Romero became archbishop of San Salvador in February 1977 not as a champion for reform but through the support of oligarchs and conservative forces in the Catholic Church. El Salvador was an overwhelmingly Catholic country in which the archbishop held enormous sway on the national stage, and tradition dictated that the Vatican's ambassador consult the military government and members of the oligarchy before the Vatican chose the new archbishop. These power brokers considered Romero a political and theological traditionalist who was too cautious to advocate major changes. Their perception of Romero was particularly significant because doctrinal changes in the Catholic Church during the previous two decades, starting with the Second Vatican Council from 1962 to 1965, had led to a radical rethinking of how the church should function. Many priests, particularly in countries like El Salvador where millions lived in poverty, took these directives to mean they should work toward the transformation of society and elimination of the underlying causes of inequality. This movement came to be known as Liberation Theology, but to many oligarchs and other conservatives, it smacked of Marxism. In 1977, the elite saw Romero as a safe choice to keep the "radical" priests in check.

Only three weeks after Romero became archbishop, gunmen murdered one of Romero's friends, Father Rutilio Grande, a trailblazing advocate of Liberation Theology. Grande, a Jesuit priest, had worked closely with *campesinos* to help them understand the Bible and organize themselves to advocate for their rights. These activities and Grande's passionate preaching were enough for right-wing extremists to brand him a Communist and a target for assassination. Grande's grisly murder affected Romero deeply, and the new archbishop took immediate, public action that belied his conservative image. Angering those who had supported him, Romero canceled all the Sunday masses throughout the archdiocese in favor of a single mass in San Salvador— a *misa única*—to show solidarity among the clergy.

From that point on, as repression continued against the church in the form of murder, torture, and threats, Romero spoke out forcefully, and his reputation grew among progressive priests, nuns, and laypeople who initially had opposed him. Romero also became a hero to Salvadoran *campesinos* as he forcefully advocated for the plight of the poor, the protection of human rights, and the need for nonviolent change in El Salvador. He repeatedly criticized the Salvadoran military for torturing and killing innocent civilians and denounced the oligarchs for underwriting the violence. An eloquent speaker, Romero used the pulpit masterfully, in particular through his Sunday homilies that were broadcast around the nation. As the repression and Romero's stature grew, Salvadorans dubbed Romero the Voice of the Voiceless.

Romero lived in constant danger, receiving numerous death threats and enduring relentless slander. Oligarch-owned newspapers painted Romero and other priests as Communists, terrorists, and traitors to El Salvador. In the face of these attacks, Romero became more strident as the bloodshed increased and the country fell apart. In February 1980, Romero wrote—and read in public— a letter to Jimmy Carter chastising the U.S. president for sending aid to the brutal Salvadoran military. On March 23, 1980, in what would be his final Sunday homily, Romero went further than ever before and called on Salvadoran soldiers to disobey the commands of their tyrannical superiors. Invoking the sanctity of God's law, Romero ordered them, "¡Cese la represión!" (Stop the repression!).[1] The next day, as Romero said mass in the Divina Providencia chapel, an assassin ended his life with a single bullet through the chest.

Despite Romero's standing and the substantial evidence against the men who killed him, no one in El Salvador went on trial for Romero's murder.

Violence, dirty tricks, a lack of political will, and the eventual enactment of an amnesty law giving immunity to the authors of the war's worst atrocities derailed the few attempts made to prosecute Romero's case. Separate investigations by journalists, human rights activists, the Catholic Church, and others resulted in the publication of detailed conclusions about the crime, but no convictions followed.

In 2001, a Salvadoran man working with a U.S.-based nonprofit organization, the Center for Justice & Accountability (CJA), got the surprise of his life in a lawyer's office in San Francisco when he spotted one of Romero's killers. An article later that year in the *Miami Herald* reported that the perpetrator, Álvaro Saravia, now lived in California. CJA, with its mandate to bring torturers and war criminals to justice, launched an investigation that gathered steam in 2002, the same year I joined the organization as a twenty-six-year-old staff attorney. The previous investigations into Romero's murder, including one by a United Nations Truth Commission, provided the primary evidence on which we relied, much of it implicating Saravia in the crime. These investigations showed that Saravia belonged to a paramilitary group run by one of El Salvador's most famous but enigmatic figures, Roberto D'Aubuisson, who had close connections to the oligarchs and later founded El Salvador's most successful political party. At CJA, our immediate goal was to harness the existing evidence and bring Saravia to justice in the United States. To do so, we would examine his role as a member of D'Aubuisson's "death squad," a term that described the phenomenon of active and discharged military figures, and sometimes civilians, working in small groups to carry out assassinations, bombings, and other violence. Our broader objective, however, was to help expose the truth and possibly stimulate change in El Salvador. This required an investigation of the oligarchs suspected of aiding the death squads and specifically the Romero assassination.

For over a year, my colleagues and I conducted a full-scale inquiry to locate witnesses who had information about the functioning and financing of the death squad that killed Romero. In partnership with Salvadoran colleagues, we interviewed people who had given secret testimony decades earlier and found others who had never spoken. We eventually put Saravia on trial in a U.S. court, but much of the evidence we collected never came out publicly, for reasons that this book will explain.

I was surprised to discover during our investigation that no one had ever written a book about Romero's murder despite the numerous volumes on his life and theology. This book presents and synthesizes the most relevant information about the Romero assassination in a way that has not previously been done. In the pages that follow, I lay out the evidence that existed prior to our case, the new facts we uncovered through our investigation, the limitations and successes of the trial against Saravia, and the repercussions of our case. In El Salvador, ongoing obfuscation and disinformation by those with selfish or sinister motives continue to obscure the truth. This book, while attempting to overcome that reality, is also a reflection of it. El Salvador remains a very dangerous place to live, and some of the evidence we collected during the investigation cannot be disclosed because the peril is too great for those who provided it. Even after the publication of this book, many facts about Romero's assassination remain hidden because witnesses still risk death if they speak out.[2]

Even in that climate, Romero is celebrated today as much as ever. His beatification, while a source of great national pride, has led to the sanitizing and commercialization of his memory, as even those who hated Romero during his life come to accept him as an important historical figure. This has led to attempts to cleanse his legacy of the pointed critiques he regularly dispensed. Appreciating Romero's brave actions, however, is essential to understanding why he died. My desire to share and analyze the available evidence, including the motivations of those who killed Romero, is the primary reason for this book.

This story is also important for people in the United States. Only some in the United States remember the story of Archbishop Romero and far fewer, particularly of younger generations, understand the determinative role our country played in El Salvador. Although our government most forcefully injected itself into the Salvadoran situation after Romero's death, through billions of dollars of aid to El Salvador's repressive military, the United States is the omnipresent elephant in the room. The U.S. role includes a decades-long foreign policy to combat Communist expansion at every turn, starting with the direct involvement of the Kennedy and Johnson administrations in developing the Salvadoran intelligence system that spawned death squads like the one that killed Romero. Other strands include U.S. politicians' embracing Salvadoran extremists as though they were simply conservative Republicans, Miami's welcoming of Salvadoran oligarchs wealthy enough to buy condominiums along tony Brickell Avenue, and the CIA's bankrolling of hard-line Salvadoran military officers. I hope this book will inspire people in the United States to educate themselves about the nation's long involvement in Central America and insist that future policies be crafted with due consideration for the human rights and basic dignity of the Salvadoran people.

The book follows the general timeline of our team's investigation but is not strictly chronological. Each chapter begins with testimony from the 2004 trial against Saravia that sets the stage for the topics examined in the subsequent pages. The early chapters weave historical background with descriptions of previous investigations that provided the starting point for our case and explain the legal developments that allowed us to hold Saravia accountable in the United States. Chapter 5 marks the beginning of a more conventional chronology of our investigation—our team's search for Saravia, the hunt for evidence about the alleged death squad financiers, and our meetings with witnesses—but with flashbacks to important events during Óscar Romero's time as archbishop. The final chapters examine the 2004 trial in Fresno, California, and the surprising post-trial developments that played out over the next six years. Through these chapters, I hope the reader will come away with a thorough understanding of not only how but why the killers took Romero's life and why they have enjoyed impunity for murdering such a beloved figure.

Archbishop Óscar Romero. Conferencia de Religiosos/as de
El Salvador (CONFRES).

(Top) Inside the Divina Providencia chapel, moments after Archbishop Romero was shot. Eulalio Pérez García / Arzobispado de San Salvador.

(Bottom) A nun prays as churchgoers try to save Archbishop Romero. Eulalio Pérez García / Arzobispado de San Salvador.

(Top) Churchgoers carry Archbishop Romero to a truck to take him to the hospital. Eulalio Pérez García / Arzobispado de San Salvador.

(Bottom) Mourners outside the San Salvador cathedral for Archbishop Romero's funeral. Copyright Etienne Montes.

Roberto D'Aubuisson. Copyright Jeremy Bigwood.

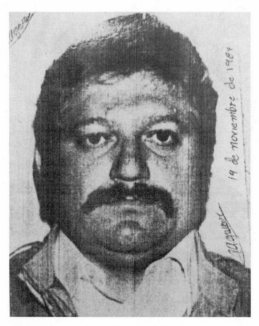

Álvaro Saravia. Photo from the Salvadoran court file.

The legal team, witnesses, and supporters at the federal court in Fresno for the 2004 trial against Álvaro Saravia. Center for Justice & Accountability.

KEY FIGURES

ÓSCAR ROMERO—Archbishop of San Salvador, 1977–80

OTHER MARTYRS

IGNACIO ELLACURÍA—Jesuit rector of the Central American University, murdered with five colleagues, their housekeeper, and her daughter in 1989

RUTILIO GRANDE—Jesuit priest, friend of Óscar Romero, murdered with two other men in 1977

ROBERTO D'AUBUISSON'S GROUP

WALTER "MUSA" ÁLVAREZ—Named by the Truth Commission as involved in the murder of Archbishop Romero, leading suspect as the shooter

EDUARDO ÁVILA—Close associate of Roberto D'Aubuisson, named by the Truth Commission as involved in the murder of Archbishop Romero

ROBERTO D'AUBUISSON—Former military intelligence official, founding leader of the ARENA political party, named by the Fresno court as the "mastermind" of the murder of Archbishop Romero

AMADO GARAY—Getaway driver for the murder of Archbishop Romero, witness in the Fresno trial

NELSON GARCÍA—Member of the security team for Roberto D'Aubuisson's group, named by Amado Garay as being with Álvaro Saravia the day of Archbishop Romero's murder

"KILLER"—National Guard lieutenant Merino Escobar, U.S. embassy source about the murder of Archbishop Romero

RICARDO LAO—Intelligence chief for the Nicaraguan Contras, allegedly paid by Roberto D'Aubuisson to arrange the murder of Archbishop Romero

MARIO MOLINA—Son of a former military president, named by the Truth Commission as involved in the murder of Archbishop Romero

NELSON MORALES—Member of the security team for Roberto D'Aubuisson's group, named by Amado Garay as being with Álvaro Saravia the day of Archbishop Romero's murder

HÉCTOR REGALADO—Chief of security for the Salvadoran legislature in the 1980s, close associate of Roberto D'Aubuisson, named on the list of people suspected of involvement in death squads that U.S. State Department officials gave to the FBI in 1983

FERNANDO "EL NEGRO" SAGRERA—Close associate of Roberto D'Aubuisson, named by the Truth Commission as involved in the murder of Archbishop Romero

ÁLVARO SARAVIA—Chief of security for Roberto D'Aubuisson in 1980, found liable by the Fresno court for the murder of Archbishop Romero

OTHER SALVADORAN MILITARY OFFICERS

NICOLÁS CARRANZA—Vice-minister of defense in 1980, found liable by a Tennessee court for crimes against humanity

JOSÉ GUILLERMO GARCÍA—Minister of defense in 1980, found liable by a Florida court for torture

NELSON IVÁN LÓPEZ Y LÓPEZ—Head of the Special Investigations Unit that investigated the murder of Archbishop Romero

ADOLFO MAJANO—Leading centrist officer on the junta after the October 1979 coup, ordered the raid on Finca San Luis

JOSÉ MEDRANO—Former chief of the National Guard, key figure in establishing the death squads, mentor to Roberto D'Aubuisson

ROBERTO SANTIVAÑEZ—Former intelligence chief and boss of Roberto D'Aubuisson, went public with allegations about the death squads and the murder of Archbishop Romero

CARLOS VIDES CASANOVA—Chief of the National Guard in 1980, later minister of defense, found liable by a Florida court for torture

BUSINESSMEN, ARENA MEMBERS, AND POLITICIANS

ANTONIO "TOÑO" CORNEJO ARANGO—Close associate of Roberto D'Aubuisson, early ARENA party member

ROBERTO "BOBBY" DAGLIO—Businessman, Álvaro Saravia's boss at the Atarraya seafood company, named on the list of people suspected of involvement in death squads that U.S. State Department officials gave to the FBI in 1983

ORLANDO DE SOLA—Businessman, early ARENA party member, named on the list of people suspected of involvement in death squads that U.S. State Department officials gave to the FBI in 1983

NAPOLEÓN DUARTE—Former president of El Salvador, longtime political rival of Roberto D'Aubuisson

EDUARDO "GUAYO" LEMUS O'BYRNE—Businessman, named on the list of people suspected of involvement in death squads that U.S. State Department officials gave to the FBI in 1983, alleged to have provided money to pay Archbishop Romero's assassin

ROBERTO MATHIES REGALADO—Businessman, named on the list of people suspected of involvement in death squads that U.S. State Department officials gave to the FBI in 1983, alleged to have provided the car later used for the murder of Archbishop Romero

ALFREDO MENA LAGOS—Businessman, early ARENA party member, named on the list of people suspected of involvement in death squads that U.S. State Department officials gave to the FBI in 1983

MARIO SANDOVAL ALARCÓN—Far-right Guatemalan politician, advisor to Roberto D'Aubuisson's group

GUILLERMO "BILLY" SOL—Businessman, early ARENA party member, former chief of the national hydroelectric company, named on the list of people suspected of involvement in death squads that U.S. State Department officials gave to the FBI in 1983

U.S. EMBASSY OFFICIALS

RICHARD CHIDESTER—Met with Álvaro Saravia in 1990, heard Saravia's account of Archbishop Romero's murder

CARL GETTINGER—Met with Killer in the early 1980s, heard Killer's account of the meeting to plan Archbishop Romero's murder

SELECT WITNESSES AND CONTRIBUTORS

LEONEL GÓMEZ—Investigator, former land-reform official, early contact for the legal team in the investigation

MARÍA JULIA HERNÁNDEZ—Head of the San Salvador archdiocese Tutela Legal human rights office, former assistant to Archbishop Romero, witness in the Fresno trial

TERRY KARL—Stanford professor of political science and Latin American studies, expert witness in the Fresno trial

ATILIO RAMÍREZ AMAYA—Judge who first investigated the murder of Archbishop Romero before fleeing El Salvador after an attempted assassination, witness in the Fresno trial

ROBERT WHITE—U.S. ambassador to El Salvador in 1980, expert witness in the Fresno trial

THE JUDGE

OLIVER WANGER

U.S. INVESTIGATORS

ROBERT "BOBBY" LEVINSON

MINTZ GROUP

THE TRIAL TEAM

ALMUDENA BERNABEU

PATTY BLUM

RUSSELL COHEN

MATT EISENBRANDT

NICO VAN AELSTYN

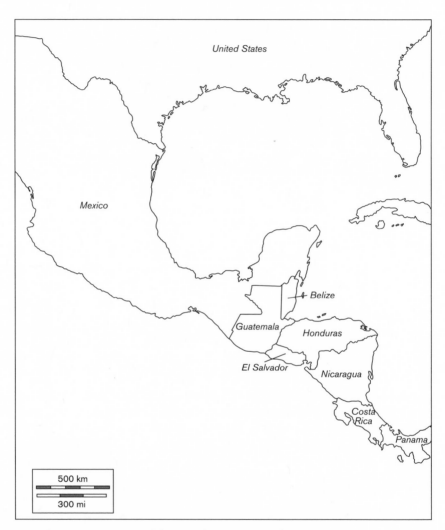

Central America, Mexico, and the United States. Copyright One Stop Map.

El Salvador. Copyright d-maps.com, http://www.d-maps.com/carte.php?num_car=1393&lang=en.

ONE

"Informational Goulash"

PRIOR INVESTIGATIONS
OF THE ROMERO ASSASSINATION

FRESNO, CALIFORNIA, USA—AUGUST 2004

Outside the air-conditioned courthouse, the summer sun scorches the city streets several floors below. August is not a comfortable time to be in Fresno, and this year is no exception. The seats behind me are sprinkled with journalists, human rights activists, and survivors of El Salvador's civil war. The chairs in the jury box to my left are unoccupied but decorated with tall photos of Óscar Romero and posters displaying headlines about his death. From his elevated seat, Judge Oliver Wanger peers down like a gargoyle hawk. His white hair and black robe convey appropriate measures of seriousness and seniority. Although the case we have put before him is unorthodox, the judge, an ex-marine, has treated it with flexibility and fairness. He insisted that the trial proceed in the largest courtroom, its high ceilings now lending a regal, if modern, feel.

Wearing a charcoal suit and muted red tie my father bought me after college, I address the aging Salvadoran man on the witness stand. He was once a judge, but he is now as far removed from that role as from his home country. Even as Atilio Ramírez Amaya testifies about the most terrifying week of his life, twenty-four years ago, he maintains a judicial stoicism.

"Where were you on the evening of March 24, 1980?" I ask.[1]

"I was [teaching] at the National University."

"How did you find out about the assassination of Monseñor Romero?" I use the archbishop's common title in Spanish.

"Around six thirty that evening . . . as I was going to my car, I heard people screaming, 'Someone has wounded Monseñor! They're saying someone killed Monseñor!' It was on the radio."

In El Salvador, a civil law country, judges have a prominent role in the earliest stages of criminal investigations, and it was Judge Ramírez Amaya's job to work with the police to gather evidence. "I headed to the forensic clinic," he says, "[but] Monseñor wasn't there. He was at the Policlínica hospital, and there was a justice of the peace on his way there."

"Why did you go?"

"I was obligated by the law to go because Monseñor was a person of high standing. As a judge overseeing criminal cases, I had to go."

"Were you in charge or was the justice of the peace in charge?"

"I was. They hadn't begun the autopsy, so I took over the case and the investigation."

"When did you arrive at the Policlínica?"

"It would have been around 7:00 P.M."

I call for an exhibit to be displayed. The photograph shows a crowd arranged in a tight horseshoe around Romero's horizontal body. His torso fills the foreground but his face, with eyes closed, recedes from the camera. The stole he wore for the mass remains draped around his neck. Everyone gathered is likewise in identifiable uniforms—nurses, nuns, doctors, even a lawyer in a suit. Their grim expressions reveal the terrible fact that Romero is already dead.

"Can you please describe the scene at the Policlínica when you arrived?"

"When I entered the room—it was smaller than this room, maybe half the size—there were about a hundred people surrounding the gurney where Monseñor's body was."

"Were there any police at the Policlínica?"

"No."

"Should they have been there?"

"Yes. They should have been there for security reasons. That's why, when I arrived, I called my secretary and I asked him to call the police and ask for backup, because there were so many people that we weren't able to work. . . . I had to make everybody leave the room." Ramírez Amaya describes the autopsy: "X-rays were taken but at first, they couldn't detect where the bullet was, so two or three more X-rays had to be taken. . . . The blood was gushing, but it was in clots. It was coagulated. They couldn't find the bullet, so the doctors, using gloves of course, had to remove all these blood clots from the body. They pressed them until they dissolved the clots one by one, and there were no clots left in the thorax. That's when the three bullet fragments were found." All the bleeding was caused by three very thin cuts in the aorta and vena cava, he says. That's when he knew the bullet was a .22 caliber with a hollow tip. "After this, I once again asked my secretary about the police so they could help us secure the evidence in bags. I was told that the police had not arrived."

I put the autopsy report on the screen. "What time did the autopsy finish?"

"The autopsy lasted over three hours, almost four hours."

"Where did you go next?"

"After that, I again spoke to my secretary to call the police so that the police could take us or accompany us to the crime scene—the Divina Providencia church where Monseñor was shot. Since the police didn't come, I, in my own car, took my secretary with me. It was just the secretary and me. We went to the church." The only people there were two of Romero's lawyers.

"What did you do at the church?"

"It is a small church, more or less the size of this room, and we went throughout the church looking for the bullet casings. We took measurements so we could know the range or distance from which the shot could have been fired. We went through the church thoroughly trying to find any type of evidence, but we found no evidence."

A little before midnight, Ramírez Amaya took his secretary to the court building. The secretary preferred to stay at the court rather than return to his house outside the capital. "Going all the way [home] was basically putting your life in danger," Ramírez Amaya says. "You could see on street corners these small tanks that were used by the army, as well as police with automatic weapons. You couldn't see a single [civilian] person out on the street, not a single vehicle." Because the police never came, Ramírez Amaya took the X-rays and bullet fragments from the autopsy to his home.

"The next day after the assassination, what did you do?" I ask.

"I arrived at my job at the Fourth Criminal Court, and I ordered the files," he says.

"Did you speak with anyone at the National Police?"

"Yes, I told my secretary to call the police so we could get together on how we were going to coordinate the investigation, but the secretary told me that the police wanted me to send [them] the evidence."

"Did you send the evidence?"

"No, I didn't send it. I spoke to the technician at the police laboratory, who was upset because I wasn't sending the evidence. He asked me if I didn't trust the police. And I told him that, indeed, I did not trust the police. I told them that if they wanted to conduct any examination as to what caliber the bullet was, they had to bring over [to my office] the microscopes and the scales and whatever else they needed to do their expert analysis."

I ask Ramírez Amaya if he had problems in the days after Romero's murder.

"On the 25th, Colonel Majano [the head of the ruling junta] appeared on television . . . saying that the assassins of Monseñor Romero would be found immediately . . . [and] they would then send those names to the Fourth Criminal Judge, which was me, for their immediate capture. Almost instantly, or moments after this press conference, which would have been around twelve noon, I received the first phone call at home. This was the first threat."

"How many phone calls did you receive?"

"Three to four phone calls were made to my home. The ones that I didn't answer were answered by my daughter. This would have been on Tuesday and Wednesday, the 25th and the 26th of March. In the phone call answered by my daughter, the voice asked her what her favorite color was, and she was told that was the color they would paint my coffin."

I ask Ramírez Amaya about the next day, March 27.

"That evening, it was about 10:15 P.M.," he says, "someone knocked at the door, asking for me, saying that a friend was looking for me. And they gave the name of this friend. I got up and I told my housekeeper to be careful, to open the door with caution. I was carrying a 12-gauge shotgun with me, out of fear since I had been threatened. In San Salvador, it was a time of incredible tension. All the people that I was somehow involved with, or coworkers, they were all fearful. Every day, as soon as the sun went down, I would get this fever." Returning to that night, Ramírez Amaya says:

> My housekeeper opened the door and two young men walked in. I had the shotgun in my hands, and I opened the door of my bedroom and I peeked to see if I recognized them. I didn't recognize them, so I told them to sit down. They didn't see the shotgun I had but when I saw them, one had a briefcase and he pulled out a machine gun. When I saw their weapon, I pulled out the shotgun, and I was about to fire at them but my housekeeper ran toward me. . . . At that moment, one of the men fired the weapon. He was trying to fire at me but since my housekeeper had run toward me, instead of the bullets hitting me, they hit her in the back and in the buttocks and she fell toward me. She fell to the ground. I wasn't able to break her fall. And then the men took off. They just hit the door hard and they left, and then they sprayed the house with bullets. . . . All this happened within five seconds, perhaps.

Then I felt as though they were walking on the roof of the house, so I started firing the gun out the windows because I thought they were trying to get into the house. About fifteen days earlier, they had killed the attorney general [Mario Zamora].... That's how the men had gotten into his house. And I was just yelling at my wife, 'Josefina, they're going to kill us, just like they did with Mario Zamora!' I gave her a pistol and asked her to start firing out the windows. We had our daughter, who was between twelve and fourteen at the time, and I threw a mattress over her. I was just crawling through my house, listening for the noises so I could fire in the direction of the noises. Then the footsteps stopped. There was this deathly silence for ten minutes when the phone rang. The voice said to me, 'Doctor, this is Eliseo Soto from the National Police.'... I knew him from [his] childhood when my mother took him in because he didn't have parents. My mother took him in and helped him. She also helped him get the job with the police.

Ramírez Amaya pauses, and I interject, "What did Eliseo Soto say?"

"He said to me, 'Doctor, you are alive,' but he was surprised to know that I was alive. And I answered him, 'Yes, I am happy to be alive.' And he said, 'Don't worry. Perhaps they were just trying to scare you.'" Ramírez Amaya is implying that Soto knew about the murder attempt ahead of time. After half an hour, family and friends came to the house, as did the night watchman. "He said to me that the police were deaf because the entrance to my neighborhood—I live in an enclosed neighborhood and you can only come in through one street—he said there were two police vehicles just outside on the street while all this was happening, while they were trying to kill me. Those police officers were just outside on the street."

"Were those officers in marked cars?"

"Yes, I was told by the night watchman that they were marked patrol units and they hadn't even moved when they heard all the firing going on." Another neighbor came over. "He said to me that what he was about to tell me, he would never repeat and he would never be a witness in any case. And he told me that during the attempt on my life, there were three people—two that entered my house and one that stayed as the driver in the getaway car. He said the man at the wheel of the car was from the National Police. And he said, 'You know that I work with the police and I know the other police officers.'"

"Did you personally know that man to work for the police?"

"Yes. Then I said to my wife, 'We have to leave the country. Otherwise, we are going to get killed. It's the police.'"

"Did anyone from the police ever arrive to investigate the attempt?"

"No, the attempt against me was never investigated by any judge or any police."

"So what happened to the housekeeper?"

"[The next day], I went to visit her at the hospital. They hadn't admitted her into the hospital. She was just somewhere on the floor in the hallway, just as we had left her."

Ramírez Amaya turns to his own situation. "I already had a ticket purchased for Saturday to go to Venezuela, to Caracas, for a criminology conference, but I couldn't go to the airport because the police had all the airports and other exits to the city secured. I was afraid to go to the airport because I figured at immigration they could detain me and take me and kill me." He left instead by boat.

"And how many years passed until you returned to El Salvador?" I ask, knowing this is the hardest question for him.

"Almost ten years," he says, tears coming to his eyes. "Almost ten years."

SAN SALVADOR—MAY 1980

Over a month after Romero died, the archbishop's murder remained unsolved. Despite the refusal of the National Police to assist Judge Ramírez Amaya's aborted investigation and their likely involvement in his attempted murder, a few police detectives did go through the motions of following leads in Romero's case, but they achieved few results. Evidence was not readily available, and there were many people in El Salvador with the motive and capability of carrying out such a crime. The U.S. ambassador to El Salvador, Robert White, initially said anti-Castro Cubans might have killed the archbishop,[2] while the CIA speculated about the "psychotic right" or "extreme leftists."[3]

On May 7, a singular event should have cracked the case wide open. A junta composed of military and civilian officials was ruling the country but barely hanging on in the face of numerous challenges. The leading centrist officer in the junta, Colonel Adolfo Majano, learned that a group of current and former military officers, all right-wing extremists, were planning a coup d'état. They would be meeting that day at a rural estate known as Finca San Luis. Majano saw the opportunity for a decisive blow against those who sought to overthrow the government, and he ordered an army unit loyal to him to arrest the group. In the short term, the raid was a success. Not only did they detain the coup plotters but they also seized weapons and numerous documents, some with damning titles like "How to Carry Out a Political Coup d'État in El Salvador."[4] As if to emphasize their incriminating nature, Colonel Majano later said that one of the key suspects tried to eat the documents as the arresting soldiers rushed in.[5]

Among the papers were several that might have solved Archbishop Romero's murder. The most damning of all the records was a daily planner, its brown cover opening to a page with the preprinted English words, "This Book is the Property of" followed by the handwritten name "Saravia Alvaro Rafael." An ex–air force captain, Álvaro Saravia was among those arrested in the raid and his datebook came to be known as the Saravia Diary.[6] The pages contained the names of suspected extremists and murderers alongside lists of weapons, expenses, and appointments but often without further details.

Several loose pieces of stationery were captured along with the Saravia Diary. When Colonel Majano's men photocopied the documents, they copied three of the loose sheets together onto one page. For years, researchers reviewing the photocopy believed the three pages went together, an assumption that seemed to implicate people in crimes they might not have committed. One sheet contains a list of some of the most prominent and wealthy people in El Salvador.[7] At the bottom of the sheet is a logo that was later reported to belong to a seafood company created by two people arrested in the San Luis raid.[8] The second piece of stationery photocopied sideways at the top of the page has different handwriting and lists a series of payments.[9] Some names, including Saravia's, are written in the ledger among other items like "housing," "clothing," "beds," "gas," "hotel," and "petty cash." The third piece of stationery, with the same handwriting as the first, carries the title "Equipo—Operación Piña" (Equipment—Operation Pineapple).[10] It bears the same logo and catalogs the following items:

1 Starlight
1 .257 Roberts
4 automatics
Grenades

_____

1 driver
1 shooter
4 security

Colonel Majano gave a copy of these notes to every member of the ruling junta and they all reached the same conclusion: Operation Piña is the assassination of Archbishop Romero. It describes a plan unlike most of the killings that were then happening in El Salvador, especially those attributed to death squads. Usually, there was no need for a sharpshooter.[11] Most murders involved machine guns and numerous bullets, not a single shot from a rifle like a .257 Roberts. U.S. ambassador Robert White, who saw the Saravia Diary, reached the same conclusion.[12] "I had knowledgeable people," White later said, "for whose political analysis and accuracy I have the profoundest respect. I gave them this document without any preparatory comments. And each one of them looked at this and said, well, this is the outline of the operation to kill Archbishop Romero."[13]

Among those arrested at Finca San Luis was Roberto D'Aubuisson, who had quickly become one of El Salvador's most notorious and feared men. D'Aubuisson, like a local and more lethal version of Joseph McCarthy, developed a public reputation for his radical—some would say fascist—views.[14] Over the years, he would come to be described as "a little Hitler"[15] and an "anarchic psychopath."[16] A chain smoker and heavy drinker, the CIA labeled him "egocentric, reckless, and perhaps mentally unstable."[17] To his backers in the business community, Salvadoran armed forces, and U.S. Republican Party, however, D'Aubuisson was charismatic, articulate and intelligent, a leader born to protect the country from the looming scourge of Communism. One month before Archbishop Romero's assassination, D'Aubuisson went on TV and denounced El Salvador's attorney general. A few days later, the attorney general was machine-gunned in his home. D'Aubuisson similarly denounced Archbishop Romero before his death.[18] More than one person later said that the handwriting on the Operation Piña page was D'Aubuisson's.[19]

Despite the Saravia Diary, the Operation Piña page, and other evidence seized from Finca San Luis, D'Aubuisson's arrest sparked a major controversy. His wealthy civilian supporters carried out public protests while his backers in the armed forces, where he still had considerable support, pushed for his release. Colonel Majano, along with members of the junta and representatives of Jimmy Carter's U.S. administration, held strong and insisted that D'Aubuisson and the others be punished.[20] After a few days, though, the majority of the military leadership turned against Majano, resulting in the release of D'Aubuisson, Saravia, and the others. There would be no punishment, much less a trial, for Romero's murder.

Amid daily bombings and murders, the U.S. embassy's young political officer, Carl Gettinger, was struggling to amass evidence about unsolved, high-profile crimes like the Romero assassination. Gettinger, a "particularly brave and resourceful American diplomat," according to then-ambassador Robert White, stumbled onto a golden source.[21] Colonel Eldon Cummings, the top U.S. military official in El Salvador, knew that Gettinger was looking into these crimes. He wanted Gettinger to meet someone who had suffered the "other" side of the violence, namely the kidnappings and targeted killings by the guerrillas.[22] Cummings introduced Gettinger to a lieutenant in the Salvadoran National Guard, the security force feared throughout El Salvador, especially in the countryside. The Guardsman's father and brother had died at the hands of the insurgents.[23]

Gettinger's first meeting with the officer revealed a dark soul. Labeling him a "badly educated individual," an embassy cable said he "used expletives to describe the current leadership in the [National] Guard, ridiculing its passivity in dealing with the current situation and pointing out several times that it was the strictures placed on the Guard in the field [fighting the guerrillas] that forced him and other like-minded security corps members to clandestinely carry out their brutal activities."[24] An official at the U.S. embassy said the officer was a "ruthless, evil guy, quixotic, tough and brutal."[25] He even confessed to Gettinger his involvement in "unauthorized operations."[26] Over the subsequent months, as his relationship with Gettinger developed, he would come to be known around the embassy by the nickname Killer.[27]

Gettinger's new source considered himself a personal friend of Roberto D'Aubuisson but he was, if possible, even more extreme. Though D'Aubuisson had asked him to join their anti-Communist efforts, Killer refused because he considered D'Aubuisson a "sell-out."[28] Killer also disliked that the oligarchs were using the military for their own purposes.[29] His credibility at that stage was uncertain, so the biggest bombshell he provided to Gettinger was hard to assess: Killer said he had participated in a meeting to plan the murder of Archbishop Romero. A November 1980 cable from the U.S. embassy to the State Department detailed the allegations. "He indicated that Major Roberto D'Aubuisson was in charge of the meeting and that it took place shortly—a day or two—before Romero was assassinated," the cable said. "According to the source, the participants drew lots for the task of killing the Archbishop. The 'winner' was an ex–National Guardsman."[30] Killer bragged that he donated the bullet used in the operation so that he could play some role, however tangential, in Romero's death.[31]

Killer's tale was particularly enlightening because, at that time, the U.S. embassy knew little about how the plot against Romero had unfolded.[32] The embassy played an important role in gathering evidence about El Salvador's most notorious crimes because the Salvadoran government was unable and often unwilling to investigate them. (As in the attempted murder of Judge Ramírez Amaya, the National Police were in charge of criminal investigations but they or their brethren in the other security forces were the ones usually committing the murders.) The U.S. government therefore tried to compile information about the worst incidents in order to pressure the Salvadorans to do something about them.

Romero's assassination was a high-priority case, but the U.S. embassy had little evidence other than the Saravia Diary. The Operation Piña page seemed to point the finger at D'Aubuisson and Saravia, but there was no proof concerning the details. At that point, Killer was an untested source, and though the U.S. embassy shared his story with Washington, he could not be trusted yet. Gettinger needed further proof of his reliability.

Everything changed a few weeks later when three nuns and one lay missionary, all U.S. citizens, were raped and killed in a remote location outside San Salvador.[33] The ghastly attacks on Ita Ford, Jean Donovan, Maura Clarke, and Dorothy Kazel shook the U.S. embassy, and gathering information about the crime became a top priority. A few months later, Killer reappeared to tell Gettinger that the National Guard had murdered the churchwomen, and he later became the lynchpin of U.S. efforts to prosecute the offenders. Throughout the next year, Killer provided details on other violent acts by the security forces and helped Gettinger develop information on those responsible for the churchwomen's deaths. Killer likewise confessed to his own participation in well-known bombings, boosting his credibility.[34]

In April 1981, Killer repeated for Gettinger the same story he had originally told concerning the Romero assassination. Killer claimed that he, Roberto D'Aubuisson, Álvaro Saravia—the keeper of the diary—and a lieutenant named Amaya Rosa were at the meeting where they planned Romero's murder.[35] Several months later, Gettinger showed Killer the Saravia Diary. Killer recognized most of the military personnel named, including himself, but very few of the civilians. While reviewing the diary, he stopped, asked Gettinger for a pen and circled a name and phone number:

Walter (Musa) . . . . 25–6514.

Killer told Gettinger that Musa had killed Archbishop Romero. According to an embassy cable, Killer said that Musa "remained as one of D'Aubuisson's henchmen inside the country and had been arrested for his participation in the Major's arms smuggling business."[36] A later U.S. embassy cable identified Musa as Walter Álvarez and described his all-too-familiar fate. "According to press reports," the document said, "several gunmen took Alvarez away from a football game on September 27, shot him several times, and left his body on the road. . . . We believe it is highly likely that the assassin of Romero is now dead by unknown hands."[37]

During the months that Killer was meeting secretly with Gettinger, the existence of the Saravia Diary became public. In April 1981, Robert White, fired as ambassador by new president Ronald Reagan a few months earlier, presented the diary to the U.S. Senate Foreign Relations Committee. White testified about Operation Piña and said that analysts had concluded that the diary contained "evidence that is compelling, if not 100 percent conclusive, that [Roberto] D'Aubuisson and his group are responsible for the murder of Archbishop Romero."[38]

A year later, a Mexican newspaper published a description of the Saravia Diary.[39] Columnist Manuel Buendía analyzed the datebook and other documents, and he accepted the conclusion that Operation Piña implicated D'Aubuisson in Romero's murder. The U.S. embassy, under a different ambassador reporting to the Reagan White House, did not agree with the allegation. "The fact of the matter," read a draft embassy cable responding to the column, "is that without an interpreter—i.e., one of the authors or someone linked very closely to them—those documents are nothing more than an informational goulash which does not explain the murder of Romero . . . nor any other specific act of rightist terrorism which has occurred in this or any other country." The draft cable continued, "There is no denying the fact that the purchases, travels and expenses outlined in the papers represent the activities of nefarious sorts who in early 1980 were engaged in ruthless actions to destabilize the [government]. But to go beyond that and state specifically, for instance, that Operation Piña was the Romero assassination plan is speculation." Although Killer had found Musa Álvarez's name in the datebook, "for the most part, the documents were hieroglyphics to him. He did not recognize Piña. . . . We still have no interpreter." The draft concluded that although "evil intent lurks throughout" the documents, "they raise more questions than they answer. Who wrote them and what they mean is not clear to us but we will continue to try to find out. Buendia, if he were honest, would do the same."[40]

WASHINGTON, D.C.—FEBRUARY 1984

Salvadoran authorities still had not charged anyone with Romero's assassination despite a newspaper account that an associate of D'Aubuisson had privately confessed his involvement in the crime.[41] Former ambassador White again testified before a congressional committee about Romero. He blamed the lack of progress in the case on the Reagan administration, not the Salvadorans. "From the first days in office," White said, referring to Killer's statements, "the Reagan White House knew—beyond any reasonable doubt—that Roberto D'Aubuisson, in addition to other crimes, planned and ordered the assassination of Archbishop Oscar Arnulfo Romero." White then told the House committee Killer's story about the meeting D'Aubuisson had chaired in which lots were drawn to choose Romero's assassin.[42] The U.S. State Department shot back that it was "well aware" of the allegations about D'Aubuisson's involvement in the murder. "The information given to us, however, was limited and incomplete," a spokesman said, "and no conclusions could be drawn from it."[43]

Through it all, Killer's real name—Lieutenant Merino Escobar—remained secret from the public.

SAN SALVADOR—NOVEMBER 1987

Despite minor developments in the case over the previous two years, no one claiming to be an eyewitness like Killer had come forward until authorities found Amado Garay hiding in Costa Rica. Garay was arrested with Roberto D'Aubuisson and Álvaro Saravia at Finca San Luis in 1980 but drew little suspicion at the time. Though his name appeared on numerous pages of the Saravia Diary, it meant little next to those of El Salvador's rich and powerful. So it came as a great surprise when, in November 1987, Garay surfaced to tell the world how he and his bosses had killed Archbishop Romero.

In two days of secret sessions before prosecutors and a judge in El Salvador, Garay testified that he was the only person, other than the assassin himself, to witness the murder from the shooter's end. Garay told the officials he was Álvaro Saravia's driver in 1980, though he occasionally chauffeured for D'Aubuisson as well. One day, Garay took Saravia to a home in the San Benito neighborhood of San Salvador. He remembered the house for its distinctive Japanese cashew trees. When they arrived, Saravia got out of the car and went into the residence while Garay stayed outside. Saravia later emerged from the house, ordering Garay to get behind the wheel of a red four-door Volkswagen and follow the lead of a second vehicle. The other car held at least two people, Garay remembered, though he was unsure of the exact number. When Garay got into the Volkswagen, he realized there was someone in the backseat. The man was about twenty-five years old, tall, thin and well groomed. He had straight black hair, a large forehead, a receding hairline, and a beard. Garay had never seen the stranger before and he would never see him again.

Trailing the other vehicle, Garay started the Volkswagen and pulled out. The driver of the lead car took what seemed a circuitous route. They passed through the Miramonte neighborhood before turning onto a dirt road with a black gate. The bearded man in the backseat, speaking with a Salvadoran accent, said they would no longer follow the other vehicle. Following his instructions, Garay turned left through the gate. Ahead lay a cobblestone street leading to a church seventy-five meters away. Garay drove forward, and the man directed him to turn around in the small parking lot. Garay did so and stopped the car a few meters from the church, but the man had Garay pull up to the front of the chapel. Inside, Garay saw a priest celebrating mass behind an altar.

The bearded man instructed Garay to pretend like he was fixing something in the vehicle. Garay played with the gearshift, lifting up the rubber casing. As he pantomimed an unscrewing motion, he heard a gunshot behind him. Startled, he turned around and saw his passenger holding a rifle through the right rear window of the car.[44] Garay noticed movement and screaming inside the church. He didn't know what had happened.

The bearded man ordered Garay to stay calm and drive away slowly. They exited through the gate and turned left toward downtown, but Garay was nervous and soon became lost. After some time, he regained his wits and found his way back to the home with the Japanese cashew trees. As he pulled into the driveway, Garay saw Saravia waiting outside the house. When they stopped, the bearded man stepped out of the car, saluted Saravia, and proclaimed, "Mission accomplished." Saravia asked Garay why they were running so late, and Garay confessed he had gotten lost. Saravia beckoned the bearded man toward the house, saying, "Let's go inside to listen to the news." The shooter did not take the rifle with him.

After some time, Garay and Saravia left, accompanied by another car carrying Nelson Morales and Nelson García, two bodyguards for Saravia and D'Aubuisson. Morales, a former National Guardsman, was the one who got Garay the job driving for Saravia.

The next night, Garay heard on the radio that Archbishop Romero had been murdered.

Two days later, Garay drove Saravia to a castle-like house across the street from the Channel 2 television station. They pulled through the front gate up a long driveway to the residence. Roberto D'Aubuisson was waiting at the door.

Saravia got out of the car and reported to D'Aubuisson, "We have already done what we planned in terms of killing Monseñor Arnulfo Romero [sic]."

"No man, you shouldn't have done it yet," D'Aubuisson said.

"You ordered us to do it," Saravia protested, "so that's why we did it."

The two men went inside. Garay remained outside but he saw other people in the house seated around a table.

Following Romero's murder, Garay began to fear for his life but kept working with Saravia for two more months while seeking opportunities to leave the job and El Salvador. He finally fled at the end of May 1980, after which his wife, still in El Salvador, received threats from people looking for Garay.[45]

These were the only details in Garay's statements to Salvadoran authorities. His testimony made no mention of his arrest at Finca San Luis. The day after his testimony, the authorities drove him around San Salvador to identify the houses mentioned in his statements. Garay hoped it would be a low-key trip, but legal procedures required the participation of many officials of different political stripes. Due to their political differences, the officials did not trust each other and all of them wanted to be present to check that their opponents did not influence Garay. The result was a conspicuous caravan of several vehicles. Garay, petrified at how visible the caravan was, wore a wig and a fake beard to hide his identity.[46]

When they arrived at the house with the Japanese cashew trees, Garay panicked. He refused to get out of the car and make a proper identification of the house. Faced with the witness's intransigence, the chief justice of the Salvadoran Supreme Court ended the exercise after receiving a message directly from the president of El Salvador: "Give each of the employees a shot of whisky and go home."[47]

Despite the indiscreet caravan of vehicles, Garay's presence in El Salvador remained a secret. He never appeared in public, and Salvadoran authorities did not charge him as an accomplice to the murder. Although his allegations would be released to the media a few days later, Garay was not there to see the erupting political firestorm. He had vanished by the time his story hit the papers. Despite Garay's testimony, none of the killers stood trial in El Salvador, and impunity endured for Romero's murder.

The most important result of the episode was the discovery that Garay's boss, Álvaro Saravia, was living in the United States.

TWO

"In Violation of the Law of Nations"

THE ROMERO ASSASSINATION COMES
TO THE UNITED STATES

FRESNO—AUGUST 2004

The time code on the courtroom TV indicates that the video was recorded one month ago. The man on the screen, former ambassador Robert White, was unable to clear his busy schedule to appear in person at our trial in Fresno. Now in his late seventies, White leans forward in his chair, reading glasses affixed. He reviews a black-and-white ID photo taken decades before in El Salvador.

The subject in the photo has the look of someone ordered by the photographer not to smile. A stocky man with a double chin, he had accumulated Salvadoran nicknames—*gordo* (fat) and *chele* (light skinned)—that fit the portrait. Another—*borracho*—dealt less with appearance than his propensity for alcohol.[1] The son of a government minister, he grew up in the 1950s attending a prestigious Catholic school in San Salvador until the Jesuit administrators expelled him for disruptive behavior. He was allowed to enroll in the Salvadoran military academy and served as a pilot in the air force.[2] Despite a continued lack of discipline, he managed to reach the rank of captain and even studied English at a military base in Texas.[3] For a while in the 1970s, he worked security for the military dictator, Colonel Arturo Molina, who took power through the familiar tactic of a rigged election.[4] By the time Ambassador White arrived in San Salvador in early 1980, the former captain was already well down the path that would one day lead him to us.

"Can you identify the person in the photograph?" asks Nico van Aelstyn, the lead lawyer on our trial team.

"Yes," White says, studying the picture. His voice is measured but authoritative. "That's Saravia. One of the principal lieutenants of [Roberto] D'Aubuisson."

"Did you ever meet Saravia?"

"I met him once that I remember. Probably met him more often than that but I certainly remember him. He was 'cashiered' from the Salvadoran military along with D'Aubuisson, but I have to tell you that … he and D'Aubuisson still met regularly with key people in the Salvadoran military."

"What is your informed opinion with regard to Roberto D'Aubuisson's role and that of Saravia in the killing of Archbishop Romero?"

White takes a breath. "I have no doubt … that Roberto D'Aubuisson was the man responsible for the planning and execution of the assassination of Archbishop Romero. I regard that as fact. Regarding the role of Saravia, I have no direct knowledge, except that he was in a sense the recorder, the secretary." White mentions the Saravia Diary. "In there, to a knowledgeable observer, there is a page that looks very much like the shorthand planning of Monseñor Romero's death."[5]

SAN FRANCISCO, CALIFORNIA—2001

Álvaro Saravia sits in a law office more than two decades after Ambassador White met him in El Salvador. The years have made him thinner—the nickname *gordo* applies less than before—but he still maintains a distinctive head of reddish hair. As he waits to get a document notarized, Saravia is unaware that another Salvadoran man in the office knows exactly who he is. Saravia is a despised figure in El Salvador, whose face was once all over the news. The other man, fully knowledgeable of Saravia's connection to the murder of Archbishop Romero, is shocked to see him. Saravia, for his part, does not realize that he has been spotted by someone who works with the Center for Justice & Accountability.

Located in the heart of San Francisco, CJA is mostly unknown outside of U.S. human rights circles in 2001. CJA is so unassuming that its name does not even appear on the office door, a detail that bespeaks the sensitivity of its mandate: suing torturers and war criminals. Despite its small size, CJA is part of a worldwide campaign to hold those who commit atrocities, like genocide and torture, accountable for their crimes. Several dictators and human rights abusers—Augusto Pinochet and Slobodan Milosevic among them—have already been caught in the international justice movement's ever-widening net. CJA focuses primarily on foreign perpetrators who committed their crimes overseas and relocated to the United States. There is no shortage of them, especially from Latin America, with military officers retiring to destinations like Miami or Los Angeles and soldiers trying to hide out in New York or Atlanta. They include high-ranking war criminals from El Salvador who received grants of asylum or help during the 1980s and 1990s from the friendly U.S. government.

Beginning in the twentieth century, there has been a long but uneven history of prosecuting perpetrators of war crimes. The concept that architects of atrocities should be brought to justice grew out of the Allied prosecutions of German and Japanese officials after World War II, including the tribunal at Nuremberg that convicted top Nazi leaders like Hermann Göring and Rudolf Hess. The Nuremberg judgment embraced a notion, groundbreaking at the time, that such heinous acts were committed by people as opposed to abstract governments such that responsibility must be attributed to specific individuals. After the war, the newly enacted Geneva Conventions required nations to pursue war criminals no matter where their abuses occurred. Later, international treaties, like the Convention against Torture, cemented the principle that countries around the world are not only authorized but also obligated to prosecute human rights offenders.

After most of the Allied military courts ended in the late 1940s, however, war crimes trials largely disappeared. One notable exception was Israel's prosecution of Adolf Eichmann, the hated Nazi official who played a central role in the Third Reich's policy of Jewish extermination in Eastern Europe. After the war, Eichmann escaped, like so many others, to South America. But when the new state of Israel became aware of his possible presence in Argentina, Mossad agents carried out months of surveillance and devised a covert operation to abduct Eichmann and smuggle him back to Israel. The plot worked and Eichmann stood trial in Jerusalem. In an important step forward for international justice, Israeli courts ruled that they had authority to hear the case even though Eichmann's crimes occurred in Europe and Israel did not exist as a country when they were committed. This was an early expression of "universal jurisdiction," the principle that certain offenses, including war crimes and genocide, are so abhorrent to the world that all nations, even those with no connection to the crimes, have the power to prosecute the offenders.

Despite the Eichmann trial, the international accountability movement remained mostly dormant in the early decades of the Cold War until U.S. courts took an unexpected lead in breaking the impunity. In 1978, Dolly

Filártiga, a Paraguayan woman who received asylum in the United States, and her family discovered that a Paraguayan police official responsible for the murder of Filártiga's brother was then living in New York. The Filártigas, with the help of the pioneering Center for Constitutional Rights (CCR), dusted off a largely unused U.S. law called the Alien Tort Statute (ATS) to sue the officer, Américo Peña Irala, in a federal court in Brooklyn.[6] The ATS, for years known as the Alien Tort Claims Act, was passed not by a modern legislature to provide justice for human rights abuses but by the first U.S. Congress in 1789 to combat piracy and affronts to diplomats.[7] The law, barely touched since the eighteenth century, still consists of only one sentence saying that federal courts can hear "any civil action by an alien for a tort only, committed in violation of the law of nations or a treaty of the United States."[8] CCR's lawyers successfully argued that this language permitted the Filártigas to sue Peña Irala for torture, by then a clear violation of the "law of nations," also known as international law.[9]

The result was a line of civil lawsuits against human rights abusers living in or visiting the United States, including former Philippine dictator Ferdinand Marcos and Bosnian Serb war criminal Radovan Karadzic. The U.S. Congress passed a second law, the Torture Victim Protection Act, to fill some gaps left open by the ATS.[10] The cases were not criminal prosecutions, so none of the offenders went to jail, but the litigation remained cutting edge because sentencing torturers and war criminals to prison terms was generally beyond reach at that time. The situation changed only in the 1990s, when the United Nations established international tribunals to respond to ethnic cleansing in the post–Cold War breakup of Yugoslavia and the genocide in Rwanda. But even as those international criminal courts took shape, ATS lawsuits in the United States sped forward because domestic prosecutors still weren't pursuing criminal charges in U.S. courts. The ATS case against Radovan Karadzic gave rise to a landmark ruling that even nongovernmental actors could be sued, opening the door to lawsuits against corporations accused of abuses overseas, a list that includes such titans as Chevron, Exxon, and Caterpillar.[11]

The revival of the Alien Tort Statute benefitted survivors of abuses committed overseas by allowing them to access U.S. courts directly when the perpetrators were present in the United States. The disadvantage, though, was that the success of ATS litigation led the United States to focus on private, civil lawsuits that resulted in money judgments rather than criminal prosecutions leading to imprisonment. In 1994, Congress passed legislation permitting the Department of Justice to criminally prosecute individuals for torture committed beyond U.S. borders, but the law only covered torture that might occur in the future; it did not apply retroactively. Other barriers were put in place, including a requirement that all torture prosecutions be approved by the assistant attorney general in Washington, D.C., thereby eliminating the discretion of U.S. Attorneys around the country to bring cases on their own. For over a decade, despite the encouragement of human rights groups, the criminal torture provision went unused.[12] Other offenses like war crimes and extrajudicial execution remained unaddressed. With no further action by Congress, the Department of Justice had no authority to prosecute those crimes when they were committed beyond U.S. borders.

The United States continued to rely on civil lawsuits and other means to address abuses even as some countries turned to criminal law to more effectively punish and deter perpetrators. The International Criminal Court came into force in 2002 and began prosecuting genocide, war crimes, and crimes against humanity committed in nations that consented to the court's authority.[13] The United States did not accede to the court. Many countries passed domestic legislation to provide their governments the power to prosecute those offenses in their national courts, but the United States focused on deporting suspected torturers and war criminals. It was a faster, easier, and cheaper way of dealing with human rights abusers but provided little accountability or redress for the survivors. When the U.S. government finally brought criminal prosecutions several years later, they were for violations of immigration laws—a suspect lying on an immigration form about having served in a foreign military, for example—and not for the underlying offenses like genocide or crimes against humanity.[14]

Whereas deportations and criminal prosecutions required action by the U.S. government, private litigation under the Alien Tort Statute could be initiated by the survivors themselves. As a result, civil lawsuits under the ATS continued and even multiplied. With the expansion into cases against corporations, and the enormous time commitment they required of the Center for Constitutional Rights and other lawyers, some human rights experts expressed a desire to create a separate organization to focus solely on ATS lawsuits against individual perpetrators. Around the same time, San Francisco psychotherapist Gerald Gray was providing counseling to a torture survivor who had discovered his torturer living in the U.S.[15] After learning of the ATS, Gray worked with several human rights lawyers, Amnesty International USA, and the United Nations Voluntary Fund for Victims of

Torture to found the Center for Justice & Accountability. CJA's mandate was simple: work with survivors and the families of victims to sue individuals present in the United States who are responsible for atrocities overseas.

From the start, CJA focused on El Salvador, thanks in large part to the efforts of Patty Blum. A clinical professor at the UC Berkeley law school, Blum founded and directed the school's International Human Rights Law Clinic. In the 1980s, she was involved in several landmark legal victories concerning U.S. refugee policy, particularly the U.S. government's discriminatory treatment of asylum applications from Salvadorans and Guatemalans escaping the civil wars in their countries.[16] The hostile stance toward these refugees was a manifestation of the Reagan administration's financing of the armies responsible for most of the carnage that forced people to flee. Alongside the hundreds of thousands of Salvadorans who overcame serious danger to reach and cross the U.S. border, some high-ranking military officers responsible for atrocities freely relocated to homes in the United States. Faced with this history, Blum and others, including members of the Salvadoran community, believed that CJA had an opportunity and responsibility to pursue these suspected war criminals on U.S. soil.

I join CJA as a new staff attorney four years after its founding and just before its first jury trial begins in 2002. The defendants in that case, who have lived in Florida for over a decade, were familiar faces to Archbishop Romero. José Guillermo García served as El Salvador's defense minister from late 1979 to 1983, the same period in which co-accused Carlos Vides Casanova ran the National Guard. When García retired, Vides Casanova took his place as defense minister. The plaintiffs are also residents of the United States but they are part of a Salvadoran diaspora who fled north to save their lives, not retire in comfort like Generals García and Vides Casanova. Juan Romagoza, Neris González, and Carlos Mauricio survived torture at the hands of the Salvadoran security forces. Years later, they have sought justice and used the ATS to sue García and Vides Casanova—"the Generals"—in a West Palm Beach court. In July 2002, the trial against the Generals concludes with a momentous $54.6 million jury verdict.[17]

Patty Blum, who is a member of the legal team, believes the victory gives CJA the credibility to commit to other cases that collectively could have an impact in El Salvador. This is important not only because of the large Salvadoran population in the United States but also because El Salvador has a blanket amnesty law, blocking the possibility of prosecutions there and perpetuating impunity for atrocities committed during the civil war. With the support of human rights colleagues in El Salvador, Patty pushes for CJA to continue with other Salvadoran investigations.[18] This includes Archbishop Romero's case, on which little progress has been made since Álvaro Saravia was spotted in the San Francisco law office in 2001.

Since starting at CJA, I have not been involved in the Generals' lawsuit, and I focus on countries other than El Salvador. Even so, once the Romero investigation starts moving, I look for opportunities to get involved. I learn that another source confirmed the sighting of Saravia in the United States. On August 1, 2001, the *Miami Herald,* knowing nothing of the San Francisco encounter, ran an article headlined "Torture Suspects Find Haven in U.S." These suspects, the paper reported, are "men such as Alvaro Rafael Saravia Marino, who arrived in Miami in 1985 on a tourist visa issued by the U.S. Embassy—even though just five years earlier authorities in El Salvador had identified him as a key suspect in the murder of Salvadoran Archbishop Oscar Arnulfo Romero." The article says that Saravia is now in Modesto, California.

News of Saravia's location, only a few hours from San Francisco, has given CJA, emboldened by the victory over the Generals, a perfect opportunity. Since we spend most of our time monitoring distant Florida for perpetrators, we relish the opportunity to pursue someone close to home. In addition, Romero's murder is one of the most emblematic crimes in El Salvador's history and no one has been held accountable. CJA also benefits from the extensive knowledge of the team that has worked on the Generals' trial, including Patty Blum and Stanford political science professor Terry Karl. While the Generals' case has focused on torture, the issues surrounding Romero's assassination spring from the same political reality: the extreme military repression in El Salvador during the 1970s and 1980s.

Throughout the rest of 2002, the CJA team, on which I play an increasing role, combs through declassified U.S. government documents, speaks with contacts, and searches public records for information about Saravia's precise location. While the suspects CJA usually pursues can be difficult to track, multiple sources have confirmed the *Miami Herald*'s claim that Saravia is in Modesto, and the records repeatedly connect him and a woman to a house on Manor Oak Drive. A few businesses in Saravia's name have used that address, as have unpaid creditors who sued him. Saravia, it appears, has not used any fake names or tried to stay underground. He is living in plain sight.

Even with our confidence about Saravia's address, we want a visual confirmation that he is actually there. My CJA colleague, Almudena Bernabeu, and I take the initiative to look for Saravia in Modesto. Originally a lawyer from Spain who spoke limited English, Almudena lived for a time in Virginia before moving to San Francisco. There she connected with some of the city's top refugee advocates and worked at an immigration law firm, which included processing numerous applications for Salvadorans. Almudena proved to be a highly intelligent and talented advocate, skills that eventually helped her find work with CJA.

The two-hour drive east from San Francisco takes Almudena and me out of the city and up the steady incline of I-580, past the rolling hills and grazing cows at the farthest reaches of the Bay Area. We turn down Highway 99, the pipeline of the Central Valley, its lanes clogged by trucks brimming with oranges, tomatoes, and onions. Among the irrigated farms whose products fill those trucks is the dusty city of Modesto, a growing metropolis of 200,000. Modesto seems like a place where someone can lie low.

We find Saravia's neighborhood without trouble and park on a street perpendicular to Manor Oak Drive. Across a vacant lot, we have a clear view of his split-level house, its sloping roof covered with Spanish tiles in the typical California style. Painted cream with brown trim, the house looks like any other on the block. The small front yard has a giant shade tree and flowering bushes. A No Solicitors sign hangs on the front door. Using binoculars inherited from my father, I get the license plate number of a white Mercury Cougar sitting on the street. For over an hour we wait, observing nothing, until a garage door opens. As the door inches upward, we can see a crowded storage space and a late-model Oldsmobile. Two women walk out from the house. We note that they are Latina and that one is probably in her fifties, the other years younger. They spend only seconds in the garage before returning inside, but they leave the garage door open. It gives us hope that we'll see more. A bit later, an older woman from next door walks into the garage, looks in the refrigerator, and wanders into the house without knocking. Several hours pass before we give up. We speak with a few neighbors—one says Salvadorans live in the house—but we don't get any more information. We decide to return to San Francisco despite not locating Saravia.

We aren't worried that we won't find him. When we eventually do, however, it is in a way we never imagined.

"The Enemy Comes from Our People"

COFFEE, ANTI-COMMUNISM,
AND THE DEATH SQUADS

FRESNO—AUGUST 2004

"Let me show you what has been marked as 'Deposition Exhibit 2,'" lawyer Nico van Aelstyn says to Ambassador Robert White on the video. "This is a copy of a telegram that, I believe, you authored and sent to the secretary of state." It is dated March 19, 1980, five days before Archbishop Romero's assassination. White confirms that while the document had several authors, it was sent out over his signature.[1] Today, the telegram looks like an artifact, but it is typical of the diplomatic cables of the time. Its block letters are sometimes uneven or fuzzy, words are misspelled, and various stamps and handwritten notes adorn the pages. A reader can almost imagine the teletype machine hastily banging the letters through the printer ribbon and onto the page. Each sheet proclaims that the contents are now "UNCLASSIFIED." It is a long cable, "something like a State of the Union address," White says, "which gave not only a summary of the actual situation but the prospects for the near-term future and what we would need to do if we were to be successful in the policies that we have outlined." The language throughout is stark.

"Why does El Salvador face a Marxist Revolution?" one paragraph asks before supplying the answer:

> That it does is the main reason for our intense concern; why it does must underlie any plan of action we develop. An extremist Communist takeover here, and by that I mean something just this side of the Pol Pot episode, is unfortunately a real possibility due mainly to the intense hatred that has been created in this country among the masses by the insensitivity, blindness and brutality of the ruling elite, usually designated 'the oligarchy.' It is hard to describe the injustice that permeates this society. Let me offer a few examples.

Magnificent suburbs full of villas right out of Beverly Hills are flanked by miserable slums right out of Jakarta where families have to walk two blocks to the only water spigot. The traditionally stark contrast between rich and poor has been intensified drastically in recent years by the immense riches that have accrued to the landowning class as a result of high prices for export crops—coffee, sugar, and cotton—produced on their vast plantations staffed by impoverished and largely illiterate day laborers. Meanwhile, the cities have been flooded with the poorest and most depressed *campesinos* who are fleeing overpopulation and rural poverty in search of work.

The paragraph concludes, "All in all, this country is a social bomb that has been ticking away for a number of years and is only now at the point of explosion."[2]

EL SALVADOR—1880 TO 1980

The threat of a cataclysmic civil war that El Salvador faced in 1980 dated back to government land policies one hundred years before. In the centuries after Spain's conquest of the New World, Spanish colonies were governed mostly at the local level and indigenous people were permitted to hold and work their agricultural lands communally.[3] The arrangement continued after the former colonies declared independence in the early nineteenth century, but two developments in subsequent decades hastened an end to this traditional *ejido* system. In the 1880s, Liberal Party reforms privatized lands previously owned by the state, the Catholic Church, and indigenous communities. The movement toward privatizing property in El Salvador was partly caused by an increasing global demand for coffee, which was grown in the highlands where indigenous communities were concentrated.[4] In 1881, the Liberal government outlawed indigenous communal lands altogether, explaining, "The existence of lands under the ownership of the [indigenous] communities impedes agricultural development, obstructs the circulation of wealth, and weakens family bonds and the independence of the individual. Their existence is contrary to the economic and social principles that the Republic has accepted."[5]

Coffee required not only large estates in the highlands but also a steady labor force. The landowners who possessed formerly communal lands enlisted the displaced indigenous population to work the plantations *(fincas)*, often through force and with help from the state. This led to sometimes-violent resistance. The state responded by creating police forces to impose the new system of forced labor. Landowners increasingly required their workers to live on the estates, and judges ensured that laborers did not leave the *fincas* before completing their duties.[6] "Thus," wrote former *New York Times* reporter Raymond Bonner, "El Salvador's economic oligarchy was born [and] the seeds of peasant revolution were planted."[7]

The next fifty years saw the dominance of the coffee barons in both the economic and political spheres. From 1898 to 1931, the Salvadoran president was always a coffee grower. It was, wrote sociology professor Jeffery Paige, "the golden age of the coffee elite," and many of the families in charge of the *fincas* at that time still maintained control in the 1970s.[8] Though a later, common reference to the "Fourteen Families" underestimated their true number (the real figure was closer to one hundred), the sentiment that a small group of people came to dominate the economy was not far off.[9]

By 1930, coffee represented 95 percent of El Salvador's export earnings, and many *campesinos* were entirely dependent on the coffee plantations for their survival.[10] The disparity between rich and poor was already extreme, but the onset of the Great Depression led to catastrophe. Coffee prices dropped dramatically and growers slashed wages and eliminated jobs. *Campesinos* were often left without options—they had no land of their own and no other work was available.[11] The observations of a U.S. military attaché describe the inequality of the time:

> About the first thing one observes when he goes to San Salvador is the number of expensive automobiles in the streets. There seems to be nothing but Packards and Pierce Arrows about. There appears to be nothing between these high priced cars and the ox cart with its bare-footed attendant. There is practically no middle class between the very rich and the very poor. From the people with whom I talked I learned that roughly ninety percent of the wealth of the country is held by about one half of one percent of the population. Thirty or forty families own nearly everything in the country. They live in almost regal splendor with many attendants, send their children to Europe or the United States to be educated, and spend money lavishly (on themselves). The rest of the population has practically nothing.[12]

As the situation for *campesinos* declined, protests became widespread, and the government responded with violent repression.[13] Against this backdrop, the Communist Party of El Salvador formed in 1930.[14] When a coup d'état brought to power a military hard-liner supported by the coffee growers and determined to end the social unrest, indigenous *campesino* groups and the

Communist Party carried out a revolt in the western coffee region.[15] For the oligarchy, the uprising "combined their two worst nightmares, Indian rebellion and Communist revolution."[16] As Michael McClintock, author of a definitive book on U.S. military involvement in El Salvador, put it, there was a fear of "International Communism, organized, resourceful, godless, unscrupulous and quite capable of leading Indian hordes into upper-class bedrooms to rape wives and daughters and slit throats."[17] But the rebellion was doomed from the start; several Communist Party leaders were captured before it began (they were later executed), and even those rebels who managed to take over rural towns for a few days could not hold out given their poor training and equipment, which mostly consisted of machetes.[18] What turned this into the most important episode of the century was not the revolt, which took approximately one hundred lives, but the military's response to it that took vastly more.[19]

The security forces of General Maximiliano Hernández Martínez not only crushed the insurrectionists but systematically eliminated the possibility that such an uprising would happen again. Some estimate that the military killed as many as thirty thousand people, primarily indigenous *campesinos*.[20] Anyone thought to be "Indian" due to physical features, clothing, or simply possessing a machete, a ubiquitous tool in the countryside, was presumed to be a rebel and killed.[21] In one town, "groups of fifty were shot at the four corners of the town every day for a month," while elsewhere leaders were hanged from trees.[22] Many indigenous people abandoned any expressions of their culture as a form of survival. After 1932, El Salvador was considered no longer to have a distinct indigenous population.[23] And, because history is written by the victors, the military regimes that followed minimized their own savagery and instead "fostered a legend of bloodthirsty [indigenous] mobs butchering thousands of middle-class citizens, and of a heroic army that barely managed to turn back the barbarian wave."[24]

In a history littered with atrocities, La Matanza—simply the Massacre— stands alone as the defining moment in El Salvador's history. So widespread was the carnage that General Martínez, who later developed strong ties with the Nazis and Mussolini, effectively ended all significant resistance to military rule for decades.[25] As Jeffery Paige has written, "The fact that El Salvador's only experience with social reform and popular mobilization ended in insurrection led by sectarian followers of the Communist International profoundly influenced popular and elite attitudes toward reform and social change."[26] This resulted in an "almost paranoic fear of communism that has gripped the nation ever since ... [and] the continual labeling of even the most modest reform movements as communist or communist inspired."[27] La Matanza also changed the way El Salvador was governed. No longer would the oligarchy rule the country. This was left to the military, with the implicit bargain that the soldiers would keep order and protect the interests of the oligarchy.[28] After 1932, the elites "traded the right to rule for the right to make money."[29]

FRESNO—AUGUST 2004

"Please state your name for the record," the court clerk says.

"Terry Lynn Karl, Terry with a *y* and Karl with a *k*." The witness's small frame keeps her partially hidden in the witness box, her short reddish-brown hair and serious face the most visible features. It is clear, though, that she is not cowering behind the short walls, because I have never seen a more confident person take the stand. Lawyer Nico van Aelstyn begins by qualifying her as an expert witness. "Professor Karl, what I would like to do—your CV is multiple pages here, twenty-five I believe, we are not going to run through the entirety of it—I would like to just cover the most pertinent points."

Karl describes her mountain of credentials—a BA, an MA, a PhD with distinction from Stanford in political science with a specialization in Latin America; an assistant professorship at Harvard and then back to Stanford, a fellowship awarded to the ten best teachers at the university, and director of Latin American studies for twelve years. The court reporter asks her to slow down, and not for the last time.

Nico turns to Karl's specific qualifications in Central America. "Could you please summarize the kinds of research that you conducted during your trips in El Salvador?"

The most important aspect of those visits was "constant interviewing," she says. "I interview everybody in El Salvador that will talk to me and I follow around people who won't talk to me until they agree to." She mentions politicians, military and police officials, and members of the governing party. "I have traveled with various presidential candidates on their presidential campaigns," Karl says. This final group "includes Roberto D'Aubuisson, who figures prominently in this case."[30]

D'Aubuisson has always been associated with Archbishop Romero's murder. D'Aubuisson and his attaché case stuffed with documents, including the

Saravia Diary, were captured in 1980 at Finca San Luis. The U.S. embassy's insider source, Killer, named him as the organizer of the Romero assassination. The getaway driver, Amado Garay, testified in 1987 that Saravia reported back to D'Aubuisson days after the crime. Ambassador Robert White, who called D'Aubuisson a "pathological killer," had "no doubt" that D'Aubuisson was the man who planned the operation to murder Romero.[31] D'Aubuisson's own career was an example of how the military dominated Salvadoran life and it explained why he and his disciples could think, half a century after La Matanza, that the archbishop had to be killed.

Terry Karl quotes a high-level U.S. government memo to explain D'Aubuisson's military roots. "Major D'Aubuisson had served much of his career as an intelligence officer with the National Guard," Karl reads. "He and several other colleagues, graduates from the [military] academy … worked directly under or in cooperation with National Guard director [José] Medrano, a notorious and powerful figure in military and right-wing civilian circles. Medrano had his protégés focus on counterintelligence and rural security; during the 1960s and 1970s, D'Aubuisson and his colleagues helped develop civilian intelligence networks and vigilante organizations controlled by the National Guard. They also engaged in illegal detentions, torture, and the killing of prisoners."

"Who was Medrano?" Nico asks.

"Medrano was a very important figure in the military," Karl says. "As head of the National Guard, he had more interaction with rural landowners than others. What Medrano did was realize—and this is one of the reasons he's considered such a hero inside the Salvadoran military—that the military itself and the security forces, as they were constituted, were not going to be able to control the situation in El Salvador [in which challenges to military rule were again taking root decades after La Matanza]. They were not going to be able to stay in power as a military regime unless they developed a more sophisticated repressive apparatus."[32]

The United States strongly supported Medrano because U.S. Cold War policy in the 1960s was obsessively focused on preventing other Cuba-style revolutions in Latin America. In addition to Fidel Castro's victory in Cuba, Soviet leader Nikita Khrushchev announced in January 1961 that the Soviet Union would start supporting wars of liberation around the globe.[33] President John F. Kennedy countered by warning the U.S. Congress that the "free world's security can be … slowly nibbled away at the periphery, by forces of subversion, infiltration, intimidation, indirect or non-overt aggression, internal revolution, lunatic blackmail, guerrilla warfare or a series of limited wars."[34] The Kennedy administration embedded counterinsurgency doctrine, the concept that unconventional military tactics were necessary to defeat unconventional enemies, in virtually every area of U.S. military and foreign policy. In short order, the U.S. Army began training foreign military forces, including El Salvador's, in guerrilla techniques, psychological warfare, and the use of "irregular" forces like civilian defense squads.[35] U.S. Special Forces helped other nations create paramilitary units to supplement the conventional armed forces, leading to what Michael McClintock calls "'guerrilla' actions *in support* of the state," including covert terrorist tactics.[36] The United States employed this strategy throughout Latin America and also in Vietnam.[37]

General Medrano told U.S. reporter Allan Nairn that his most important paramilitary and intelligence institutions in El Salvador "grew out of the State Department, the CIA, and the Green Berets during the time of Kennedy. We created these specialized agencies to fight the plans and actions of international communism." They included the Nationalist Democratic Organization (ORDEN), a rural spy network of around 100,000 at its peak, whose leaders were trained by the U.S. military and the CIA. Medrano, with significant U.S. government involvement, created ORDEN to "indoctrinate" *campesinos* against communism. "You discover the communist by the way he talks," Medrano said. "Generally, he speaks against Yankee imperialism, he speaks against the oligarchy, he speaks against military men. We can spot them easily." Medrano flew frequently to CIA headquarters, and the U.S. government sent him to Vietnam, where he traveled with the U.S. Army, the Green Berets, and CIA agents. In 1968, Lyndon Johnson awarded him a presidential medal "in recognition of exceptionally meritorious service."[38]

During the 1960s, though, there was no Communist insurgency for Medrano and his compatriots to fight in El Salvador, only a growing number of popular movements calling primarily for nonviolent change concerning the numerous political and social issues plaguing the country. The Communist Party, having managed to survive clandestinely in the decades since La Matanza, was again gaining strength but was not advocating for revolt.[39] In 1970, as military repression and intransigence continued despite widespread calls for reform, a splinter group, believing that peaceful change was no longer possible, abandoned the Communist Party to begin an armed insurgency. Another breakaway group followed two years later. These groups, though small in numbers and separated by ideological differences, were the most prominent forces engaged in guerrilla tactics throughout the 1970s. They carried out audacious kidnappings, mostly of wealthy and powerful Salvadorans, resulting in the payment of more than $50 million in ransom over the course of the decade.[40] The names of their targets read like a roll call of the Salvadoran oligarchy: Hill, Simán, de Sola, Escalante, Sol Meza.[41] Unlike those men, other victims were never released, their bodies disposed of by their captors. These brutal methods, combined with bombings of businesses, government offices, and embassies, spread terror among the oligarchs, who increasingly felt unprotected by the Salvadoran state. Some believed that even a government run by the military wasn't enough to eliminate the "terrorist" threat.

The Salvadoran military, rather than reforming, saw the leftist bombings and killings as justification for continuing its ruthless and counterproductive tactics. National Guardsmen and other soldiers, wishing to hide their complicity in atrocities or instill an extra measure of fear among the population, took off their uniforms and carried out operations in plain clothes. A succinct term came to describe these extralegal groups for what they were—death squads—and their targets were not limited to insurgents but encompassed anyone perceived as "subversive" for belonging to unions or student organizations, attending demonstrations, or disagreeing with the government. The death squads sometimes gave themselves menacing names like White Hand (Mano Blanca) and White Warriors Union (Unión Guerrera Blanca), and made public declarations to further intimidate the population. Reflecting on a situation he had helped create, General Medrano later said, "In this revolutionary war, the enemy comes from our people. They don't have the rights of Geneva. They are traitors to the country. What can the troops do? When they find them, they kill them."[42] In that mission, Medrano labeled Roberto D'Aubuisson, a rising star in the military intelligence community, one of his "assassins."[43]

"[D'Aubuisson] was an extraordinarily ambitious, very intelligent, and clever person," Professor Terry Karl testifies. "He always wanted to rise high in the ranks. So one of the things he did in this period of time, which actually sets him apart from all the others, is he had some extensive training outside El Salvador."[44] D'Aubuisson attended the International Police Academy in Washington, D.C.,[45] and studied counterinsurgency techniques in Taiwan.[46] "This was extremely important for Roberto D'Aubuisson," Karl says. "He is the only one who had this kind of training. No one else went. He was the only one who was really interested in ideology and in models of how to rule. . . . He was a deeply, deeply—and I'm not using this word loosely—fanatical anti-Communist."[47]

D'Aubuisson's anti-Communist ideology was in line with many of El Salvador's wealthy landowners who detested, perhaps more than any other issue, a growing demand for a national land redistribution program. "El Salvador had at this time one of the highest concentrations of landownership worldwide, not just in Latin America, but also worldwide," Professor Karl explains. "And that meant that there was a situation in which there were some very wealthy Salvadorans, and the great majority of Salvadorans were extremely poor. . . . It was still primarily a rural country. And that meant that—it's not my estimate, this is the estimate of economists—about 70 percent of the people lived far below what we call an absolute poverty line. . . . It is the issue of the concentration of land that is one of the major issues that provokes the kind of violence that we see in El Salvador during this period." This was not just a political issue but a military issue. "There is a debate inside the military between what I refer to as 'hard-liners and reformists.' The reformists are people who believe that some type of land reform has to occur, even if it's very, very small. And even if it's a very, very small one, of at least massive properties that are unoccupied and are not being worked, that at least those should be broken up. Hard-liners do not believe in any form of land reform and they are absolutely violently opposed to it, as are, really, all of the leading landowners."[48]

By 1979, the exasperated reformists were planning a coup d'état. Junior officers, many at the level of major, captain, and lieutenant, wanted to kick out the hard-line military government, implement some land reform, and remove their colleagues, like D'Aubuisson, who were responsible for oppressing the Salvadoran people under the guise of stamping out "subversives." Many of the coup plotters looked south to Nicaragua, where leftist Sandinista rebels had just overthrown a recalcitrant dictatorship. The junior officers foresaw a similar fate in El Salvador if the status quo persisted. They saw that repression had not worked.[49] When the coup finally commenced on October 15, 1979, it appeared a triumph. The junior officers easily elected their leader, Colonel Adolfo Majano, to head a civilian-military junta, and the cabinet had a progressive bent. Although the militant guerrilla groups viewed the government skeptically, the composition of the new administration was even more chilling for the oligarchs. They suddenly foresaw the real possibility that a land-reform program, one of the signature pledges of the new junta, might break up their vast estates and diminish the unchecked power of their protectors in the National Guard and other security forces.

"Majano makes clear that they are going to kick out of the military the most repressive hard-liners," including D'Aubuisson, Karl continues in her testimony. "They are going to have to get out of the military. They are going to be 'cashiered.' They are going to be pushed out of the military."[50] On his way out, following the orders of hard-line commanders who managed to keep their posts, D'Aubuisson absconded with military intelligence files on suspected Communists and "subversives." Wearing "dirty coveralls, a Caterpillar hat, and five days growth of beard," D'Aubuisson fled to neighboring Guatemala with a copy of the files.[51] From there, the stolen records would form the basis for targeted paramilitary and death squad activities, including bombings and assassinations, inside El Salvador.[52] Though now based in Guatemala, D'Aubuisson made clandestine excursions back into El Salvador to enroll sympathetic military officers in his anti-Communist crusade. One of the people in his audience was Álvaro Saravia. Though Saravia had also been cashiered, his active-duty friends still let him into the military barracks where Saravia listened to D'Aubuisson deliver impassioned, patriotic pitches to recruit the men to his paramilitary cause.[53] Over a shared bottle of rum with D'Aubuisson, Saravia accepted an offer to serve as D'Aubuisson's chief of security and thereby pledged himself anew to the bloody salvation of El Salvador.[54]

Though D'Aubuisson's many trips into El Salvador were secret, he simultaneously built a platform as a public spokesperson for El Salvador's Far Right.[55] Under the auspices of a new civic organization, the Broad National Front (FAN), D'Aubuisson and like-minded members of El Salvador's oligarchy held press conferences and produced television programs denouncing people they considered Communists and enemies of El Salvador.[56] "He was an unusual man," Ambassador White later said. "He would go on TV and actually threaten people by name, and he couldn't have done that, of course, if he didn't have the support of the people who owned the TV station. So he believed that he had, and I'm sure he did have, the support of a great many people of wealth and power in the country."[57] D'Aubuisson taped many of these TV spots at an air force base in Guatemala, and the recordings were flown into El Salvador on private airplanes or carried in overland.[58]

While FAN was becoming the public face of the anti-Communist cause, lurking behind its facade were the shock troops of the movement: the death squads. Though D'Aubuisson was not the only organizer of Salvadoran death squads—they existed throughout the military—he was the commander of one of the most brazen units. D'Aubuisson's group maintained connections to active-duty security forces, a fact the hard-liners repeatedly denied even as they supported D'Aubuisson's outfit as a way to undermine the progressive coup and its military leader, Colonel Majano.

Professor Karl calls for an exhibit to be displayed on the courtroom screen. The grisly photo shows several bloated corpses with their heads either missing or destroyed. They are dressed only in underwear. Bones are scattered in the background and several skulls seem to be staring at the camera. "The name of it is El Playón," Karl says. "It is a body dump area. It is important to note that there is only one way to get to El Playón. There is only one road leading to it and that road has a military guardhouse at the front of it. . . . So in order to get to this spot, you must go through a military checkpoint." She had her own experience with El Playón. "The day I was there, I saw nine bodies. They were in a pile. . . . The top body was a woman who had had her left breast cut off and was naked. There were other bodies. I could tell that their faces were destroyed and I saw signs of torture on the bodies. So this is a representation to the kind of work that I personally witnessed that death squads did."[59]

Karl describes the motivation of the military hard-liners and the death squads:

> They are afraid of two things. They are afraid that they are losing control of the military . . . the reformers are going to be in power in the military, and the military is not going to be reliable any more to fight land reform. The military won't be reliable [in fighting the Communist threat]. It might decide to leave power and let there be democratic elections. They are very worried about the reliability of the military as an institution if reformers control the decision-making process. They know they are going to fight this. These are people who are extremely, fanatically against any form of reform. . . . So they develop a strategy that I call "inside-outside." And what I mean by that is they decide to fight inside the military to try to get the chief positions within the military back from Colonel Majano, from the reformist faction of the military. But at the same time, just in case that fails, they set up an apparatus outside the military. [They have D'Aubuisson] operate outside the military as a form of security and to help set up an apparatus just in case the military, as an institution, falls under the control of reformers.[60]

Within just a few months, the inside-outside strategy worked, as the military hard-liners outfoxed Majano and the progressive junta. Rather than abuses by uniformed troops and plainclothes death squads coming to an end, the killings actually increased. In January 1980, all the civilian members of the junta resigned in protest. The crumbling of the brief political experiment ushered in an *annus terribilis,* one of the bloodiest years in El Salvador's bloody history. Although a second junta formed to include a centrist political party, the Christian Democrats, this did not improve the situation because D'Aubuisson, FAN, and the military hard-liners despised centrists too. "There is an ideology that is extremely strong in this group," Karl says. "They believe very, very strongly that the key enemy is not, in fact, the Communists, but it's the moderates . . . meaning Christian Democrats, that open the door for Communism. That's what they believe. If the door is slammed shut you are safe. But if somebody opens it a little bit, the people behind them can push through."

Karl tells a favorite story about D'Aubuisson. "One of the things I most remember him saying to me, he was talking about moderates being Communists, basically. He would name people. He would say, 'You know, [Christian Democrat politician Napoleón] Duarte is a Communist.'"

Nico interjects, "Didn't you say the Christian Democrats were very anti-Communist?"

"Yes, so that was strange to me," Karl says. "So I would say, 'You know, they have this platform, the Christian Democrats. They are anti-Communists. . . . They have always been the opposition to Communism. So how can you say they are Communists?' And he would say, 'You know, the thing is you can be a Communist without knowing you are a Communist.' . . . He would pick up a watermelon, because a watermelon is green and the color of the Christian Democratic party is green. And he would cut open the watermelon"—with a machete—"and say, 'See? Green on the outside, red on the inside.'"[61]

The Christian Democrats had an enemy in Roberto D'Aubuisson but a strong ally in the U.S. administration of Jimmy Carter. The situation in El Salvador in early 1980 was critical for the United States. The revolution in Nicaragua the year before had overthrown dictator Anastasio Somoza—a longtime U.S. ally—and brought the left-wing Sandinistas to power, increasing the importance of neighboring El Salvador to U.S. foreign policy.[62] The Carter White House feared that if revolutionary forces in Nicaragua could bring down a military government, the same could occur in El Salvador, resulting in a third Marxist government in the United States' backyard.[63]

With the Christian Democrats sharing power with El Salvador's armed forces, President Carter sent a new ambassador to the country. Robert White had a reputation for standing up to dictators and speaking his mind more than most diplomats.[64] White believed the greatest threat to stability in El Salvador was from the Far Right—the oligarchs, Roberto D'Aubuisson, and the military hard-liners—rather than the Far Left guerrilla forces.[65] White thought that undermining the Far Right would strengthen the center, including the Christian Democrats, thereby decreasing the chances of a takeover by a Marxist guerrilla insurgency. "Washington wants something to the right of Nicaragua," White said. "My job is to make that happen."[66] The U.S. government, seeking to play a greater part in El Salvador, wanted to give him latitude to take on the extreme right.[67] In White's Senate confirmation hearings, Senator Jacob Javits told him, "While theoretically you may be an ambassador and buried in the bureaucracy, you are a proconsul so far as we are concerned." It wouldn't work for White to be a passive ambassador. "You really have to be an activist and take a chance with your career," Javits said. "If not, this just isn't going to go."[68]

White arrived in El Salvador in March 1980 with those instructions to reinforce the Christian Democrats and others in the political center against the guerrillas on the left and the extremists on the right like D'Aubuisson. In response, D'Aubuisson and his FAN associates stepped up their verbal assault on the U.S. government's role in El Salvador and particularly its support for the reform program that seized land from the oligarchs. In a television appearance, D'Aubuisson denounced the United States for being the Christian Democrats' "foreign godfathers" who would eventually send the "Marines and Green Berets" into El Salvador.[69] In a FAN press conference from Guatemala, D'Aubuisson accused the United States of supporting Communism and thereby creating chaos that would lead to a civil war and provide the pretext for U.S. military intervention.[70] Documents later seized from D'Aubuisson called Robert White a "left-wing socialist" and a "loyal spy" of the United States.[71]

Despite White's mandate to strengthen the center, his arrival did little to quell the repression in El Salvador. The Carter administration also exacerbated the situation by continuing a contradictory policy. Even as White sought to undermine the Far Right, the U.S. government was providing aid to the Salvadoran military that remained under the control of rightist commanders. The assistance was minimal compared to the largesse that President Reagan bestowed in later years, but it still signaled support for the Salvadoran armed forces at a time when they were killing thousands of civilians.

After a few weeks in country, White transmitted to the State Department the extensive analysis of the situation in El Salvador that he later read in his testimony in our case. The cable was dated March 19, 1980, five days before Archbishop Romero's assassination. White wrote:

The immediate threat to the junta is from the ultra-right. Backed by the great fortunes of at least some members of the oligarchy, and abetted by the acquiescence and participation of some members of the armed forces, a wave of violence against moderates has been underway for several weeks and is reaching a decisive stage. The junta must end right-wing terrorism if it is to win international support and lure away from the ultra-left those moderates who want to see structural change and an end to oppression.... For the ultra-right, it seems clear that these acts of terror are designed to eliminate or radicalize the relatively moderate elements on the left and preclude a moderate solution. For the ultra-left, the goal is to provoke rightist assassinations or a wholesale massacre that will outrage the population and kick off a national insurrection.

Then came White's most prophetic statement, "Probably the most serious threat to a moderate solution would be the assassination . . . of Archbishop Romero, the most important political figure in El Salvador and a symbol of a better life to the poor."[72]

———

FOUR

"The Door of History"

ARCHBISHOP ROMERO AND THE CATHOLIC CHURCH IN EL SALVADOR

FRESNO—AUGUST 2004

"Please state your name for the record," the clerk says.

"William Louis Wipfler."

"Thank you. You may take the stand."

Father Wipfler sits in the witness chair. Despite his short stature, he has a commanding presence, and his black clothes and white collar—standard attire for an Episcopal priest—mask an energetic personality and vibrant sense of humor. His silver beard gives him an appearance both serious and kind.

"How did you come to know Monseñor Romero?" Nico van Aelstyn asks.

Wipfler tells the court about a letter he received from a concerned writer in 1977, just after Romero was selected archbishop of San Salvador. "He felt that Archbishop Romero was two things," Wipfler says. "Too conservative . . . and also too young." From the stand, Wipfler seems like he has been transported back to that time. "That was the beginning of my knowledge of the archbishop," he says. "But when Father Rutilio Grande was murdered . . ."[1]

EL SALVADOR—MARCH 1977

Grainy photographs show a white Volkswagen Safari with a dark top, tilted at a 45-degree angle and propped up with a stick, the tropical sun casting a shadow on the dirt road. The front of the car faces a wire fence strung through logs, separating the crime scene from the sugarcane fields beyond. A dead man hangs out the back left door, his arm reaching nearly to the ground, as a helmeted National Guard soldier looks on from a short distance, his distinct leather boots visible behind one of the fence posts. Two other bodies slump in the front seat.

This carnage on March 12, 1977, was the work of gunmen who surrounded and fired into the car numerous times at short range, peppering the driver with at least a dozen bullets.[2] The driver, either dead or panicked, lost control of the vehicle, flipping it on its side. Two passengers may have died in the initial torrent or when the killers finished them off after the crash. Children who had been riding in the backseat managed to escape, either through astonishing luck or the executioners' perverted sense of decency. When nearby residents arrived at the scene, the car's engine was still running, the wheels spinning wildly. In 1970s El Salvador, there was nothing uncommon about this kind of death squad murder, but what made the incident unique was that the driver, and primary target, was a priest.

Rutilio Grande was the Jesuit pastor of the Aguilares parish, a short distance north of San Salvador, where large sugar plantations dominated the region's flatlands. Most of the area's poor *campesinos* worked in the cane fields and resided on the rocky slopes of the neighboring hillsides.[3] The local economic system mirrored the national reality in which a handful of wealthy families owned virtually all the land and the National Guard used intimidation and force to maintain the system. As one Jesuit priest wrote, "It was not necessary to tell the *campesinos* that they were oppressed or who their oppressors were. Both were evident."[4] Grande, along with fellow Jesuit priests, wanted to overturn the status quo in Aguilares by empowering *campesinos* to demand their own change, and he sought to do so through the lens of Catholic theology, which had just undergone a revolutionary transformation.

From the time of the Spanish conquest in the sixteenth century, the Catholic Church had enjoyed a privileged place in the social order of Latin America. Priests arrived with the earliest *conquistadores* and the church quickly became one of the largest landholders in the New World, with some religious orders even benefiting from a system of slave labor. While some clergy, including the pope on occasion, complained about the worst of the abuses the Spanish inflicted on the conquered indigenous populations, the Latin American church remained docile and conservative. Although church and state were separate, the Catholic hierarchy was dependent on the imperial government for its wealth and lofty status.[5] The church was, according to Professor Thomas Kelly, author of a leading biography of Rutilio Grande, "an uncritical chaplain to colonial power."[6]

The prevailing theology, in Latin America and the Vatican, was that the church's domain was limited to the spiritual plane whereas the state was the steward of the present-day material world. While the church did not ignore the concerns of the downtrodden, it focused on charity and filling immediate needs rather than addressing the underlying causes of inequality and oppression. The preoccupation was saving souls for the afterlife rather than alleviating human suffering on earth.[7] In El Salvador, this doctrinal mind-set generally aligned the Catholic leadership with the wealthy and powerful while demanding obedience from the general population.

By the twentieth century, the Vatican seemed out of step with the modern world's embrace of political concepts like democracy and liberalism, and this was exacerbated by the church's emphasis on hierarchy, the favored status for ordained clergy, and the spiritual inferiority of laypeople.[8] The result was a two-tiered system in which the laity occupied, according to a papal encyclical of the time, "an honorable, if often a lowly, place" and were encouraged to "pay due honor and reverence" to the "more exalted" clergy.[9] True holiness, the church taught, resided only in ordained members of the hierarchy.[10]

This is the church in which Óscar Romero grew up and studied. Romero was born in 1917 in Ciudad Barrios, a remote mountain community without electricity and accessible only on foot or horseback. His father was a postmaster and telegraph operator, so although the family's income was modest, the Romeros were not *campesinos* like the majority of Salvadorans. Romero was a quiet and studious child who apprenticed with a carpenter, but he was always drawn to the Catholic faith. At the age of thirteen, Romero left to enter the seminary in the larger city of San Miguel. Quiet and reflective prayer became a sanctuary for Romero during that time, a practice he would continue his entire life.

In 1937, Romero went to Rome to complete his studies. He stayed despite the beginning of World War II, and through food shortages and constant air-raid sirens, he managed to finish his clerical education. He became a priest in 1942, but before he could finish additional doctorate work, Romero's bishop summoned him back to El Salvador. Romero spent most of the next twenty years as secretary of the diocese of San Miguel. He worked long hours and developed a reputation for being strict about Catholic formalities and the behavior of priests.[11] He was recognized for his speaking skills and parishioners followed him on local radio, where he discussed lessons from the

Bible. Romero knew the large landowners in San Miguel and he asked them for contributions for those in need, but social issues were not a top priority for him.[12] As leading biographer Roberto Morozzo della Rocca has written about him during those years, "Romero was neither conservative nor progressive."[13]

Romero was still in San Miguel when the Catholic hierarchy convened the Second Vatican Council in 1962. The conference, which lasted until 1965, radically overhauled the Catholic Church. Vatican II, as it became known, threw out many of the antiquated tenets of Catholic theology and reoriented the church toward the people who filled its pews. While not dismantling the hierarchy, Vatican II emphasized the role of laypeople and included them among the "people of God."[14] The council also overturned the notions that the world is static, the church is separated from earthly issues, and suffering will be rewarded in heaven.[15] Rather, the council stated, it was mistaken to think and act as if "earthly activities" were "utterly foreign to religion, and religion were nothing more than the fulfillment of acts of worship and the observance of a few moral obligations. One of the gravest errors of our time is the dichotomy between the faith which many profess and their day-to-day conduct."[16]

The church committed itself to "more humane and just conditions of life and directing institutions to guaranteeing human dignity," and it did so by recognizing the social and economic realities of the world. "In the midst of huge numbers deprived of the bare necessities of life there are some who live in riches and squander their wealth," the council declared. "Luxury and misery exist side by side. While a few individuals enjoy almost unlimited freedom of choice, the vast majority have no chance whatever of exercising personal initiative and responsibility, and quite often have to live and work in conditions unworthy of human beings."[17] The council called for "strenuous efforts" to "remove as quickly as possible the immense economic inequalities ... connected with individual and social discrimination."[18] The new emphasis on alleviating poverty later came to be known as the "preferential option for the poor."[19]

In 1967, two years after the conclusion of Vatican II and its drastic realignment of Catholic theology, Pope Paul VI issued *Populorum progressio* (On the development of peoples), a document highlighting that the quest for human fulfillment, including spiritual fulfillment, can only be achieved through liberation from oppression. According to Professor Kelly, "If Vatican II redefined how the church understood itself and its mission to the world,

Populorum progressio tried to apply this redefinition concretely in those areas of the world where wealth, opportunity, and freedom were lacking."[20] The encyclical touched on concrete issues, including ones at the heart of El Salvador's reality. "If certain landed estates impede the general prosperity because they are extensive, unused or poorly used, or because they bring hardship to peoples or are detrimental to the interests of the country, the common good sometimes demands their expropriation," wrote Paul VI.[21] But even as he quoted Saint Ambrose in saying that "the earth belongs to everyone, not to the rich," the pope clearly emphasized the interplay between material development and spiritual development, thereby separating Catholic teaching from economic theories like Marxism.[22]

The next year, 1968, the bishops of Latin America met in Medellín, Colombia, and published several documents applying Vatican II to the realities of the region. Unmistakably aligning the Latin American church with the poor, the bishops called for action, saying it was "a time full of zeal for full emancipation, of liberation from every form of servitude."[23] Following the dictates of Vatican II, they rejected the church's previous single-mindedness on eternal salvation and disregard for worldly issues, even going so far as to call for the strengthening of labor unions and *campesino* organizations.[24] The bishops also acknowledged the negative way in which many perceived the church—"that the hierarchy, the clergy, the religious are rich and allied with the rich"—and tasked themselves with modesty and humility.[25] In emphasizing that charity alone was not enough, they called for "criticism of injustice and oppression in the struggle against the intolerable situation that a poor person often has to tolerate."[26] Medellín was, in the words of U.S. journalist and author Penny Lernoux, "one of the major political events of the century: it shattered the centuries old alliance of Church, military, and the rich elites."[27]

At the time of the Medellín conference, Óscar Romero had recently left his post as parish priest in San Miguel to become secretary of the Bishops Conference for El Salvador. At the Jesuit seminary in San Salvador, Romero became friends with Rutilio Grande. In 1970, when Romero became a bishop, he asked Grande to be the master of ceremonies. Reflecting the demands of tradition, the ceremony was extravagant. Romero carried the bishop's staff, complemented by his intricately designed garments, and wore a tall miter on his head. The audience, themselves clad in suits and white dresses, included El Salvador's president and many of the country's elite. The ceremony failed to reflect Medellín's call for modesty, and some members of the clergy believed that Romero was still wedded to the old ways, unsympathetic to the more progressive dictates of Vatican II and Medellín. Romero actually welcomed Vatican II and Medellín but he was not, in the words of biographer James Brockman, "ready to draw from the church's pronouncements all the conclusions that others were drawing."[28]

The same year, Grande penned an article that demonstrated differences between his and Romero's thinking at that time. "It is often said by some," wrote Grande, "that the priest should not get involved in economic or social matters. If he does, he will be called a communist. They will give the following reasons: if you are an engineer you shouldn't get involved with morality, in the same way a priest should not involve himself in economic or social matters. But the comparison is not valid, for while technical things pertain to the engineer and the economist, etc., social and economic realities are necessary to be human, they pertain to all people, and are thus a part of morality."[29] In looking at the situation in El Salvador, Grande called for an overhaul of society, though not from a Marxist perspective. "We need people convinced of the necessity of modifying the existing structures and who will do so despite the greatest enemy—human selfishness," Grande wrote. "To change the structures, alone, would only promote a harmful revolution."[30] Among other changes, Grande called for land reform in El Salvador.[31]

In 1972, Grande had the opportunity to put theory into practice as a parish priest in Aguilares, and the actions he and other young Jesuits implemented came in line with what is known as Liberation Theology.[32] A key focus for the Jesuits was the education of poor and oppressed residents of the area through *concientización,* the raising of consciousness that their intolerable condition was not predestined and could be changed.[33] In this context, the influential Grande and the team of Jesuits began a process in Aguilares that was replicated throughout El Salvador. He and other priests traveled to the small towns of the parish to meet with *campesinos* and held long discussions about the Bible's New Testament and how it applied to the experiences of the people there. The villages created Ecclesial Base Communities, selecting leaders and holding regular meetings, and their improved organization led, through marches and strikes, to demands for reforms.[34] A local woman summed up her feelings about Grande's leadership by saying, "What I remember about him most of all is that one day he asked me what I thought. . . . No one had ever asked me that in all of my 70 years."[35]

The work of Grande and the other Jesuits drew attention. In 1975, a group calling itself the Conservative Religious Front distributed leaflets accusing them of being agitators and "subversives" who had thrown away their faith in God and stirred up class divisions.[36] The same year, El Salvador's military president denounced "liberationist clerics" and in another parish, the National Guard detained and tortured a priest.[37]

By this time, Óscar Romero had been installed as the bishop for the diocese of Santiago de María. His actions there showed a willingness to address governmental abuses, but he took a cautious approach. Before arriving in Santiago de María, Romero had served as editor of the newspaper for the archdiocese of San Salvador, and some believed the content during Romero's tenure had ignored social topics that might be considered controversial. When an editorial waded into more turbulent waters, it did so by denouncing "demagogy and Marxism" in "pamphlets and literature of known red origin" being distributed by a Jesuit high school.[38] The newspaper defended the Medellín conference but argued against its dictates being taken to extremes in articles such as "Medellín, Misunderstood and Mutilated." In response, a journal at the Jesuit Central American University—with which Romero later came to be linked—criticized Romero's newspaper as supporting the status quo and appealing only to those "satisfied with the present situation."[39]

As bishop of Santiago de María, though, Romero was directly confronted with government repression against the people of his diocese. In June 1975, when National Guardsmen murdered five *campesinos* in the community of Tres Calles, Romero denounced the massacre in his homily, calling it an attack on human rights, and complained to the local National Guard commander. Five days later, he wrote a letter to the military president but made no other public condemnation, a cautious strategy he then justified in a memo to the other Salvadoran bishops. According to James Brockman, "Romero's explanation of his actions shows he still believed that the public authorities were not responsible for the crimes of their subordinates and would remedy abuses." Romero thought "he must avoid the embarrassment of speaking out on behalf of victims who might prove to be subversives or criminals."[40]

Romero's attitude toward the more progressive strains in the Salvadoran church remained skeptical, though he recognized the problems the country faced. He penned a memorandum highly critical of various "politicizing" influences in the church, particularly the Jesuits, even as he labeled the military government "repressive" and the country's inequality "cruel."[41] A few months later, Romero gave an interview to one of El Salvador's largest papers and said, "We must keep to the center, watchfully, in the traditional way, but seeking justice." He advocated for the role of priests to be "religious and transcendent," although he cautioned that "the government should not consider a priest who takes a stand for social justice as a politician or a subversive element when he is fulfilling his mission in the politics of the common good."[42]

Meanwhile, Rutilio Grande continued his pastoral work in Aguilares as repression against priests grew more intense with the arrest and torture of Father Rafael Barahona, the bombing of a parish house, and the military government's new campaign of deporting foreign clergymen. In February 1977, Grande delivered probably his most famous sermon in protest against the recent expulsion of a Colombian priest. "What is at stake here is the fundamental question of what it means to be Christian today," Grande said. "If you are a poor priest or a poor catechist in this country from our community, you are slandered, threatened, taken out secretly in the night. . . . It is practically illegal to be Christian in our country." Grande squarely blamed those in power. "The world around us is radically rooted in an established disorder, to which the mere proclamation of the gospel is subversive. . . . Woe to you, hypocrites, who call yourselves Catholics but inside are full of filth and evil!" Grande reminded the congregation that Jesus's radicalism would not be tolerated in El Salvador. "I am fully aware that very soon the Bible and the Gospels will not be allowed to cross the border," he said. "All that will reach us will be the covers, since all the pages are subversive. . . . So that if Jesus crossed the [Salvadoran border], they would not allow him to enter." They would accuse him of being "an agitator, of being a Jewish foreigner, who confuses the people with exotic and foreign ideas." Instead, the powerful want "a mute Christ, without a mouth," or a "God in the clouds" who leaves them alone. But, Grande said, "this is not the Christ of the Gospel! This is not the young Christ, thirty-three years old, who gave his life for the noblest cause of humanity!"[43] Grande's Jesus would have denounced the established powers the same way Grande did.

Amid the turmoil and repression of early 1977, the minister of defense, through yet another fraudulent election, won the presidency, perpetuating the armed forces' unbroken political control over the country. Two days later, the Vatican named Óscar Romero the new archbishop of San Salvador to replace Monsignor Luis Chávez, who had served for nearly four decades and embraced the shift in church doctrine spelled out in Vatican II and Medellín. In deciding on the new archbishop, and following tradition, the papal nuncio, Rome's ambassador to El Salvador, had consulted about forty members of the oligarchy and government. Their opinion was unanimous in favor of

Romero, whom they perceived as conservative and noncontroversial. The clergy preferred someone the elite opposed, Bishop Arturo Rivera Damas, who was a strong advocate against repression, but the Holy See chose Romero.[44] Rivera was told that he was passed over in favor of Romero because the Vatican did not want "anyone who is going to oppose the government."[45]

The new archbishop, however, was not blind to the wave of repression against Catholic priests. The day after he was installed, Romero went to the presidential palace and demanded the release of Father Barahona from prison. According to Tommie Sue Montgomery, author of *Revolution in El Salvador,* the president said to Romero, "I will release Barahona but you cannot ask us to treat [priests] any differently until they go back to their basic business which is religion. These priests of yours," the president said, "have become politicians and I hold you responsible for their behavior." Romero replied, "With all due respect, Mr. President, we take our orders from someone higher."[46]

A few weeks later, Romero called a private meeting to discuss the issue of persecution against the church despite his continued hesitancy to address the topic publicly. The priests in attendance, many of whom faced oppression every day in their parishes, were adamant in their views but Romero was more tentative. Rutilio Grande, who knew Romero well, spoke up and said, "Monseñor, I have many sheep. They live up in the hills. I have sent them up to the hills so that they can be all right. So if you say that there is no persecution, I'm going to call them down to the valley."

"Well, no, no, it is better that they stay up in the hills, where they stay hidden," Romero said.

"Then there is still persecution?" Grande asked rhetorically. Romero did not answer, and the meeting ended inconclusively.[47]

Grande was murdered two days later. Romero went to Aguilares that evening and saw the bodies of his friend and the other two victims laid out on tables, wrapped in white sheets.[48] He decided to say a mass for them in Aguilares even though it was late at night. The tragedy of the moment—the nascence of Romero's rise to a position of tremendous responsibility, the bloodied corpse of his friend before him, the knowledge that a death squad, and perhaps even the institutional military, had declared open season for killing priests—weighed heavily on Romero.

Some who knew Romero say the killing radically altered his thinking, while others claim it was simply a tipping point for the already evolving archbishop.[49] Regardless, Grande's assassination laid bare for Romero the fanaticism of those who labeled priests Communists and terrorists for supporting poor *campesinos,* and it starkly depicted the repression awaiting those who spoke out against injustice. Whether or not he had a conversion, there is no doubt that from that moment, Romero became a dedicated champion for the poor and oppressed. While preaching at Grande's public funeral, Romero spoke repeatedly of Christian "liberation," a concept that was not merely political or economic but also spiritual.[50] The same day, in an inflammatory act in such a Catholic country, Romero declared that he would boycott all government events unless the state did everything possible to solve Grande's murder. Romero cancelled every mass in the archdiocese the following Sunday in favor of a single celebration, a *misa única,* in San Salvador's cathedral. The decision brought vocal opposition from members of the oligarchy, who called it a provocation, and from the papal nuncio, who thought it contrary to Catholic doctrine, but Romero held fast that the solitary mass was a needed demonstration of church unity.[51]

The next Sunday, March 20, 1977, brought a packed cathedral and tens of thousands of worshippers filling the plaza outside. Romero, normally a gifted speaker, sounded uncomfortable as he began preaching. A priest in attendance said the new archbishop seemed "reluctant to go through the door of history that God was opening up for him." But Romero found his voice as he thanked the priests of the archdiocese, acknowledging the danger they faced, and he mentioned Grande's name to thunderous applause. Invoking the solidarity he felt in the cathedral and the defiant role into which he was now casting himself, Romero pledged to his clergy, "Whoever touches one of my priests touches me."[52]

From that day, the emboldened archbishop publicly denounced the military government for atrocities, filling his sermons with details of the latest killings and showing his clear support for the largest segment of the Salvadoran population: the poor. The traditional, oligarch-owned media usually avoided covering government abuses, so the broadcasts of Romero's Sunday homilies over the archdiocese's radio station were often the only source for information about atrocities committed by the security forces and the death squads. For that, the station's transmitter or antenna would be bombed ten times in the next three years.[53]

The situation only grew worse for the Catholic Church during Romero's next few months as archbishop. In May, a death squad killed another priest along with a fourteen-year-old boy. A shadowy group calling itself the White

Warriors Union claimed responsibility for the assassination, saying it was in retaliation for the recent murder of El Salvador's foreign minister by leftist guerrillas. Romero, in an example of the worlds he was attempting to bridge, presided over both funerals. Even so, he did not shy away from publicly criticizing the military government over the situation. "I would like to address my words from here to the president of the republic," Romero said, "if what he told me yesterday by telephone was sincere, that he would be concerned to investigate this murder, just as he would be concerned . . . about that of his foreign minister. The life of [the foreign minister] was sacred but so was the life of the priest who is lost to us today, as was the life of Father Grande." Despite the president's promises to investigate, Romero said, "we are still far from knowing the truth."[54] The same month, fliers began circulating with the slogan "Be a patriot, kill a priest."[55]

In June, the White Warriors Union made international news by sending Salvadoran priests and newspapers a document titled "War Order No. 6" that proclaimed, "All Jesuits without exception must leave the country forever within 30 days of this date. . . . The immediate and systematic execution of all Jesuits who remain in the country will proceed until we have finished with all of them." The Jesuits, backed by international support and pressure on the Salvadoran government, refused to leave, and the deadline passed without retribution.[56] A few years later, Romero himself would get a threat letter—among the hundreds he received—from the White Warriors Union, mailed to him in a Defense Ministry envelope.[57] Many would later assert that the leader of the group was Roberto D'Aubuisson.[58]

The attacks on the church came not only from faceless death squads but also through columns and advertisements, *campos pagados,* placed in El Salvador's largest newspapers by organizations representing the interests of landholders and the oligarchy, most prominently the Eastern Regional Agricultural Front (FARO) and the National Association of Private Enterprise (ANEP).[59] This "shrill campaign," as a former U.S. ambassador called it, did not necessarily call for violence against the clergy but harshly slandered priests, including bishops like Romero and Rivera, and often called them Communists.[60] The worst was a smaller tabloid, *La Opinión,* that in December 1977 carried the headline "Monseñor Romero Directs Terrorist Group," subtitled "Archbishop Great Ally of Agents of Subversion."[61] In just a few months, Romero had gone from being the consensus choice of the oligarchy to a primary target of their vitriol and condemnation.[62]

"Who did [Robert D'Aubuisson] perceive at that time to be the enemy of his faction within El Salvador?" Nico van Aelstyn asks Professor Terry Karl.

"I think the way D'Aubuisson thought is that anybody who wasn't his very close friend was his enemy. And the reason I put it that way is that his enemy was a broad umbrella of anybody who wasn't a hard-line military officer. And that umbrella was focused primarily, in my view, on the Christian Democratic Party, as a party, and on the church."

"On the church itself?"

"On the church, absolutely." Karl explains:

> I don't quite know how to express the visceral animosity to the changes that were going on in the church. . . . I took a delegation of congressmen and senators from Massachusetts to El Salvador, who were trying to learn about El Salvador. And they asked the man who was the president of the [Salvadoran] Chamber of Commerce this question. They said, "Sir, is it the Cubans, the Soviets, and Nicaraguans that are causing problems here in El Salvador?" This was in Spanish. . . . And the landowner said, "No, it is not the Cubans, it is not the Soviets, it is not the Nicaraguans." And so a senator, who was Catholic, said, "So who is it who is causing these problems here in El Salvador, sir?" And the landowner said, "Es la iglesia." "It's the church." . . . I actually did the translation at this moment, so when I turned to the delegation and said, "It's the church," they started saying, "He didn't say that. You must have misunderstood." And I said, "No, he says the Catholic Church is causing all the problems." And they said, "No, you must have misunderstood." So we were having this conversation in English on the side and it turned out that the landowner spoke perfect English, so he turned around and said to the senators and delegation there, he said, "No, no, congressmen. It's the church. It's the Catholic Church."[63]

EL SALVADOR—1977

As damaged as his standing became among many in the oligarchy, Romero's relationship with the military government was equally bad. When *campesino* families in Aguilares, Rutilio Grande's former parish, took over a plantation whose owner had evicted them from the small plots they traditionally leased, the National Guard forced the occupiers out and, after a confrontation led to deaths on both sides, the soldiers ransacked the town. The National Guard converted the church into a barracks, shooting up the tabernacle and scattering the communion hosts on the ground. When Romero arrived to assess the situation, the National Guard denied him entry to the church and briefly arrested the military chaplain whom Romero sent as a messenger.[64]

Several days later, an exasperated Romero wrote to the military president, "I do not understand, Mr. President, how you can declare yourself before the nation a Catholic by upbringing and by conviction and yet allow these unspeakable outrages on the part of the Security Forces in a country that we call civilized and Christian." Seeking an explanation for the maddening refusal to let him enter the Aguilares church, Romero asked a question that would have seemed absurd in many places, but not in El Salvador: "Can it be that even the person of the Archbishop endangers the security of the state?"[65] One month later, when the National Guard's occupation of Aguilares finally ended, Romero went to the town to say mass. He began his homily by lamenting, "It has become my job to tend to all the wounds produced by the persecution of the Church—to record the abuses and pick up the bodies." After the service, the archbishop invited the congregation to lead a procession to, in the words of a priest who was there, "purify the places that the National Guard had profaned." When some of the remaining soldiers saw the march, they blocked the road and pointed their rifles at the parishioners. Romero, at the back of the procession, shouted *"¡Adelante!"* and the people moved forward as the soldiers yielded.[66]

Romero understood the importance of documenting the widespread human rights violations in El Salvador and providing legal support to the country's most vulnerable. To carry out this dangerous work, he looked to Socorro Jurídico. When Romero became archbishop, Socorro Jurídico was a legal aid office providing free services to those who could not afford lawyers. After the murder of Rutilio Grande, it was the only law office that dared to help people affiliated with the Catholic Church. Romero respected the courage and skill of the young lawyers and students, and he invited them to work under the auspices of the archdiocese. The office quickly evolved from a legal aid clinic into a human rights organization investigating murders, disappearances, and arbitrary detentions. Romero used Socorro Jurídico's evidence extensively in his homilies.[67] According to its first director, Roberto Cuéllar, the group documented the abuses carefully "so [the government] could never claim that his denunciations were made up."

As Romero confronted the repression, his stature grew at home and abroad. Adoration for him soared among El Salvador's poor, and a group of

British parliamentarians nominated him for the Nobel Peace Prize. But that positive foreign attention reflected a view far different than the coverage Romero received in El Salvador from the country's right-wing news media. At the same time, Romero was dealing with a troubling split in the hierarchy of the Salvadoran church. While Romero, as archbishop of the most populated region of the country, was most prominent among the Catholic leadership, he did not have any formal authority outside his archdiocese. By 1978, the majority of the Salvadoran Bishops Conference was aligned against Romero, with four of the bishops opposed to the course he had charted and only Bishop Rivera supporting him. The other bishops, unable to mask their disdain for the perceived radicalization of their colleague, occasionally denounced him in public. Romero sometimes responded in kind, resulting in the unseemly airing of ecclesiastical dirty laundry, including through correspondence sent directly to the Vatican.[68]

Violence continued in waves during 1978 and into 1979, including a massacre of over two dozen demonstrators on the stairs of San Salvador's cathedral, and Romero received near-daily threats. One came in a letter mailed to the archdiocese, addressed to Romero and signed by "the Falange," a group taking its name from Franco's fascist movement in Spain. A bold swastika dominated the left side of the page. "The swastika, symbol of the bitter enemy of Communism, is our emblem," the author wrote. "We have a long list of priests, teachers, workers, students, and employees, whom we will be eliminating. You, Monseñor, are at the head, among the group of clergy that at any moment will receive thirty bullets in the face and chest."[69]

Even though many in the oligarchy despised him, Romero still maintained relationships with wealthy Salvadorans and met with the families of those who were kidnapped by left-wing guerrillas.[70] He also comforted those on the other side of the growing divide, the *campesina* mothers whose sons were disappeared by the security forces. He visited rural parishes and endured National Guard searches, sometimes being forced to put his hands on the roof of his car like a criminal.[71] Romero mediated labor strikes at factories, called on the popular organizations to stop their occupations of churches, and denounced as "spies" the government agents who taped his Sunday homilies.

When reformist officers carried out the coup d'état in October 1979, Romero was sympathetic to their agenda and gave the new junta every opportunity to succeed.[72] Even as the security forces and death squads intensified their campaign of terror, he backed the new government in hopes that it could pull the country back from the abyss, a position that put him at odds with many on the political left and in the popular organizations.[73] Romero, though, preferred to reform the junta without seeing its complete elimination, and he tried in vain to broker a compromise between the civilian and military members who were increasingly in conflict. Yet even as he sought a resolution, he publicly called for José Guillermo García, the defense minster at the head of the armed forces, to resign.[74] Instead, it was the civilians who left the government in disgust in January 1980.

The second junta, pairing the military with the centrist Christian Democrats, did not garner great favor from Romero, and he began to speak out more forcefully in February as bodies literally piled up in the streets. Romero detailed the horrors in every one of his Sunday homilies. "Many bodies with signs of torture have appeared in different areas of the country," he said on February 24. "Each day an average of six bodies are found, but these bodies are unable to be identified. . . . Some of the bodies are marked with the initials of criminal groups of the extreme right." He gave specific examples, like the bodies of two men being thrown out of a moving car. "They were tortured and their throats were cut. . . . During the month of February at least fifty *campesinos* have died after being tortured or machine-gunned."[75]

Romero harshly condemned the oligarchs and the security forces for the worsening situation. "There are among us those who sell the just ones for money and the poor for a pair of sandals," he said. "Those who pile up spoils and plunder in their palaces, who crush the poor, who bring on a reign of violence while reclining on beds of ivory."[76] Romero called out Roberto D'Aubuisson by name. Quoting a program aired on the archdiocese's radio station, he said, "We want to single out the intervention of Mr. D'Aubuisson for what it is, defamatory and filled with lies. We hope that the armed forces are able to see the lack of truthfulness in this man who wants to call a torturer a national hero, who doesn't want to take responsibility for those who have been disappeared, assassinated or tortured. One who confuses the words of the [paramilitaries] with the reality of their threats and assassinations and puts forth false testimony that doesn't fool even the dumbest person."[77]

Even as he denounced the military and the oligarchs, Romero did not spare the Christian Democrats, who were now the only civilians in the junta. He criticized their presence in the government for "covering up the repressive nature of the current regime."[78] In return, some Christian Democrats considered Romero a political neophyte, a man more gullible than realistic. One described him as "easily influenced by the masses" with "a really romantic conception of social justice."[79] Some in Jimmy Carter's U.S. administration concurred with the Christian Democrats, who were close allies of the White House. Carter's assistant secretary of state for inter-American affairs, William Bowdler, characterized Romero as a "weak archbishop, strongly influenced by an idealistic but naïve Jesuit cadre." He recommended that the U.S. government try to get Romero sent to the Vatican to give El Salvador a break from his scathing Sunday homilies and allow the pope to "talk to him about [the] role of the Church in El Salvador."[80] U.S. national security advisor Zbigniew Brzezinski complained directly to the pope about the archbishop's lack of support for the second junta.[81]

Romero only complicated matters by penning a letter to President Carter protesting the United States' plan to send riot-control equipment and advisors to El Salvador, which he then read in his Sunday homily. Describing his fear of an "arms race in El Salvador," Romero lectured the U.S. president, "Your government's contribution, instead of favoring greater justice and peace in El Salvador, will undoubtedly sharpen the injustice and the repression suffered by the organized people, whose struggle has often been for respect for their most basic human rights." He continued, "If you truly want to defend human rights, I ask you to not allow this military aid to go to the Salvadoran government, and to guarantee that your government will not intervene directly or indirectly with military, economic or diplomatic pressure to determine the destiny of the Salvadoran people."[82] The letter did not block the military assistance, but it gained Romero greater support in many Salvadoran circles for his willingness to challenge the seemingly omnipotent Yankees.[83]

During the final month of Romero's life, the situation in El Salvador deteriorated on all fronts. A bomb successfully destroyed the transmitter for the archdiocese's radio station.[84] The junta implemented a first phase of land reform but simultaneously imposed a state of siege. This led to a capture of large estates that infuriated the oligarchy but also fostered greater repression in the countryside, dismaying *campesinos* and the Left.[85] A death squad killed the attorney general, a Christian Democrat, after Roberto D'Aubuisson publicly denounced him as a Communist. D'Aubuisson likewise threatened Romero on television, warning, "You still have time to change your ways."[86]

Amid escalating violence and political tension, new U.S. ambassador Robert White arrived in San Salvador. White's task was to hold the middle together and help prevent a civil war that would lead to a Marxist takeover. White, in a blunt assessment of the Salvadoran reality, advised the U.S. State Department, "It is vital to understand that no moderate government can succeed without the support of Archbishop Romero and the Church."[87] But Romero had lost confidence in the junta, and with each passing week, his preaching became more strident. Knowing that hundreds of thousands tuned in to his Sunday homilies on the radio, he continued to call on the oligarchs to reform, saying, "Let them not keep killing those of us who are trying to achieve a more just sharing of the power and wealth of our country. . . . But let it be known that no one can any longer kill the voice of justice."[88] He also criticized the armed guerrillas, particularly for their killings, but he put their actions in context compared to those of the government security forces. "We do not overlook the sins of the Left also," he said. "But they are not in proportion to the amount of repressive violence."[89]

Romero understood the danger he faced by speaking out.[90] He often drove his car alone to avoid additional casualties should anyone make an attempt on his life, but he refused the protection of bodyguards.[91] On March 10, a sacristan in the Sagrado Corazón Basilica found a briefcase near the altar where Romero had said mass the previous day. The case contained an undetonated bomb with over seventy sticks of dynamite.[92]

On March 16, Romero's Sunday homily ran almost two hours. "You are the principal protagonists in this hour of change," he told the oligarchs. "On you depends in great part the end of the violence." To the recalcitrant segment of the armed forces, he said, "Do not be obstructionists. In so historic a moment for the nation you are performing a sad role of betrayal." Confirming his allegiance with the nonviolent Left, he explained, "Someone criticized me as if I wanted to lump together in one sector the popular forces and the guerrilla groups. The difference is always very clear in my mind. To the latter, and to those who advocate violent solutions, I appeal for understanding that nothing violent can be lasting."[93]

Vehement though these words were, Romero intended his homily of the next week, March 23, to go further still. The day before the Sunday mass, Romero conferred, as he did every week, with a group of trusted clergy, and he stunned them by announcing his intention to call on government soldiers to disobey the immoral orders of their superiors. The priests, having experienced repression first-hand and fully aware of the numerous threats against Romero, counseled him against such a drastic step. They foresaw the rage such a challenge would incite among the military, the oligarchy, and the death squads. Romero listened to their arguments, but he retired to write the homily without indicating whether they had changed his mind.[94]

Father Bill Wipfler testifies that he arrived in El Salvador with a delegation of U.S. religious leaders on March 21, 1980, and they saw Romero the next afternoon, the same day Romero met with his own advisors.[95]

"He was very welcoming and very grateful," Wipfler says. "He was saying that the moral fiber of the society was falling to pieces. He described some of the things that were being done, like the cutting off of the fingertips of people and pouring acid on their faces so that the victims could not be identified, and bodies left nude and so on."

"Did he indicate that this was a worsening of the human rights situation then?" Nico van Aelstyn asks Wipfler.

"He said it was getting deeper into the 'barbarity.' That was the phrase he used. . . . Then he did something which was very moving to all of us. He asked [Franciscan priest] Father McCoy to come celebrate mass the next day with him. . . . He asked Tom Quigley from the U.S. Catholic Conference to read one of the scripture readings and asked me, a non–Roman Catholic Protestant Episcopalian, to read one of the other readings. We felt that was a considerable honor, to be asked to participate in his Sunday mass."

The next morning, March 23, the Sagrado Corazón Basilica overflowed with people. The larger cathedral was unavailable due to repairs. "We arrived early," Wipfler says. "It was already full. People were gathering in the streets because there were loudspeakers just outside the church so that people could hear the mass and the sermon."

"Was that different from church services you had experienced in the U.S.?" Nico asks.

"That was when attendance was falling off in [U.S.] churches and one might find that there was lots of room to sit down in most cases. [But] in the Basilica, there were no chairs. The congregation stood except for the elderly—there were some pews left in the front—but the remainder of the church was just an open space, and everyone stood."

"Throughout the entire service?"

"Throughout the entire service. We happened to be the dignitaries who were present for the event, so we sat toward the altar. The altar was in the center, and we were on the side . . . within a few feet of the altar."

"Did you hear Monseñor Romero's sermon that day?"

"I did."

Our technician presses play on his computer and Romero's voice fills the courtroom. His words are measured, his tone surprisingly calm, as he analyzes the day's readings.

Wipfler describes Romero's methodology. "There was always this marvelous use of the biblical readings for the day that were then applied to the contemporary situation. . . . It was that marvelous biblical presentation about the Exodus and the return and how El Salvador is coming back from its exodus."

"There are traditionally other portions of his homilies?" Nico asks.

"Yes, the two other parts are always the catalog . . . of human rights violations, and then some conclusion that was a moral demand or an ethical requirement."

Romero's calm but insistent voice returns. "And something very horrible, very important, on this same day, Thursday the 20th, the *campesino* Augustín Sánchez was found alive. He had been captured by fifteen soldiers from Zacatecoluca who handed him over to the [security forces]. . . . They held him for four days, torturing him without food or water, with constant beatings and suffocation." Romero goes through other abuses committed during the week before he concludes, "Without its roots in the people, no government can be effective, much less so when it seeks to impose itself by the force of bloodshed and pain."

As the recording stops, Nico turns to Father Wipfler, "It sounded like there was applause at the portion there. Is that right?"

"Yes," Wipfler says. "I happen to come from a very traditional religious community. And I was rather startled by the fact that about ten times during the sermon—it's only happened once to me—but ten times during his sermon, at least, he was applauded. And people, as I said, were on their feet. It was an amazing thing to see that kind of a response occurring throughout this sermon."

"You mentioned that there was usually a third portion of the sermon?"

"Yes. The third portion is always this kind of ethical obligation that everyone has . . . and that was always at the end of the sermon."

Over the speakers, we hear Romero arrive at the defining moment of his life. Ignoring the previous day's advice from his inner circle, he delivers the lines that sealed his fate and his legacy. "I would like to make a special appeal to the men of the army, and in particular, to the troops of the National Guard, the police, the garrisons. Brothers, you are part of our very own people. You kill your own *campesino* brothers. In the face of an order to kill given by a man, the law of God that says 'thou shalt not kill' must prevail." The audience explodes into sustained applause.

"No soldier is obliged to obey an order contrary to the law of God."

More applause.

"No one has to comply with an immoral law."

Now they clap after every line.

"It is time now that you recover your conscience and obey its dictates rather than the command of sin. The church, defender of the rights of God, of the law of God, of human dignity, of personal dignity, cannot remain silent before such an abomination. We want the government to take seriously that their reforms mean nothing if they come bathed in so much blood."

The audience, sensing the escalation in Romero's words, continues clapping as he speaks.

"In the name of God, then, and in the name of this suffering people whose cries rise to heaven more tumultuously every day, I beseech you, I beg you, I order you, in the name of God, stop the repression!"

The applause builds, rolling through the Basilica and echoing in our courtroom. Romero's words hang in the air. They are among the most famous in the history of El Salvador.

When silence returns, Nico turns back to Father Wipfler. "Do you recall your reaction when you heard Monseñor Romero speak those words at the end of his homily?"

"Yes. I turned to Mr. Quigley, who was sitting beside me, and I said, 'I don't think that the military is going to let this one pass by.'"

The remainder of the mass went by normally, Wipfler says, "but then I was rather startled by the fact that the archbishop . . . was the only one that gave communion. He gave communion to absolutely everyone in the congregation. It took more than a half an hour. He walked through the church and gave communion to every single person in the church. I think a lot of them would have felt cheated if it would have been by anybody else."

"How did that communion portion of the service end?"

"This is a very hard part for me. He came back . . . Excuse me." Wipfler tears up.

He came back from giving communion. I am not a Roman Catholic. I had not presented myself for communion. . . . I had my eyes closed. I was praying for the church and for the people. And I heard a voice. It was the archbishop. He said, "Would you like to receive communion, Father?" And I said, "Yes." And he gave me communion. I was very moved. It was an incredible gesture. . . . And I only realized later, when I was preaching a sermon later that week at home, that I was the last person ever to receive communion from the archbishop, because he died before he finished the mass the next day. And that's always been a very important treasure in my life.

FIVE

"A Bed to Drop Dead In"

THE SEARCH FOR ÁLVARO SARAVIA AND
THE DEATH SQUAD FINANCIERS

FRESNO—AUGUST 2004

Judge Wanger is stern but not hostile as he quizzes Nico van Aelstyn. "It is stated under oath that the Center for Justice & Accountability, which is an institute that is located in San Francisco, California, had done background investigation to locate the defendant, and he is named Álvaro Rafael Saravia in the complaint," the judge says. "As of 2001, there was a report that the defendant was resident in Miami, and that there were family members in Miami. . . . The defendant then moved to California to . . . Manor Oak Drive, Modesto. . . . I just want to confirm with you the additional evidence that gives you the confidence to know that this was the place of residence of the right Saravia."

"Yes, Your Honor," Nico says, anticipating the question for which we have long prepared. "We have no doubt about that."[1]

SAN FRANCISCO—AUGUST 2003

My CJA colleagues and I still have not seen Álvaro Saravia in Modesto, but we can't wait much longer to file a case against him. The legal deadline, imposed by a statute of limitations, is fast approaching and as we draft the paperwork necessary to initiate the lawsuit, we decide that the lack of visual contact with Saravia is not fatal. We aren't pursuing a criminal prosecution, for which the perpetrator's presence is essential, because criminal charges aren't possible under U.S. law. Our civil lawsuit under the Alien Tort Statute only requires proof that the defendant has connections to the local area, and we feel sure that

Saravia's numerous links on paper to the Manor Oak address will be enough to convince the court. We move ahead without the visual proof.

We have also reached an agreement with a private law firm to serve as CJA's cocounsel. The firm, Heller Ehrman, possesses the experience, staffing, and money to litigate what promises to be a complex case, something CJA can't do alone. Founded in 1890, with over six hundred lawyers from Anchorage to Beijing, representing clients like Microsoft and Sony, Heller is the cream of the crop, but the partner taking the case, Nico van Aelstyn, is not the stereotype of a corporate lawyer. Nico specializes in environmental law and has a history of political activism, particularly about El Salvador. During law school in the 1980s, he was arrested for protesting U.S. support for the Salvadoran military that was then dropping white phosphorus—a highly painful and potentially lethal chemical—on civilian areas during the civil war. When the war ended, Nico went to El Salvador as an observer for the first nationwide elections, and he monitored polling stations in San Miguel, the province where Archbishop Romero was born. He later connected with CJA through Patty Blum, with whom he had worked on cases of Central American asylum seekers.

Joining the team from Nico's firm is senior associate Russell Cohen. Originally from Canada, Russ, like Nico, is very smart, with a sharp memory and impeccable instincts. His straitlaced appearance masks a wonderful personality and a rebellious streak that runs in the family. His grandfather was once a leader in Canada's Communist Party, before quitting after he learned about Joseph Stalin's horrific crimes. In just a week, Russ has immersed himself in every detail of the Romero case, and the fact that he does not speak a word of Spanish and has no previous experience in Central America matters little to his capabilities.

On September 12, just ahead of our deadline, CJA and Heller Ehrman file the lawsuit against Saravia in Fresno, the federal court closest to Modesto. That night, a process server rings the doorbell at Saravia's house on Manor Oak Drive, but there is no answer. The following day, a neighbor says he has never heard of Saravia, but a woman named Inés Olsson lives in the house with a young man. This matches the public records in our files. When the process server returns to the house, the young man, who turns out to be Olsson's nephew, answers. Only he and Olsson live at the address, he says, though he has heard Olsson mention a "Mr. Álvaro."[2]

The next day, Inés Olsson is home but she insists to the process server that Saravia has never lived there. She has only met Saravia once, she claims, and he was just a friend of a friend who used her address to receive mail. Olsson accepts the court documents but calls Nico the next day to protest. Almost immediately, she contradicts her story. Saravia used to live at her house, she admits, and he registered several businesses there but she hasn't seen him in months and doesn't know how to contact him. Olsson disparages our case as "old news" that people should just forget. When a *Modesto Bee* reporter visits the Manor Oak home, a woman, who refuses to provide her name, tells the reporter, "I know [Saravia] very well." The woman, who we assume is Olsson, calls the lawsuit "very ridiculous." She implies that Saravia is living in hardship. "The poor guy does not even have a bed to drop dead in."[3] His apparent situation is in sharp contrast to the lives of the people whose interests he used to serve in El Salvador.

FRESNO—AUGUST 2004

"In that period of time," Judge Wanger asks the expert witness, Professor Terry Karl, "let's just take October [1979] through the assassination, if he was being compensated, who was Saravia compensated by?"

"It's a question that there has been a great deal of attention on," Karl says. "First of all, there are a group of wealthy Salvadorans located in El Salvador, in Miami, and in Guatemala who are helping to finance these activities, although that financing goes directly to Roberto D'Aubuisson, who subsequently pays it out. And you will see . . . that Mr. Saravia then becomes in fact the record keeper and paymaster." Karl also mentions money coming from the military high command, a kidnapping-for-profit ring, and perhaps, narco-trafficking.

"And from this," the judge says, "I infer that the best information you have is that the money went to D'Aubuisson from either the landowners, I will call it the oligarchy, or the military high command, and there is evidence that Saravia was then compensated by D'Aubuisson?"

"That's right."[4]

SAN SALVADOR—JANUARY 1981

Many of the cables going from the U.S. embassy in San Salvador to the State Department in Washington, D.C., carried provocative titles, but this one—

"Millionaires' Murder Inc.?"—was more alarmist than usual. The dispatch cited "a highly respected Salvadoran lawyer who has been well and favorably known to the embassy for many years." He told an embassy official that "a group of six Salvadoran millionaire émigrés in Miami have directed and financed rightwing death squads here for nearly a year, that they are trying to destroy the moderate reformist government by terrorizing its officials as well as the businessmen who cooperate with its reform program."

These "Miami Six" allegedly ran their enterprise with ruthless determination, as the telegram described:

> The lawyer then said that he was leaving [El Salvador] because he had resisted intense pressures from the ultraright for six months but he was now certain that they would kill anyone who stood in the way of their plan. . . . He said he had spent the last three days talking to wealthy people here who have been interrogated and threatened in Miami. . . . These men have been called to Miami and seated at the end of a long table, facing the "Six," and made to answer such questions as "Why are you contributing to the Communist victory by keeping your business open?" . . . Then it is carefully explained to them that to rebuild the country on a new foundation it must first be destroyed totally, the economy must be wrecked, unemployment must be massive, the junta must be ousted and a "good" military officer brought to power who will carry out a total "limpieza" (cleansing), killing three or four or five hundred thousand people, whatever it takes to get rid of all the Communists and their allies. Then and only then can the wealthy elite return to preside over the reconstruction of the country on a new foundation where the rights of property will be secured forever.

As the lawyer left, he reminded the embassy official, "All are in Miami, hatch plots, hold constant meetings and communicate instructions to D'Aubuisson."[5]

If the lawyer was telling the truth, the cable reflected what everyone in El Salvador intuitively knew, that death squads like D'Aubuisson's could not have existed without funding.[6] Though the men on the ground, like Saravia, were true believers and zealous anti-Communists, the people who had the most to lose from the junta's land reform or a takeover by leftist guerrillas were the oligarchs who dominated El Salvador's economy.

While the cable, and the names it contained, remained secret, U.S. ambassador Robert White soon told the media that rich Salvadorans were funding the death squads from Miami. Several of the wealthy expats, who had already banded together and hired a Washington, D.C., public relations firm, responded publicly. "We don't eat children. We're not savages," said Alfonso Salaverría, whose family was one of El Salvador's most important coffee producers.[7] "We are not oligarchs in the sense of exploiters. We developed our country. . . . We are like the pioneers of the United States."[8] Orlando de Sola, whose family owned coffee and sugar mills, said, "The day I need to kill someone, I wouldn't send someone else. I'd do it with my own hands."[9]

SAN FRANCISCO—SEPTEMBER 2003

Despite the denials that date back decades, there is circumstantial evidence that some wealthy Salvadorans provided direct support to D'Aubuisson's and other paramilitary groups. If true, this could implicate them, even if indirectly, in the Romero assassination. At our deadline for filing against Saravia, we don't feel we have enough proof to bring anyone else into the case, but alongside Saravia's name, the court papers list "Doe 1" through "Doe 10" as placeholder defendants. We hope to have sufficient evidence later to specify who they are. Under the jurisdictional rules, we can't sue anyone without strong U.S. connections, so we will examine those Salvadorans who still own businesses and homes in U.S. cities. Gathering proof about anyone who underwrote D'Aubuisson's death squad—and possibly the murder of Archbishop Romero—will be our primary focus for the next year.

Our best evidence, better even than the Miami Six cable, is the Saravia Diary seized at Finca San Luis in May 1980, two months after the assassination. Its pages, and the loose sheets captured with it, are filled with recognizable Salvadoran names. In addition to Alfonso Salaverría, they include men like Ricardo Simán, the president of a major department store chain;[10] Francisco Guirola, a D'Aubuisson confidant detained in Texas while carrying suitcases stuffed with nearly $6 million in cash;[11] and Orlando Llovera, a man later arrested for running a kidnapping ring.[12] But their inclusion in the diary does not tell us precisely what contributions they made. Did they provide financing for the death squad? Did they have meetings with D'Aubuisson? Were they part of his ostensibly political organization, FAN? The description of the Saravia Diary as "informational goulash" was correct at least in its ability to conclusively answer those questions.

The arrest of D'Aubuisson, Saravia, and other extremists at Finca San Luis caused an immediate backlash among D'Aubuisson's supporters. A group of mostly well-to-do women, known as the Frente Femenino, demanded D'Aubuisson's release. Because the military commander who ordered the Finca San Luis raid, Colonel Adolfo Majano, was openly aligned with the U.S. government, the Frente Femenino blockaded the residence of U.S. ambassador Robert White. White had to enlist the U.S. Marines to ram through the barricade.[13] The protests, along with maneuvers by hard-liners within the Salvadoran armed forces, succeeded in springing D'Aubuisson, Saravia, and the others from jail in spite of the incriminating evidence against them. Some of the freed men fled to Guatemala to regroup.[14]

In Guatemala, D'Aubuisson's team deepened a relationship with a key anti-Communist figure, Mario Sandoval Alarcón, who was a former vice president of Guatemala and the founder of a political party he called "the party of organized violence."[15] According to Sandoval, when D'Aubuisson and the others first met him in 1979, they only cared about weapons and paramilitary activities, but Sandoval advised them against being "only a terrorist organization."[16] To push their agenda, Sandoval told them to become politically active, and D'Aubuisson took the guidance to heart. Though D'Aubuisson's links to violence did not abate, he began building a political movement through an ambitious plan to convert FAN—his organization that held press conferences to denounce Communists and traitors—from a collection of angry oligarchs into a national party. Borrowing from the name and platform of U.S. Republicans, D'Aubuisson later dubbed his new political force the Nationalist Republican Alliance, known by its Spanish acronym, ARENA.[17]

D'Aubuisson and some of his devotees, armed with weapons and nationalist fervor, began returning clandestinely to El Salvador to organize supporters throughout the countryside, tapping into the vast spy network that D'Aubuisson and others in military intelligence had developed throughout the 1970s.[18] At the same time, D'Aubuisson's wealthy civilian compatriots established relationships in the United States through influential conservative circles, including the Heritage Foundation and the office of Senator Jesse Helms.[19] In mid-1980, just a few months after the Finca San Luis raid, D'Aubuisson even joined them on a trip to Washington, D.C., embarrassing Jimmy Carter's administration by his open presence in the country.[20] The State Department revoked D'Aubuisson's visa and forced him to leave.

In El Salvador, the situation worsened. Even with strong U.S. support for the centrist members of the Salvadoran government, the spiraling violence did not stop, largely because the civilians and military moderates in the government could not control the hard-liners who ran the security forces and the death squads. Even as the government implemented needed policy reforms, the military repression continued unabated.

Priests and others linked to the Catholic Church remained targets. In November 1980, an "anti-Communist brigade" left a threat letter on the door of a parish house in Chalatenango, the home of U.S. Maryknoll nuns Ita Ford and Maura Clarke, who worked with *campesinos* in the surrounding countryside. The letter showed a drawing of a bloody knife thrust into a skull accompanied by the words, "In this house there are Communists. Everyone who enters here will die. Try it and see."[21] A few weeks later, as Ford and Clarke were driving with Ursuline nun Dorothy Kazel and lay missionary Jean Donovan, National Guardsmen intercepted them and took them to a remote area. The soldiers raped and murdered the four churchwomen before burning their van. The entire operation was preplanned.[22]

By coincidence, Kazel and Donovan had eaten dinner at the house of U.S. ambassador Robert White the evening before. Their deaths would dominate the remainder of White's short tenure in El Salvador. The murders made headlines in the United States, and the Carter administration quickly dispatched a high-level team to investigate. The U.S. government also suspended payment of aid to the Salvadoran military but, typical of President Carter's contradictory policies, resumed it a month later out of fear that the Salvadoran government would be overthrown by Marxist rebels.[23] The resumption came despite Ambassador White's assertion that "it will be a rare person who will not conclude that [Salvadoran] security forces killed the churchwomen and that high officials were involved in the cover-up."[24]

By this time, White's days as ambassador were numbered. Ronald Reagan had defeated Jimmy Carter in the presidential election, and Reagan's arrival promised to end whatever remained of Carter's emphasis on human rights in U.S. foreign policy, including, at least for a time, an abandonment of White's strategy of taming El Salvador's Far Right.[25] This was particularly true when on January 10, 1981, four days after the "Millionaires' Murder Inc.?" cable and ten days before Reagan's inauguration, the unified guerrilla armies in El Salvador, their ranks swelling with leftists who had given up on the peaceful negotiations Ambassador White was pushing for, launched a major offensive that plunged the country into all-out civil war.

Shortly after, the new Reagan administration recalled White from his post, and Secretary of State Alexander Haig took the rare step of forcing White out of the Foreign Service. White blamed the firing on his refusal to follow Haig's order to use official channels to obfuscate the Salvadoran military's responsibility for the murder of the U.S. churchwomen.[26] White had written in a cable, "I will have no part of any cover-up."[27]

Haig replaced White with a new ambassador, Deane Hinton. With El Salvador now in an open civil war, the Reagan administration reasserted its support for the Salvadoran high command, something that would be more far more contentious if it turned out the military was involved in killing the churchwomen. Ambassador Hinton quickly staked out a position that the leadership of the Salvadoran National Guard had no role in the crime. "As I read the evidence and as I understand the society," Hinton said, "there's no reason for orders [from the top commanders]. Suspicious women coming in from [Nicaragua]; one of the 'fellers' always thought that Jean Donovan was attractive; they had money. It just got out of control. You got a bunch of barbarians. I don't think they needed orders."[28] In March 1981, Secretary Haig enraged the churchwomen's families by telling Congress, "I'd like to suggest to you that some of the investigations would lead one to believe that perhaps the vehicle that the nuns were riding in may have tried to run a roadblock, or may accidentally have been perceived to have been doing so, and there'd been an exchange of fire."[29] Haig's statement ignored the FBI's own evidence that the churchwomen were shot execution-style in the back of the head.[30]

Around the same time, the Reagan administration issued a white paper titled "Communist Interference in El Salvador." The report focused on Soviet and Cuban support for the Salvadoran guerrillas and concluded, based on documents allegedly captured from the rebels, that the armed resistance was a "textbook case" of foreign Communist aggression.[31] In other words, the insurgency was not a homegrown rebellion based on decades of repression but a calculated plot controlled from abroad. The white paper, despite later being discredited, became the basis for a major escalation of U.S. military involvement in El Salvador.[32] The Reagan administration portrayed El Salvador as the place where the line had to be held against Soviet and Cuban advances. "We believe that the government of El Salvador is on the front line in a battle that is really aimed at the very heart of the Western Hemisphere, and eventually us," Reagan proclaimed.[33] U.S. funding to the Salvadoran military skyrocketed. From 1946 to 1979, the U.S. government had provided the Salvadoran armed forces a total of $16.7 million. In just the first year of Reagan's presidency, military aid was $82 million, and it grew significantly in subsequent years. Reagan increased the number of U.S. military advisors stationed in El Salvador from twenty to fifty-five, and the U.S. Army provided training to numerous Salvadoran officers.[34]

In its first year in office, the Reagan administration explicitly abandoned human rights as a factor in its Central American policy and provided aid to El Salvador without conditions.[35] In December 1981, the Atlacatl Batalion, the first elite army unit trained by Reagan's new military advisors, murdered at least seven hundred civilians in and around the community of El Mozote. Before even learning about the massacre, the U.S. Congress tried to put a check on Reagan's actions. Congress tied future military funding and the presence of military advisors in El Salvador to a requirement that every six months President Reagan certify that the Salvadoran government was making a significant effort to safeguard human rights.[36] One congressman said, "This vote represents a decisive repudiation of the blank-check military policy of the Reagan administration in El Salvador."[37] The first reports of the El Mozote massacre appeared in U.S. newspapers on January 27, 1982. The next day, Reagan delivered his first certification that the Salvadoran military was making a concerted effort to protect human rights.[38]

While underwriting the Salvadoran military, the White House pushed hard for legislative elections in 1982 to legitimize the Salvadoran government that, at that point, was still a military-civilian junta. The new, elected assembly would choose a provisional president. During the campaign, the United States strongly backed the Christian Democrats, who won a plurality.[39] Even so, two right-wing parties held enough seats collectively to control the selection of the president. One of them was the surprisingly successful ARENA party headed by Roberto D'Aubuisson, who was positioned to assume the presidency.[40]

The Reagan administration, worried that D'Aubuisson's selection would enrage the U.S. Congress and jeopardize support for military aid to El Salvador, directly lobbied the politicians and the Salvadoran military for a different solution.[41] The Salvadoran high command, concerned their millions in U.S. assistance could disappear, stepped in and imposed their own man as president, a banker who had not even run in the election.[42] D'Aubuisson felt betrayed by Reagan and the Salvadoran high command, but he accepted his consolation prize: being head of the new legislature.[43] The Reagan administration, realizing it was stuck with D'Aubuisson in a position of power as a result of elections the United States had championed so fiercely, began rehabilitating D'Aubuisson's image.[44] D'Aubuisson, for his part, appointed his friend Héctor Regalado as chief of security for the legislative assembly. Regalado promptly began running a death squad out of his office.[45]

SIX

————

"ARENA's Achilles' Heel"

OUR FIRST TRIP TO EL SALVADOR

FRESNO—SEPTEMBER 2004

"What is the significance of this page?" Nico van Aelstyn asks about a single photocopy of three small sheets of stationery seized with the Saravia Diary in 1980 at Finca San Luis.

"This is an extremely important page," Professor Terry Karl testifies. "These are three pieces of paper that are Xeroxed on the same page. Colonel Majano [who ordered the raid that netted the documents] told me that they were Xeroxed on the same page because they were clipped together." The first is the famous Operation Piña page allegedly describing the operational details of the Romero assassination. The second sheet, to the left of Operation Piña, shows a list of names. "It includes some of the most prominent land-owning families of El Salvador. For example, the name Ricardo Sol Meza, the name Alfonso Salaverría. These are very prominent. These are families that are considered among what we once called the Fourteen Families." The government officials Professor Karl interviewed concluded that the names belonged to the financiers of the assassination.

"Do you have any opinion as to whose handwriting is on [these two sheets]?" Nico asks.

"Yes," Karl replies. "I am familiar with that handwriting. I think that's Roberto D'Aubuisson's handwriting."[1]

SAN SALVADOR—SEPTEMBER 2003

To launch our full-scale investigation into the families that financed D'Aubuisson's death squad and possibly Romero's murder—the "big fish" we hope to catch in our case—Nico van Aelstyn, Russell Cohen, and I go to El Salvador two weeks after filing the lawsuit. The contrasts between my non-profit reality and the customs of a corporate law firm surface even before our trip begins. Nico and Russ reserve flights in business class while I buy a coach seat on a cheaper airline. They also decide to stay at the elegant Camino Real hotel. In addition to being one of San Salvador's finest establishments, the Camino Real is the place from which, in 1980, driver Amado Garay and the gunman departed to kill Archbishop Romero. I choose team cohesion over budgetary prudence and bad karma, and I book a room there too.

Our most promising lead in El Salvador is a man we don't fully trust. Two sources have told us he is the person most likely to lead us to the "bad guys," those insiders we will ultimately need, but the introductions come with a warning that getting straight information from him will require patience. Depending on whom we ask, Leonel Gómez is either a human rights hero or a pawn of the U.S. government. Many of our activist colleagues, certain that Gómez is a CIA asset, tell us to avoid him, but U.S. officials love him for his ability to get information no one else can. Ambassador Robert White has encouraged us to contact him. Speaking an impeccable, almost folksy English, Gómez knows how to work with *gringos*. He possesses a keen under-standing of the U.S. political system; counts congresspeople, ambassadors, and Washington insiders among his friends; and is not shy about dropping their names into conversation. We know the risks in dealing with him, but with his investigative experience, we reason that the potential payoff is high.

A heavy metal gate swings open, revealing a modest San Salvador home and our host waiting in the driveway. Dressed in shorts and a gray T-shirt that barely covers his substantial torso, Gómez strokes his silver mustache and greets us with a slight grin. He leads us inside to a living room wallpa-pered in books, some neatly shelved, others stacked with abandon. A framed AK-47 hangs on the wall. Wasting no time, Gómez dives into a monologue about the realities of El Salvador. The next three hours pass in a torrent of uninterrupted speech as Gómez, almost without a breath, throws out names, anecdotes, suppositions, and strategies, rarely pausing to distinguish the true from the speculative. Our lawyerly instincts to cross-examine are muted by his domineering speech. I feel disoriented, like being caught in a Salvadoran thunderstorm without an umbrella.

"Billy Sol is key," Gómez declares as we scribble the name in our notebooks.

Guillermo "Billy" Sol Bang is in his tenth year as head of the national hydroelectric company, one of the largest government-owned entities in El Salvador. Years later, "Don Billy" will face corruption charges stemming from his time as director of the company, but the charges will be dismissed.[2] Like many oligarchs, Sol attended college in the United States and then returned to El Salvador to pursue business interests, including a successful rice plantation, ranching, and coffee cultivation.[3] He was not spared suffering during the 1980s. The government seized his large estate, he was shot during a 1982 attack, and he was kidnapped toward the end of the civil war.[4] His own words reveal Sol as a hard-liner. "Terrorism cannot be fought with conventional methods," he told the *Los Angeles Times*.[5] The solution, he said, is to "destroy it," and for that "you need excellent intelligence. D'Aubuisson is excellent on that. He's U.S.-trained."[6] Rodolfo López Sibrián, a member of D'Aubuisson's group who was implicated in murder and arrested for kidnapping, publicly alleged that Sol allowed his house to be used as a clandestine jail for kidnap victims.[7] Sol was also a founder of the ARENA party.

Leonel Gómez now characterizes Billy Sol as a critical financier for the ultraright. He claims that Sol was a middleman between the oligarchs and the "thugs" like Álvaro Saravia. This is an interesting allegation. We already know that Sol was on the list of people suspected of involvement in death squads that State Department officials gave to the FBI in 1983.[8]

Gómez transitions to someone we know more about, Héctor Regalado, and says that Regalado got some help from Billy Sol when he was down on his luck. Regalado was D'Aubuisson's chief of security in the 1980s who ran a death squad out of the legislature.[9] We also know that he bears a macabre nickname: Dr. Death.[10] CIA sources said that Regalado, a dentist by trade, used his medical tools to craft special bullets.[11] A former DEA agent accused him of testing his instruments directly on prisoners.[12] We have read that Regalado even organized his own death squad out of a Boy Scout troop.[13] In 1980, Regalado met up with D'Aubuisson and Saravia in Guatemala, where they we were running paramilitary operations, and Regalado was closely linked to D'Aubuisson from that time on.[14]

For us, the most important point about Regalado is that many people in El Salvador believe he is the man who shot Archbishop Romero. This understanding has its roots in a 1987 criminal investigation that marked the first serious attempt to hold someone accountable for Romero's murder. The getaway driver, Amado Garay, testifying in secret, implicated D'Aubuisson in the assassination. A few months later, in early 1988, Garay reviewed a lineup of photos and identified Regalado as the person who most resembled the shooter.[15] The next year, just ahead of presidential elections, a TV program orchestrated by the Christian Democrats announced that Garay had fingered Regalado as the assassin.[16] Although the claim was politically expedient for the Christian Democrats because Regalado was closely tied to their nemesis D'Aubuisson and his ARENA party, the charge nonetheless stuck.[17]

Later investigations cast serious doubt on the identification of Regalado. It turned out that officials had altered the photo that Garay reviewed. Regalado was clean shaven in the picture but because Garay had testified that the shooter had a beard, investigators used a marker to draw a beard on the photo.[18] Also, if a public letter by Regalado is to be believed, the picture was taken in 1969, eleven years before the assassination. Investigators found no compelling evidence of Regalado's involvement in the crime.[19]

"Regalado is not the shooter," Leonel Gómez proclaims. This is no surprise to us.

"I talked with Regalado," he says. Now he has my attention.

According to Gómez, Regalado, whatever his sins, could no longer bear the weight of being branded as Romero's murderer. He is distraught with the way his life turned out. Despite his years of commitment to the anti-Communist cause, he was not celebrated by the Right as a hero like Roberto D'Aubuisson. Regalado, it appears, reached out to Gómez in an attempt to absolve his name and relieve his guilt.

Gómez says that a priest joined him in the conversation with Regalado, and the priest is waiting to speak with us. He is outside the capital but we will immediately go to see him. Following Gómez's car, we head out of San Salvador but our pace is agonizingly slow. Whatever his other attributes, Gómez is the world's pokiest driver. As we climb into verdant hillsides, the light begins to dim in the distance and a thickening haze gathers. Though hidden from our view, coffee plants responsible for so much of El Salvador's pain occupy the slopes around us. A steady rain starts to fall, and the trees seem to close in on us as the road narrows and darkness completely descends. Not sure where we are going, not fully trusting Gómez, and aware that we are investigating a case that has previously gotten people killed, the unspoken apprehension in our car is as dense as the fog outside. Breaking the long silence, our driver mutters something to me in Spanish.

"What did he say?" Russ asks from the backseat.

"He told me this road is notorious for bandits and kidnappings," I answer. The nervous quiet returns for the rest of the trip.

We finally arrive at a small house near the side of the road and follow Gómez inside. The man waiting for us in a white guayabera shirt would appear more at home tanning on the beach than serving poor parishioners in a rural church. The priest's perfect hair gives him the look of a gracefully graying Hollywood actor, but his life has been nothing like a movie star's.

Following the *padre* inside, Leonel Gómez sets the stage for our conversation. Again in his pontificating style, he tells us it took him five years to get close to Héctor Regalado. Eventually, Regalado said he wanted to be at peace with the church, and he asked Gómez to put him in touch with a priest. The *padre* says he was aware of Regalado's involvement in the death squads, so he was frightened when Gómez showed up that first day with the notorious figure. Though they had two meetings, Regalado never went into many details with the *padre,* and the conversation was superficial and self-serving. Regalado claimed to know people involved in Romero's assassination but he insisted he had nothing to do with the operation. He showed the *padre* some documents he sent to the U.S. State Department that allegedly proved his innocence.

The *padre* and Gómez elicited information from him by posing "true" or "false" questions. Gómez describes the process:

"Billy Sol is key."

"Yes."

"Billy Sol is dangerous."

"Super dangerous."

The *padre* arranged for Regalado to speak with a bishop in San Salvador. Regalado, though, was evasive in the face of pointed questions. The *padre* didn't know all the details of their conversation, but he heard that Regalado's excuse was that the bishop had tried to interrogate him. The *padre* believed that Regalado only wanted to know what the church thought about him. He had no interest in justice or truth.

Before we leave the *padre*'s house, he gives us some stern advice about the timing of our case: a presidential election is just around the corner in March 2004, and if we aren't careful, the lawsuit will look like a political attack against the Right. The ARENA party has been in power for well over a decade, but because of the evidence against D'Aubuisson, the Romero assassination remains, as a U.S. embassy official called it, "ARENA's Achilles' heel."[20] For years, politicians in the center or on the left have used Romero's death to score political points against ARENA. The *padre* tells us that to be credible we have to prove that the lawsuit is untainted by politics. And ARENA still has the power—and no doubt the incentive—to "neutralize any effort to clarify the truth." We have to be careful.

The *padre*'s message of caution runs through my mind the next day as we visit the place that forms the backdrop for our entire endeavor: the chapel at Divina Providencia where Romero was murdered. The grounds surrounding the A-frame church, teeming with tropical trees and plants, are as lush as I imagined. One of the diminutive Carmelite nuns, dressed in modest white, her hair draped in a veil, delicately opens the chapel for us. Having seen the black-and-white photos of the assassination, I notice the interior is similar to how it appeared in 1980. Like so many homes and offices in El Salvador, a murder was not enough to take the place out of commission, and priests still say mass from the spot behind the altar where Romero collapsed to the floor.

After seeing the church, we walk across the lane to the tiny house where Romero lived. The nuns preserved the home after Romero's death, and the space now serves as a modest museum. The contents, including the type-writer on which Romero edited his homilies, reflect the austerity of his life. The vestments from his final mass, still stained with blood, hang in the glass-enclosed closet while pictures of the assassination and his funeral cover the walls. The enduring loss from his death over two decades ago is palpable. I cannot shake the feeling even as we return to our truck and drive away. It stays with me all the way back to San Francisco.

SEVEN

Baby Robbers, Mad Bombers, and Other Assorted Criminals

SARAVIA'S ESCAPE TO MIAMI BRINGS
U.S. FOREIGN POLICY FULL CIRCLE

FRESNO—AUGUST 2004

"Was there any current information that was developed by your investigators as to the then whereabouts of the defendant [Álvaro Saravia]?" Judge Wanger inquires.

"No, Your Honor," Nico van Aelstyn says. "We could not tell. In addition to Inés Olsson, there was a second person at the residence who also spoke to the process server, a young man who said that he knew who Mr. Saravia was. . . . But, no, we did not ascertain the immediate whereabouts of Mr. Saravia. We did confirm to our satisfaction that he had been there not long before and that he continued to have communications and relations with those at that address."

"And did the owner or the person in control, Ms. Olsson, confirm that Saravia had lived there?"

"Oh, yes, she did. Yes, she did."

SAN FRANCISCO—OCTOBER 2003

A few weeks after Nico, Russ, and I return from El Salvador, Saravia's time for responding to the lawsuit passes without a reply. Going into the case, we envisioned the possibility that Saravia might not hire a lawyer to defend himself, but we were always confident that we would find him. We have so much data tying him to Inés Olsson's address in Modesto that we almost assumed he would be there waiting for our process server. While we continue to disbelieve Olsson's varying stories, we do come across some clues hinting that Saravia might not be around.

Beyond Modesto, we try to cover our bases in Miami, where Saravia used to live and where his ex-wife and children still reside. We line up a Spanish-speaking investigator there, who suggests we draft letters to Saravia in English and Spanish that can be left with the family and others. It might open a channel of communication if indeed Saravia is around. The idea is smart but tricky because Saravia is the defendant in our case. "We cannot promise Saravia safety, a deal, immigration status—nothing," Russ cautions in an e-mail. "But, of course, we would like to start a dialogue, and hopefully these letters will provide some evidence of that." We keep the wording simple but hint that we want to know about the death squad financiers, whom we still consider the big fish in the case:

Dear Mr. Saravia,

As you may know, you have been named a defendant in a lawsuit filed in federal court in California relating to the assassination of Archbishop Oscar Arnulfo Romero. We know there are others who also were involved in the assassination. The lawsuit identifies these other individuals as defendants as well without naming them. As the legal representatives of the plaintiff, we would like to speak with you about this case and about the other individuals who were involved.

Almudena Bernabeu, our team's native Spanish speaker, signs the letter. It carries the date November 13, 2003.

EL SALVADOR—1982

As Héctor Regalado took on the role of chief of security at the legislature, the activities of D'Aubuisson's previous security chief, Álvaro Saravia, were less clear. U.S. State Department documents indicated that Saravia remained with D'Aubuisson after the 1982 elections and continued to work in security,[1] while other reports said he had already distanced himself from the ARENA leader.[2] Some claimed that Saravia was dismissed because he fought with members of the group, even punching D'Aubuisson on one occasion.[3] Whatever the truth, Saravia's path from that point became less about ideology—if indeed it ever was—and more about trying to get by. In 1983 or 1984, Saravia became chief of security for the Atarraya seafood company.[4] Atarraya's owner, Roberto Daglio, was one of El Salvador's most powerful oligarchs who had fled to Miami. He was named in the January 1981 State Department cable as one of the Miami Six who allegedly financed D'Aubuisson's death squad activities.[5]

According to testimony in our records, Saravia's employment with Atarraya greatly improved his financial situation, as he and his family moved into a house owned by Daglio in an upscale San Salvador neighborhood. They paid very little rent even though Saravia brought in a salary of almost 3,000 colones (about $600) a month, a respectable sum at that time for El Salvador. But Saravia's old demons remained, and in the spring of 1984, Atarraya fired Saravia for poor performance as a result of his drinking. One night, Saravia came home drunk and when his wife, Lorena, would not let him into the house, he broke down the front door. Lorena soon took the children and moved to Miami, and the company kicked Saravia out of the residence. By 1985, he was back to maintaining a meager existence on the outskirts of San Salvador.[6]

Saravia's diminished lifestyle did not alter his criminal propensities. A judicial investigation in 1985 revealed that Saravia was likely involved in the kidnapping and death of a Salvadoran businessman.[7] Saravia now ran the risk that an arrest in the kidnapping case might also lead to charges in the assassination of Archbishop Romero.[8]

By 1985, even as the civil war continued, the political landscape in El Salvador had changed in a way that brought renewed hope that Romero's death might be investigated properly. A new judge was in charge of the Romero file, and the Christian Democrats had replaced D'Aubuisson's ARENA party and were in control of the Legislative Assembly. Though no witnesses had yet testified on the record that Saravia was involved in Romero's murder, the capture of his diary at Finca San Luis had always made him a prime suspect. Fearing arrest, Saravia managed to flee to the United States. He arrived in Florida in October 1985, reunited with his wife and children, and settled into a home on the western edge of Miami.[9]

While Saravia tried to blend into the South Florida community, the government of El Salvador, now controlled by D'Aubuisson's rivals, the Christian Democrats, began a concerted inquiry into Romero's murder. The Salvadoran government deployed a U.S.-funded investigative unit to uncover evidence that might lead to the killers. The investigation led to Costa Rica, where the getaway driver, Amado Garay, was in hiding. Garay implicated Saravia in the murder.

Saravia, perhaps sensing the net closing around him even in Miami, offered to speak with Salvadoran officials in exchange for a large sum of money. In mid-1987, Salvadoran media reported on Saravia's involvement in the Romero assassination. According to a U.S. State Department cable, Saravia's version of events was that he and Roberto D'Aubuisson, along with D'Aubuisson's close friend Fernando "El Negro" Sagrera and a former National Guardsman, Víctor Hugo Vega Valencia, had planned Romero's murder. Saravia said that on March 24, 1980, the group saw a newspaper advertisement announcing that Romero would be officiating a mass, and D'Aubuisson told Saravia to put a plan together to kill the archbishop that evening. Saravia then contacted a National Guard officer named Molina, who gave them a rifle and found a shooter.[10]

For the first time, one of the insiders had described the decisions made the day of Romero's murder, but Saravia's attempts to procure money from the Salvadoran government failed. Instead, he became the primary target of the investigation. By October 1987, Salvadoran authorities were preparing to bring Garay, the getaway driver, to testify in El Salvador. Knowing that the Salvadorans would charge Saravia and seek his return to stand trial, the U.S. government arranged for his detention in Miami.[11] The U.S. embassy also worked with Salvadoran officials to make certain their request for Saravia's extradition would meet U.S. legal standards.[12] Garay testified in secret on November 19 and 20, and a Salvadoran judge issued an order for Saravia's arrest on November 24. U.S. Marshals took Saravia into immigration custody on deportation charges for overstaying his visa, while U.S. federal prosecutors in Miami got their own warrant based on the Salvadoran extradition request.[13]

Saravia's close links to D'Aubuisson, still one of El Salvador's most influential politicians, made the stakes of the case extraordinarily high. Saravia's diary showed that he could potentially implicate dozens of prominent Salvadorans, particularly ARENA members, in death squad activities. The ramifications of Saravia's extradition were, according the U.S. embassy, "potentially enormous."[14]

From the start, U.S. officials knew that D'Aubuisson and his ARENA colleagues had no intention of allowing Saravia to be extradited for trial in El Salvador. They involved themselves in his legal defense. When Saravia called his former boss from a Miami prison, D'Aubuisson gave reassurances that he would take care of everything.[15] The U.S. embassy in San Salvador received information that Saravia's prestigious Miami lawyer was being paid "in the range of a half million dollars," even though Saravia was "penniless," and that someone might have transferred a large sum of money to Saravia's bank account to cover the costs.[16] The embassy speculated that the funds could have come from an ARENA kidnap-for-profit ring.[17] In a cable to Washington, U.S. ambassador William Walker cautioned, "Those supporting Saravia will exhaust every means legal and less so to prevent Saravia's return."[18]

The U.S. government was nervous that Salvadoran authorities, even those who wanted Saravia behind bars, would fail to put together a strong prosecution case, and Saravia would be released upon returning to El Salvador. U.S. Democrats, now holding majorities in both houses of Congress, kept a close eye on the proceedings, knowing that the Reagan administration needed their support to keep millions of dollars in aid flowing to the Salvadoran military in the ongoing civil war. The White House understood that if Saravia returned to El Salvador only to be set free, the "fallout on the Hill [would] be awesome."[19] But even with all the maneuvering in Miami and Washington, the most significant roadblock to Saravia's extradition was the Supreme Court of El Salvador. Its chief justice was a leading figure in a political party traditionally aligned with the Salvadoran military, and his refusal to permit the prosecution of human rights cases had already resulted in repeated conflicts with the U.S. embassy.[20] If the Salvadoran Supreme Court got a hold of Saravia's file, it could scuttle the entire case.

SAN SALVADOR—APRIL 1978

Ten years before Saravia's extradition case, Archbishop Romero took on the Supreme Court, criticizing its role in perpetuating impunity throughout the judicial system. In an April 1978 homily, Romero cataloged the numerous problems in the criminal courts, "where the judge does not allow lawyers to attend with their defendants, while the National Guard is allowed to be present and intimidate the accused, who often bears marks of torture." Romero was direct. "A judge who does not report signs of torture and lets himself be swayed by its effect on the testimony of the accused is not a just judge.... What does the Supreme Court of Justice do?" He singled out the president of the Supreme Court for causing "a great part of the malaise of our country" and applauded those lawyers who were "putting their finger on the sore."[21]

The Supreme Court did not take kindly to the scolding and sent Romero a protest letter that it also leaked to the press. "I most respectfully beg Your Excellency to express the names of the 'venal judges' to whom you referred in the homily," the court's secretary wrote, despite the fact that Romero had not used that phrase.[22] Responding during Sunday mass, Romero expressed frustration at the court's focus on "venal judges" while ignoring his broader message about "a social evil" rooted in the system. Romero turned the court's language around, saying, "I believe the concept of venality is fulfilled by any functionary who receives from the people a salary to administer justice and instead becomes the accomplice of injustice, moved by sinful purposes." Romero's retort ended the public feud.[23]

SAN SALVADOR—NOVEMBER 1987

The day after Álvaro Saravia's arrest in Miami, D'Aubuisson publicly called the getaway driver, Amado Garay, a "false witness." Even though there was no warrant against D'Aubuisson, and he was protected by immunity as a sitting legislator, he filed a habeas corpus petition in San Salvador seeking to invalidate the warrant and extradition request against Saravia.[24] The maneuver allowed the Salvadoran Supreme Court to take the Romero file away from the investigating judge, and it gave the chief justice control over the proceedings. For good measure, Saravia's representatives in El Salvador also submitted their own habeas corpus claims.[25]

The extradition case in Miami moved at a leisurely pace until August 1988.[26] On the same day that a U.S. magistrate scheduled a hearing, an administrative judge in El Salvador appointed by the Salvadoran Supreme Court to investigate Saravia's habeas corpus petition issued an advisory opinion arguing that the arrest warrant was invalid and should be revoked. Mere hours after the nonbinding decision was delivered to the Salvadoran Supreme Court, a copy arrived on the fax machine of Saravia's Miami lawyer. The fax sheets identified the sender as a shrimping business in El Salvador. The company's board of directors, it turned out, included D'Aubuisson and three fugitives then fleeing indictments for their involvement in a kidnapping-for-profit ring. The general manager of the company was D'Aubuisson's close friend Negro Sagrera. Based on these facts, the U.S. embassy concluded that D'Aubuisson and his allies were strongly influencing, if not controlling, the judicial process in El Salvador. An exasperated Ambassador Walker sent a cable to Washington detailing the steps taken by the "D'Aubuisson mafia" to disrupt Saravia's extradition proceedings. "The swiftness with which the administrative judge's advisory opinion arrived in D'Aubuisson's hands and was sent from his office suggests collusion," Walker wrote. Abandoning any pretense of diplomatic language, Walker concluded that the fax "clearly links the Saravia defense to an entire realm of coup plotters, death squad chiefs, kidnappers, baby robbers, mad bombers, car thieves, and other assorted criminals."[27] D'Aubuisson later admitted the fax was sent from his office.[28]

The ploy did not affect the U.S. case, however, as the Miami judge simply found that the advisory opinion did not invalidate El Salvador's original extradition request, and she ruled that U.S. prosecutors had provided sufficient proof to meet the legal standard for extradition.[29] But as the U.S. process was playing out, El Salvador's Supreme Court continued to review Saravia's petition to quash the Salvadoran arrest warrant. In December 1988, the Supreme Court, in an obviously political decision, invalidated the arrest warrant by ruling that the original request for Saravia's extradition had been improper. The court decided that Garay's testimony, which provided the basis for the arrest warrant, was lacking in credibility because it was given more than seven years after the assassination and conflicted in one aspect with the testimony of another eyewitness. The judges ruled that Garay was covering up the truth and his testimony therefore had no value.[30] (The court's opinion about Garay contrasted with the conclusion of the U.S. government, which knew that Garay had passed several lie detector tests and found his testimony "convincing.")[31] With the Salvadoran arrest warrant and extradition request invalidated—meaning that El Salvador was no longer asking for Saravia's extradition—the federal court in Miami had no legal basis for holding Saravia. Although there were deportation charges still pending against him, Saravia was able to post bond and go free.

The U.S. government was furious with the ARENA party and the Salvadoran Supreme Court, and U.S. officials accused D'Aubuisson of obstructing justice.[32] Ambassador Walker warned that ARENA's role in the case would be interpreted as "another disturbing indicator that the party does not believe in the vigorous pursuit of the truth in human rights matters."[33] Plans were put in place for U.S. vice president Dan Quayle to pull aside the chief justice during an upcoming trip to San Salvador and express that the United States blamed him for the extradition's failure.[34] But whatever the level of scorn from the United States, D'Aubuisson and ARENA had achieved their goal of blocking Saravia's return to El Salvador and with it the best hope for finally holding someone accountable for the murder of Archbishop Romero.

In Miami, Saravia was suddenly free, and he returned temporarily to live with his wife and children, but his usual problems continued to plague him. Following an old pattern, he started drinking, and Lorena kicked him out. Saravia also faced deportation charges that were unaffected by the rulings in the extradition case. At some point, to slow the deportation process, Saravia applied for asylum and claimed he would face persecution if he returned to El Salvador.[35] The notion was hardly out of bounds; given the information he possessed, Saravia likely would have been a target.

A U.S. embassy official in San Salvador, Richard Chidester, found out about Saravia's predicament. Chidester was by then an old hand on Latin American issues, having spent nearly a decade representing the U.S. government in the region. He was also close with Leonel Gómez, who had learned about Saravia's immigration situation and saw an opportunity to squeeze Saravia for information. Chidester took the initiative to contact Saravia, who was shaken at hearing from the U.S. embassy but agreed to meet. In May 1990, the men sat down in Miami, but Saravia almost immediately asked for money, somewhere around $250,000. Chidester rejected the demand and ended the meeting.[36]

A few days later, Saravia called Chidester and said he wanted to explore collaboration with the U.S. government regardless of compensation. Chidester laid down the rules: if they were going to do this, Chidester wanted to know everything, particularly about the Romero assassination. They met again on May 14, with Saravia's lawyer present, and this time Saravia was ready to talk. His story provided the insider details that the getaway driver, Amado Garay, had not been able to give. On the morning of March 24, 1980, Saravia said, he had been at a house in San Salvador's Escalón neighborhood.[37] Ten people were there, including Roberto D'Aubuisson, Captain Eduardo Ávila and Negro Sagrera.[38] Ávila had a newspaper announcing that Romero would say a mass that night, and Ávila suggested it would be a good time to kill the archbishop. D'Aubuisson agreed. One of their compatriots, the son of a former president, knew a shooter, so D'Aubuisson ordered him to contact the marksman. D'Aubuisson then put Negro Sagrera in charge of the operation and left for a trip. A half hour before the evening mass, Sagrera, the shooter, and two others met in the parking lot of San Salvador's Camino Real hotel to finalize the plans and from there, the shooter went to the church and killed Romero. The gun he used, Saravia said, was an M-16, and the shooter's compensation was 1,000 colones, the equivalent of $200.[39]

Chidester found Saravia's account convincing, and the proffer was enough to get a postponement of Saravia's impending immigration hearing, but then the initiative stalled.[40] The State Department uncovered information that, due to Saravia's "lack of discretion," some "ultrarightists" might have sent someone to the United States to threaten or kill Saravia.[41] Chidester also had to return to El Salvador, and when he tried to involve the U.S. Department of Justice to take the case further, officials there showed little interest.[42] With Chidester back in El Salvador and Saravia in Florida, the relationship dissolved, and Saravia's revelations remained confidential, recorded only on the pages of classified U.S. government documents. Another potential break in the Romero case was squandered. For Saravia, his immigration problems were temporarily pushed off but not resolved, and his next step, he soon decided, would be to leave Miami.

SAN SALVADOR—1992

Both El Salvador's long civil war and Roberto D'Aubuisson's life were coming to an end. Diagnosed with throat cancer, D'Aubuisson died in February 1992 just one month after the Salvadoran government, again led by ARENA, and the guerrilla army signed a peace agreement. The rebels' radio station called the passing of D'Aubuisson, their hated foe, "an act of divine justice in this moment of national reconciliation," but one key provision of the peace accord would prevent D'Aubuisson from truly resting in peace.[43] The agreement called for the creation of a Truth Commission to investigate "serious acts of violence" committed during the conflict, and the Romero assassination became one of the commission's "illustrative cases." When the groundbreaking report came out in 1993, D'Aubuisson's name, along with Saravia's, was front and center. With an important exception, the commission's version of the Romero assassination was remarkably similar to what Saravia had told Richard Chidester in 1990:

> Former major Roberto D'Aubuisson, former captain Álvaro Saravia, and Fernando Sagrera were present on March 24, 1980, at the home of Alejandro Cáceres in San Salvador. Captain Eduardo Ávila arrived and told them that Archbishop Romero would be celebrating a mass that day. Captain Ávila said that this would be a good opportunity to assassinate the archbishop. D'Aubuisson ordered that this be done and put Saravia in charge of the operation. When it was pointed out that a sniper would be needed, Captain Ávila said he would contact one through Mario Molina. Amado Garay was assigned to drive the assassin to the chapel.

The parking lot of the Camino Real hotel was the assembly point before proceeding to the chapel. There, the bearded gunman, carrying the murder weapon, got into a red four-door Volkswagen driven by Garay. At least two vehicles drove from the Camino Real hotel to the scene of the crime. Outside the main entrance to the chapel, the assassin fired a single bullet from the vehicle, killing Archbishop Romero. D'Aubuisson ordered that 1,000 colones be handed over to Walter Antonio "Musa" Álvarez, who received the payment in question, as did the bearded assassin. Álvarez was abducted in September 1981 and was found dead not long afterward.[44]

The Truth Commission also concluded that the Salvadoran Supreme Court had "played an active role in preventing" Saravia's extradition from the United States to El Salvador, thereby ensuring impunity for those responsible for Romero's death.[45] Only five days after the release of the report, however, the Salvadoran Legislative Assembly, still dominated by ARENA, passed a sweeping amnesty law immunizing virtually everyone fingered by the Truth Commission.[46] There would be no prosecutions, and two weeks later a Salvadoran judge granted Saravia amnesty and closed the already moribund criminal case against him.[47]

What almost no one knew at the time was that the Truth Commission's version of the Romero assassination was nearly identical to Saravia's account because Saravia had been their key witness.

EIGHT

"You're Making a Lot of Noise"

LOOKING FOR EVIDENCE
ON THE DEATH SQUAD FINANCIERS

FRESNO—SEPTEMBER 2004

"Has there been any prosecution of Roberto D'Aubuisson or Mr. Saravia, to your knowledge?" Nico van Aelstyn asks.

"There has not been any prosecution," Professor Terry Karl answers, "but there have been further attempts to discover what happened in the Romero assassination from Mr. Saravia." Karl summarizes the peace process leading to the creation of the Truth Commission. "As part of this investigation, Mr. Saravia was interviewed in New York for the Truth Commission, and he had an attorney with him, although it was no longer the same high-priced attorney that he had in Miami. So he is now operating in a different way," she says. "He gave a series of statements to the Truth Commission in secret. Those statements are recorded. There are summaries of them and there are transcripts of them, and I have seen most of them. Not all."

"Is there anything of particular note that you want to mention about these documents before we move on?"

"I would just like to say that in those testimonies, they are the fullest statements that I have seen of Mr. Saravia's discussion of the Romero assassination."[1]

SAN FRANCISCO—FALL 2003

I read the transcripts of Álvaro Saravia's testimony to the Truth Commission with great interest.[2] They show that Saravia provided several clues to the commission but not always with the clarity we would like, particularly concerning the alleged financiers. For example, Saravia told the commission that D'Aubuisson received money, vehicles, and housing from, and met regularly with, several people whose names were well known throughout El Salvador.[3] The money D'Aubuisson received also went to buying weapons, Saravia said, but without indicating whose money was used for which purchases.

The key for us in sorting through the evidence is to distinguish between those who supported only ostensibly "political" action—the vitriolic public relations campaign of FAN and the later development of the ARENA party—and those who provided money for paramilitary purposes. To many Salvadorans, there is no distinction between the two, and many believe that D'Aubuisson supporters who claimed to donate to the former had no problem if it went to the latter. For us, any names of early FAN or ARENA members provide possible leads, but we will need concrete evidence that might only come through firsthand witness testimony. And even if we find proof of payments for death squad activities, we still hope to identify those who specifically financed Romero's assassination.

On this point, Saravia's Truth Commission testimony gives clues about those allegedly involved in the conspiracy against Romero.[4] Saravia told the commission that the red Volkswagen Passat that Amado Garay drove to the church was donated to D'Aubuisson's group by Roberto Mathies Regalado, a leading entrepreneur in El Salvador and later a fugitive in one of the largest fraud cases in the country's history.[5] The day after Romero's murder, Saravia said, there was a meeting at the house of Eduardo "Guayo" Lemus O'Byrne, a successful businessman in the poultry industry and a former president of the National Association of Private Enterprise (ANEP).[6] Lemus O'Byrne was present with his brother and other guests, Saravia said, and it was at this meeting that D'Aubuisson ordered the disposal of the red Volkswagen.[7] Saravia also told the commission that the 1,000 colones D'Aubuisson provided to pay the shooter likely came from Lemus O'Byrne.[8] More broadly, Saravia emphasized to the commission that the D'Aubuisson squad's responsibility for Romero's murder was well known among its financiers, and the assassination gave the group prestige and made it is easier to raise money.[9]

With all Saravia knows about the suspected financiers, we would love to talk to him. "We know there are others who also were involved in the assassination" was the enticement we used in the letter we left for Saravia in Modesto and Miami, but until we locate him and learn whether he is willing to talk, we have to pursue other means to investigate the financiers. We retain some high-powered allies to do just that. The Mintz Group, a private-investigation company, is the creation of its namesake, James Mintz, a former in-house investigator for a Washington, D.C., law firm. Its skilled experts have extensive law enforcement contacts and the ability to track individuals. From the moment we contact the Mintz Group, its investigators show great interest in the case and the company even waives the fees it normally charges.

In October, Russell Cohen e-mails our team with an intriguing strategy for Mintz's pursuit of the financiers, whom we refer to as the Does. "On the broader circle of Doe defendants, I asked Mintz how they could help us there," Russ writes. The Mintz investigator has asked for "a concise list of possible defendants, which she can share with a Florida-based former-FBI 'friend.'" The ex-FBI contact is so sensitive that we aren't allowed to know his name.

EL SALVADOR—LATE 1983

In a pivotal time in El Salvador's civil war, the issue of the death squads played a central role in U.S. policy toward the Salvadoran military. The conflict had been raging for almost three years. U.S.-trained officers deploying U.S.-made weapons populated the Salvadoran armed forces.[10] The guerrilla army had grown in strength and occupied portions of the country.[11] Even as the U.S. Congress continued to accept the White House certifications that El Salvador was making progress on human rights, it had become more assertive in scrutinizing the situation.

Congress exerted greater control by rejecting or limiting Reagan administration requests for increases in military aid to El Salvador (although the assistance it approved remained significant). With Congress holding the purse strings and showing greater concern about the Salvadoran military's terrible human rights record, the Reagan administration knew it would have to pressure El Salvador's commanders to clean up their act. The alternative might be the catastrophic elimination of all U.S. assistance, thereby risking a guerrilla victory in the civil war.[12] Repeated showdowns between Congress and the White House kept El Salvador in the headlines, with commentators and politicians regularly debating whether the United States was dragging itself into another Vietnam.[13]

Through a more aggressive policy of curtailing abuses, Reagan dispatched Vice President George H. W. Bush to San Salvador in December 1983 with a list of military officers linked to the death squads. Bush demanded that the

Salvadoran commanders relieve them of duty immediately and prosecute them.[14] The Reagan administration simultaneously tried to minimize Roberto D'Aubuisson's power and influence. The State Department turned down D'Aubuisson's request for a visa to the United States,[15] and U.S. officials publicly denounced the Salvadoran death squads with which D'Aubuisson was so often linked.[16]

The same month that Vice President Bush went to El Salvador, the *Albuquerque Journal* and *Los Angeles Times* ran a series of in-depth stories exposing the death squads, their civilian backers, and their patrons in the military hierarchy. The accounts, written respectively by Craig Pyes and Laurie Becklund, quoted D'Aubuisson extensively and pointed to him as the central figure in the strategy of deploying death squads to combat changes to the status quo. The articles also detailed the extensive contacts between conservative U.S. Republicans, members of the Salvadoran oligarchy, and D'Aubuisson.[17]

The timing of these events was critical because El Salvador was preparing to hold presidential elections in March 1984, with D'Aubuisson running for the ARENA party against Christian Democrat Napoleón Duarte. Despite Republican ties to D'Aubuisson, the Reagan administration faced the same situation as in 1982: D'Aubuisson's election would cause the U.S. Congress to shut off all military aid, with disastrous consequences for the war effort. The White House thus actively supported the Christian Democrats' campaign to defeat D'Aubuisson.[18] But moving away from D'Aubuisson and ARENA was not easy, because critics persisted in reminding the public about Reagan's earlier failures.

Robert White, the former ambassador whom Reagan had forced out of the Foreign Service, was particularly outspoken. "For three years," White declared shortly before the Salvadoran election, "the Reagan administration has pretended it did not know that death squads and military butchery are intrinsic features of the government and military of El Salvador. For three years, the administration has known the names and involvement of wealthy Salvadoran exiles living in Miami, Florida, who organize, fund and direct right wing death squads."[19]

In congressional hearings, White condemned D'Aubuisson's ARENA party and blamed the Reagan administration for failing to contain D'Aubuisson earlier. "ARENA is a violent Fascist party modeled after the Nazis," White testified. "The founders and chief supporters of ARENA are rich Salvadoran exiles headquartered in Miami and civilian activists in El

Salvador." He gave the essential information from the January 1981 "Millionaires' Murder Inc.?" cable in which a U.S. embassy source alleged that the Miami Six oversaw D'Aubuisson and the death squads. "The administration of President Carter classified Roberto D'Aubuisson as a terrorist, a murderer, and a leader of death squads," White said. "Shortly after President Reagan took office, this administration overturned this policy and began the process of rehabilitating ex-Major D'Aubuisson. No longer was he a pariah. . . . In a very real sense, the Reagan administration created Roberto D'Aubuisson the political leader."[20]

White also named the Miami Six: Enrique Altamirano, publisher of one of El Salvador's largest and most conservative newspapers;[21] Luis Escalante, a banker and victim of kidnapping; Arturo Muyshondt, another banker; Roberto Daglio, a businessman and Álvaro Saravia's old boss; and two brothers from the coffee-growing Salaverría family. The accused men reacted swiftly. Arturo Muyshondt and Julio Salaverría made statements from El Salvador asserting they had never lived outside the country and therefore could not have been members of the Miami group. Roberto Daglio denounced the charges from Miami.[22] One month later, when White returned to Congress for further testimony, Muyshondt and his lawyer confronted the former ambassador. White was forced to say that the embassy's source must have been mistaken in naming Muyshondt.[23] A libel suit Muyshondt filed the same day against White was later dismissed.[24]

SAN FRANCISCO—FALL 2003

The Mintz Group's ex-FBI contact is already working his network to get information about suspected death squad financiers, but he still is not prepared to interact directly with our legal team. We ask Mintz to convey to him that this is not a one-shot deal. We want his help on future matters. We hope that if he sees there will be ongoing work for him with the Heller Ehrman law firm, he might feel more comfortable cooperating with us on the Romero case. Mintz representatives have a meeting scheduled with him in New York and they promise to convey our wishes. We keep our fingers crossed.

Though others started higher on our list, our strongest information on alleged financiers is starting to point to two men: Billy Sol and Roberto "Bobby" Daglio. Sol is the focus of the theories of our contact, Leonel

Gómez. He has been mentioned by known death squad leader Héctor Regalado, and he was named on the list of people suspected of involvement in death squads that U.S. State Department officials gave to the FBI in 1983. Daglio, we know, once employed Álvaro Saravia as head of security at the Atarraya seafood company. Saravia's testimony to the Truth Commission linked Daglio with Roberto D'Aubuisson, as did the testimony of the getaway driver, Amado Garay.[25] The U.S. embassy's source also named Daglio as one of the Miami Six, though Daglio disputed that publicly and in an interview with the FBI.[26]

We have learned about another witness against Daglio. According to our documents, a former colleague told the Truth Commission that Daglio operated death squads, and the colleague said that he saw grenades and machine guns hidden in Daglio's house.[27] Without eyewitness testimony on the record in our case, we don't yet have enough evidence to name Daglio as a defendant, but these allegations are moving us closer to that possibility. Leonel Gómez knows the witness, and Gómez agrees to help us approach him through contacts on Capitol Hill who were instrumental in getting the man to come forward. To that end, Gómez is traveling to Boston for a conference that will include some of the top U.S. players on Salvadoran issues. He encourages me to join him there.

We are already less dependent on Gómez, particularly for contacts in Washington, D.C., and we remain nervous about being publicly associated with him. But when we get word that Gómez might bring the witness to Boston, we decide that I should go. I talk to Gómez privately and he mentions the potential impact of our case. "You're making a lot of noise," he says. "People on the Far Right are scared. You're a bunch of young lawyers energetic about investigating the Romero case and they're unsure how far you'll go. The key is to show people that you're serious and you'll follow through on this. That's how you'll get people to talk."

Even with these encouraging words, Gómez falls flat on the primary reason for my trip. He doesn't bring the witness against Daglio, and he confesses that he can't put us in touch with the man because it's too big a favor to ask. Gómez instead insists on a strategy of going through members of Congress, something he promises to advance when he goes to Washington, D.C., after the Boston conference. Several days later, though, Gómez tells me by phone that he doesn't have much to report. He offers yet another plan for talking to Daglio's old colleague that involves inviting the man to dinner and hoping that, after a few drinks, he will open up to the young female member of our legal team, Almudena Bernabeu. Prevalent though *machismo* is in Salvadoran society, it does not sound like much of a strategy.

WASHINGTON, D.C.—1984

Two decades before working with us, Leonel Gómez was involved in an episode that produced alarming accusations about the death squads in El Salvador. A month after Ambassador White's 1984 testimony on the Miami Six, an anonymous but high-ranking former officer in the Salvadoran armed forces made sweeping allegations in the U.S. media about the involvement of Roberto D'Aubuisson and El Salvador's top commanders in death squad activities. The accusations first appeared on the front page of the *New York Times* weeks before the Salvadoran presidential election in which D'Aubuisson was a leading candidate. Among the details was a claim that the money for death squad operations came from Salvadorans living in Miami. The Romero assassination, the officer said, was "planned and carried out by Mr. D'Aubuisson with money from exiles in Guatemala and under the protection of General [José Guillermo] García and Colonel [Nicolás] Carranza," the minister and vice-minister of defense at the time.[28] Because "D'Aubuisson did not have a reliable team of Salvadoran killers" he "used veterans of Nicaragua's deposed National Guard" for the Romero operation, the officer claimed.[29]

He seemed motivated to speak out because of D'Aubuisson's run for the presidency. He called D'Aubuisson an "anarchic psychopath" who would lead El Salvador into "uncontrollable violence." The officer worried that a D'Aubuisson victory "might provoke a break between the United States and the Salvadoran Government, thereby possibly aiding the insurgent guerrillas."[30] In that, he was on the same page as the Reagan administration, which needed to keep military aid flowing by distancing itself from D'Aubuisson. But the officer's anonymous interviews, including one with Walter Cronkite on CBS News, were actually engineered by opponents of Reagan's policies, including Leonel Gómez and former ambassador Robert White.[31]

A few weeks later, another front-page *New York Times* article tied the U.S. government directly to a top Salvadoran hard-liner. The *Times* reported that the CIA was paying $90,000 a year to Colonel Carranza.[32] Unnamed U.S. officials confirmed for the *Times* the anonymous officer's information about the link between the CIA and Carranza, whom U.S. diplomats referred to as a "fascist" and "the Gestapo."[33] The next day, just two days from the presidential election, Carranza denied any relationship with the CIA, and D'Aubuisson held his own press conference to denounce the officer who had made the allegations.[34] D'Aubuisson also called Carranza "a good man, a good soldier, a good Salvadoran."[35]

Despite the negative press, D'Aubuisson survived in the election to take on Duarte in a second round of voting set for early May. Several days later, the Salvadoran government fired the diplomat running its New Orleans consulate on the belief that he was the anonymous source who blew the whistle on the death squads.[36] The fired consul, Roberto Santivañez, once served at the highest levels of Salvadoran military intelligence, including as D'Aubuisson's boss.[37] Santivañez himself was believed to be involved in abuses, possibly even the Romero assassination.[38] This background bolstered Santivañez's credibility but his timing and the funding he received from supporters cut against it.[39] A year later, Santivañez went public. At a press conference in March 1985, he repeated and supplemented some of his earlier accusations, including that Salvadoran oligarchs in Miami had made the decision to kill Archbishop Romero. They tasked D'Aubuisson with passing along the order, Santivañez said. The assassination was planned in Guatemala, and Ricardo Lao Castillo, working directly for D'Aubuisson, received $120,000 to arrange the killing.[40]

Lao was an intelligence chief for the Contras, the collection of far-right forces then fighting to overthrow Nicaragua's leftist Sandinista regime. The allegation about Lao's involvement in Romero's assassination was explosive because at the time, the Reagan administration was financing the Contras in violation of U.S. law.[41] (Álvaro Saravia later told the Truth Commission that Lao once received $40,000 from D'Aubuisson's civilian backers.[42] And the commission reported that D'Aubuisson came to know Lao while D'Aubuisson was in exile in Guatemala.)[43]

Santivañez repeated many of these allegations in a documentary film shot around the same time. "It's decided in Guatemala that the objective is Monseñor Romero," Santivañez claimed.[44] "The death squads go and carry out the action in combination with Nicaraguans," Santivañez recounted, "possibly using a .223 [rifle]. . . . I also know that there were two Nicaraguans that participated, and members of Salvadoran security gave them cover." His sources were Salvadorans involved in intelligence, he said, though they did not personally participate in the assassination.

Santivañez said they killed Romero "with the singular idea of creating such chaos that would permit the removal of the junta . . . putting in a new junta in which [Defense Minister] García and [Vice-Minister] Carranza might participate. At that time, D'Aubuisson was following orders directly from Colonel García and Colonel Carranza."

"And in the case of D'Aubuisson, he participated directly? He gave the order to kill?" the filmmaker asked.

"There is not the slightest doubt that the person responsible for giving the order was D'Aubuisson. Now, the group of people that makes the decision is undoubtedly the group of capitalists."

"And in the case of General García and Colonel Carranza, had they been abreast of the decision?"

"Obviously," Santivañez continued, "General García and Colonel Carranza had to be abreast of this decision, they had to be informed of this decision because the death squad enters a dead-end street [where the chapel is located]. They assassinate Monseñor Romero and leave calmly. . . . There was coordination with all the [military] units in El Salvador."

"And in the case of the CIA, they were informed immediately? Taking into account that Carranza—"

"If we take into account that Colonel Carranza was on the CIA's payroll," Santivañez interrupted, "the CIA had to be informed of this assassination at the time. If not, [Carranza] was lying. But I don't think he was lying to them because he continued working for them."[45]

Even though Santivañez was willing to make such stunning charges about the CIA and his old Salvadoran colleagues, he didn't do it out of love for Archbishop Romero.

"And what had been the attitude about Romero's statements in his last sermon?" the filmmaker asked.

"In his homilies, Monseñor Romero was quite aggressive and he was instructing the troops that when an officer gave them orders to shoot Salvadorans that they should not shoot them." Santivañez found Romero's words intolerable. "It was an intrusion."

SAN SALVADOR—JANUARY 1980

Romero was an "intrusion" for the Salvadoran military not only because he called on soldiers to disobey their superiors but also because he criticized those superiors directly, including García and Carranza. On January 6, in his Sunday homily, Romero reflected on the crisis the country faced after most of the progressive members of the government resigned. "Their protest was against the high command of the armed forces which . . . had abandoned the spirit of [the reformist coup of] October 15th . . . to continue serving the interest of the economic oligarchy," Romero said, quoting a report aired on the archdiocese's radio station. Romero agreed that the high command's approach "prefers the repression of people over the proposed reforms as a way of resolving their problems." Going beyond mere criticism, Romero concretely called on García to resign as minister of defense. "His continued presence," Romero said, "signifies to the outside world that he is a tainted element of the government and the armed forces."[46] In his diary, Romero called García a "figure of the repression."[47]

SAN FRANCISCO—JANUARY 2004

The wind gently shakes the trees above our table on the patio of the Arlequin Cafe as Félix Kury pensively puffs on his cigar. A therapist, professor, and dedicated activist, Kury has been involved with CJA since its early days. He was instrumental in building CJA's original El Salvador case, the successful Florida lawsuit against General García and another former defense minister, Carlos Vides Casanova. Before that groundbreaking case began, Kury met with torture survivors about being plaintiffs in the civil action. He later became the director of the Clínica Martín-Baró, named for the Jesuit priest who pioneered the field of Liberation Psychology that analyzes people's psychological needs through an understanding of the repressive context in which they live. Kury hosted Martín-Baro in San Francisco in 1988, the year before he and five other Jesuit priests, along with their housekeeper and her daughter, were assassinated in San Salvador by the U.S.-trained Atlacatl Batalion. Many years before, Kury was an altar boy for Óscar Romero.

Kury was also responsible for connecting Almudena Bernabeu with CJA. During Almudena's early days in San Francisco, Kury introduced her to CJA's founding director, Gerald Gray. By now, Kury and Almudena are old friends, while I am just beginning to learn the value of Kury's insights. He has become a sounding board for us as we navigate the complexities of such a sensitive investigation. As we sit at the Arlequin, we are just a few weeks away from returning to El Salvador.

Kury pulls the cigar out of his mouth, leans forward, and speaks in a low voice, mixing his calm Spanish with occasional English. "CJA has had to work long and hard in El Salvador to gain a good reputation, but you've done it," Kury says. Our new lawsuit in Tennessee against Colonel Carranza, filed on behalf of survivors accusing him of crimes against humanity, has helped. "Now you've got some political capital, especially with the important human rights figures in El Salvador." I listen closely, waiting for the admonishment I know is coming. "But when it becomes known that you're working closely with Leonel Gómez," he says, "you'll lose that political capital, and key people won't talk to you anymore. This will jeopardize not only the Romero case but also the Carranza case. And Carranza could end up being important for the Romero investigation."

Kury reaches the crux of his analysis. "Gómez has a big mouth," he says, "and it will quickly become known if you end up meeting people like Héctor Regalado. When that happens, you will have already alienated the people who can help you far more than Gómez. And his idea that Almudena will be able to go to a casual dinner with someone who has information about the death squad financiers and suddenly charm him into talking is absolutely wrong." Kury pauses. "The only reason someone like that will talk is because you've given him a reason to do so. A really compelling motivation, like fear or revenge. And even if Gómez can get you to Héctor Regalado, that son of a bitch will lie to you."

"The other problem," he continues, "is that Gómez can't assure your safety. Talking to the bad guys is a very dangerous thing. The people you would alienate by working with Gómez are alive today for the simple reason that they know people who can protect them. They couldn't have done the things they've done without people looking out for them, people on the Right. If you have them watching out for you, you'll be much safer than if you're going it alone with Gómez." I agree, but to this point Gómez is the only person who has even hinted at being able to arrange meetings with insiders. "These other people can absolutely get you to the bad guys," Kury says, as though reading my mind. "It is infinitely safer to do it through them. The problem, of course, is that you can't do it over the phone. It has to be in person."

Kury gives us a lot to think about, and he is the first person who has provided a sound reason why our working with Gómez is not just counterproductive but dangerous. Others have told us not to trust Gómez but they have never given us an alternative. I e-mail the legal team an account of our meeting with Kury, and Nico van Aelstyn's reply sums up so many of the concerns we face. "The bottom line is if [others] can deliver witnesses, I'd drop [Gómez] and jump to [them] in an instant," Nico writes. "It's a question of getting the job done. . . . And in the end (as your email acknowledges in passing when describing the long road to establishing CJA's credibility in El Salvador), nothing builds credibility like success. It's really simple: we've got to win this case."

In mid-January, we finally learn the identity of the Mintz Group's secret ex-FBI contact who is looking into the death squad financiers. His name is Robert "Bobby" Levinson, and our introduction to him comes with a few words of caution. Levinson is an international operator, Mintz tells us, and he spent his career tracking the Russian mafia. His world is one where the sands are always shifting, so he is tough and perhaps difficult, but he can get results. Levinson authorizes Mintz to tell us his name and expresses that he wants to work with us if we can convince his employer to let him do so on a pro bono basis.

While we wait for the authorization, we debate the many areas in which we need Levinson's help. We want him to have a follow-up conversation with an insider source he has found concerning our list of suspected financiers and hard-line military officers. We think this is where Levinson can help most, but as the weeks pass and we wait for an answer, our list of topics for him grows. By the time we speak with him again, the list will include a subject we could have not imagined just a few months before.

NINE

"You Know Better Than to Ask That"

THE SEARCH FOR THE GETAWAY DRIVER

FRESNO—AUGUST 2004

"Let's go back to [Amado] Garay," Judge Wanger says about the getaway driver. "If Garay returned to El Salvador and got on a witness stand and implicated himself under oath, if he did that in my courtroom, I would order him taken into custody. Did he do that under a grant of some kind of amnesty or immunity in the Salvadoran court when he was there?"

"He says he was the driver in this action," Professor Terry Karl answers. "He did not, in the documents that I have seen, go as far as to locate himself in a range of actions. That's the first answer. The second—"

"Well," the judge interrupts, "that makes him a coconspirator, an aider and abettor."[1]

SAN FRANCISCO—2003

Garay's status as a coconspirator is the reason we want to find him. He was a member of Roberto D'Aubuisson's group and one of the only eyewitnesses to Romero's assassination, and because he has already testified maybe he will again. Even without knowing his whereabouts, we have pinned our hopes on Garay precisely because everyone else is a tougher bet. Many D'Aubuisson insiders are already dead. Some who are alive have publicly and repeatedly denied any involvement in violence. Any others, we assume, are unlikely to talk. Beyond Garay, we have prior, detailed testimony about the assassination from only one other man: Álvaro Saravia, our defendant on the lam.

We begin looking for Garay using the few documents we have. Salvadoran police records show he was born near Quezaltepeque, a city north of San Salvador, and that a doctor lives at Garay's old address there. After fleeing El Salvador in 1980, Garay landed in Costa Rica as a political refugee where, according to the documents, he ran a juice stand and a bar called the Copa Cabana. Other than his nickname, Mario, this is all we know.[2] We start by calling Costa Rican immigration officials but they give us nothing so we ask a colleague there for help. She can't find the juice stand or the bar, but someone does tell her that those establishments were once owned by a Salvadoran man and his wife. That is all she gets. As time marches on, we uncover few other leads. By the end of 2003, the trail is completely cold and we have almost given up hope of finding him.

In January 2004, Almudena Bernabeu goes to El Salvador to establish relationships that might pave the way to insider witnesses about the death squad financiers. These sensitive meetings are best held only in Spanish, without the disruption of an interpreter. I am the only other Spanish-speaking member of our team, but a medical emergency prevents me from traveling so we ask David Esquivel to go. David is our cocounsel in the Tennessee lawsuit against Colonel Nicolás Carranza. The son of Cuban immigrants, David is fluent in Spanish, and he and Almudena can interview witnesses for the Carranza case alongside meetings on the Romero work.

At the end of the trip, Almudena and David go to Garay's hometown of Quezaltepeque as a shot in the dark. They know there is no hope of finding him there, but they think the journey might produce a lead or two. The man who drives them there, Paulino Espinoza, is the director of the Cultural Center of the Central American University, as well as an accomplished musician and devoted follower of Archbishop Romero. Paulino is becoming a trusted friend in our investigation, driving us to meetings, serving as a sounding board, and keeping an eye out for us. Paulino decides to bring his colleague Eduardo "Guayo" Quijano along for the ride. Guayo has already driven Almudena and David to a few appointments during their trip, and it turns out that Guayo is from Quezaltepeque.

As they wind out of San Salvador and up through the mountains, Guayo tells them about his life growing up. His father died young and Guayo was raised by his uncle. For many years, Guayo says, the uncle was a supporter of the Farabundo Martí National Liberation Front (FMLN), the political party formed by the guerrillas after the civil war ended. Recently, though, Guayo's uncle has become far more conservative and he is now a fanatic for ARENA, the party of the late Roberto D'Aubuisson. In between stories in the car, Guayo pesters Almudena about why they are going to Quezaltepeque, his hometown. Almudena is evasive, fearful that any disclosure could jeopardize their covert mission, but as she dodges his questions, she thinks about the urgent need to find Garay, our best prospect for an insider witness.

Almudena knows that our records reveal that a doctor, the husband of Garay's stepdaughter, now lives in Garay's old house in Quezaltepeque. Almudena hopes to locate him by arriving in town and talking to strangers until she finds someone who knows where the doctor lives. But as Guayo hounds her about why they are going to Quezaltepeque, she reasons that although she doesn't know him well, he isn't a stranger. If Paulino brought him along, he can be trusted. It would be better to talk to him than a person on the street, and Quezaltepeque is far from safe. Corpses have been showing up there as a result of recent gang violence.

Still trying to hide the reason behind her question, Almudena asks Guayo if he knows the doctor. He laughs and asks, "Why do you want to know?"

Almudena sidesteps and tries to mask Garay's identity. "The doctor's name is in the documents I have."

Guayo turns around and looks at her, a smile coming to his lips. "That's my uncle," he says. "That's the man who raised me."

David, knowing that Guayo has a unique sense of humor, thinks Guayo is joking. But he is serious, and Guayo realizes that if Almudena is there to investigate the Romero assassination and she is asking about the doctor, she must be looking for Garay. Guayo knows him too. "Garay is the stepfather of my uncle's wife," Guayo says. They are related. The news hangs in the air before Almudena gathers herself and springs into action, urging Guayo to call his uncle. Happy to oblige, Guayo takes out his cell phone and dials the number. The doctor answers. "I'm on my way to Quezaltepeque with some friends," Guayo says, and his uncle invites them to drop by.

Navigating Quezaltepeque's bumpy roads and potholes, Paulino drives straight to the house and Guayo's uncle comes out to greet them. With presidential elections only two months away, the doctor's home reflects his new political orientation, as posters of ARENA's candidate decorate the walls. His daughters come in wearing red, white, and blue ARENA wristbands, and he serves his guests *agua de coco* as the youngest girl sings a campaign tune glorifying D'Aubuisson's party. The visitors try to hide their discomfort.

Despite the doctor's hospitality, the person they really want to see is his wife, Garay's stepdaughter. "She's at the market," he says, "but she'll be home soon." In El Salvador, they know, "soon" has no fixed meaning, so Almudena tries to kill time by engaging the doctor about his transformed political views. He praises the virtues of ARENA as the clock continues to tick and Almudena grows anxious. Unable to wait, she decides to tell the doctor why they are there. She moves to the edge of the couch, leans forward, and begins describing CJA's work, the same stump speech we have delivered countless times. When she finishes, she decides to take the plunge. "I'm looking for Amado Garay," she says.

The doctor remains silent for some time. As he crafts a careful reply, his words emerge in polite but formal tones. Using Garay's nickname, Mario, he details the difficulties his wife has endured over the years. Life is not easy, he says, with a notorious stepfather like Garay. Measured though he is, the doctor lets slip that Garay is not in Central America. As he continues to talk, he implies that Garay is in the United States. Almudena, listening intently, sees this as a useful confirmation but not a big surprise until the doctor, in his cryptic monologue, hints that Garay is under the care of the U.S. government. It dawns on Almudena that Garay is in the witness protection program.

Struggling to stay calm, Almudena takes the tiny thread of information and tugs at it. Under a barrage of questions, the doctor confirms that the family has traveled to the United States several times to see Garay and his wife, but they have never learned exactly where Garay lives. They fly to Miami, the doctor says, where "agents" transport them to a second city, which is different on every visit. On the first trip, for example, they all met at a hotel near the Kansas City airport. When the doctor's wife speaks to her mother on the phone, they can't discuss the weather for risk of disclosing their location. ("You know better than to ask that," the mother warns.) The doctor suggests to Almudena that the Salvadoran government negotiated Garay's arrangement directly with the United States. Almudena begs him to contact Garay on our behalf, but the doctor refuses to commit. After so many questions, he is becoming impatient, and even though his wife still has not returned, it is clear he wants his visitors to go. Having learned far more than they ever expected, Almudena, David, Paulino, and Guayo gather their things and thank the doctor.

As they walk back to the truck, they pass a woman carrying grocery bags. She smiles. Guayo, without saying a word to his colleagues, stops to talk with her as the others continue on. At such a late hour, they are in a hurry to get back to San Salvador. The truck's engine is running when Guayo catches up and climbs in. As they drive out of town, he says that the woman with the bags is the doctor's wife, Garay's stepdaughter, the one they came to see. But they don't turn around; there's no time and their message has already been delivered. Quezaltepeque has given them more than enough.

Although we are stunned to hear the news from Almudena, our pragmatic team immediately begins to strategize about what to do next. Just knowing Garay is in witness protection gets us only so far. Now there is a potentially impenetrable obstruction between us and Garay: the U.S. government. Will U.S. officials let us speak with him? Will this weaken our chances of getting him to testify? Will this cause other government agencies, like the CIA, to take note of our investigation? No one on our team has the slightest clue about the witness protection program. We do not even know which branch of government administers the program.

We eventually turn to Bobby Levinson, the Mintz Group's ex-FBI contact, for help. Although we think maybe the U.S. Marshals Service, not the FBI, runs witness protection, we still assume the FBI played a role in getting Garay to the United States in 1987. We hope Levinson might have contacts that can help. In early March, we compile a memo of the investigative areas in which we want his assistance. The final section seeks advice on how to approach the witness protection program. In addition to Garay, we include the name of Roberto Santivañez, the former intelligence officer who spilled the beans on his old compatriots in the Salvadoran military. We speculate that if Santivañez is still alive, he might also be in hiding. "Any information about these individuals could be extremely helpful," the memo concludes.

After almost a month, Levinson comes through with a solid strategy. A colleague made some discreet inquiries in Washington, D.C., on our behalf. He learned that if we make a request in writing to a particular official, there's a good probability we'll receive confirmation that the people we're looking for are indeed in witness protection. We might be able to take their testimony, though it would require a subpoena.

Two days later, by phone, Levinson seems to confirm that both Garay and Santivañez are in the program. "I would've been told if nothing was there," he says to Russell Cohen. It seems like a dream come true until Levinson clarifies in a further call that he did not receive definite confirmation that the two men were under protection. He only meant to say that we might receive helpful information if we contact the right official. Unsure what this means, Russ and Nico van Aelstyn draft a letter to the official and send it off.

More than three weeks pass with no answer, and when we tell Levinson he expresses genuine surprise. He was under the impression we would receive an immediate reply. He offers to speak with his source to find out about the holdup, but he is unable to reach the source for over a week.

On Levinson's advice, Nico and Russ call the witness protection program. Several tries to the phone number are unsuccessful. When we finally get a more direct phone number, Russ connects with someone only to be told that the man to whom we have addressed our letter is no longer the head of witness security. Bewildered, Russ pleads with the person for another name, but the furthest the man will go is to say, "We'll see if we can do that." Russ hangs up the phone in frustration, puzzled that Levinson uncharacteristically gave us the out-of-date name. Even so, at least we have a phone number and we have spoken to someone, so now we can beg, plead, and cajole as much as necessary. But after a few days, all Nico can report to the team is "some curious and as yet insubstantial communications with the witness protection folks." With so little progress, Nico wonders if we might need to enlist the support of allies on Capitol Hill.

WASHINGTON, D.C.—MARCH 1980

Capitol Hill was not always kind to Archbishop Romero's message of peace. Less than twenty-four hours after his assassination, a subcommittee in the U.S. House of Representatives began hearings on President Carter's proposed military aid package to El Salvador that Romero had criticized publicly before his death. The military assistance was so important for the Carter administration, and Romero was such a prominent voice, that the acting U.S. ambassador, James Cheek, had met with the archbishop in February 1980.[3] Romero rejected Cheek's explanation that the military assistance was nonlethal and designed to address only deficiencies in the Salvadoran Army. Romero recorded in his diary that he told Cheek the aid could result in "greater repression of the people."[4]

The day after Romero's murder, some U.S. congresspeople wanted to postpone the session on military assistance, but the Carter administration pushed for it to continue. Witnesses testified the same day. The subcommittee did delay the vote until after Romero's funeral. But the following week, a majority of subcommittee members ignored Romero's pleas and approved the military aid package to El Salvador.[5]

We need to speak to Amado Garay because he is the only eyewitness against Saravia who might cooperate with us. With our pessimism growing about the witness protection program, Russ finally catches a break when a sympathetic official connects him with the program's general counsel. The man is friendly, but their conversations have a surreal air. Because he represents a service based on secrecy, the counsel refuses to offer any real information and cannot confirm whether Garay and Santivañez are in the program. Russ is forced to couch his responses as conditional hypotheticals.

"If someone were in witness protection," Russ asks, "what would I do?"

"Well," the man says, "if someone were in witness protection, what one would do would be to . . ." He gives no hint about Garay or Santivañez yet he seems to want to help. He leaves Russ with a promise to look into the matter, but even his affable tone gives little reassurance, and Russ concludes that our inquiry is dead.

———

TEN

"A Rabid Anti-Communist"

MEETING WITNESSES FROM THE ARENA PARTY

FRESNO—AUGUST 2004

"Was Romero a political person?" I ask the witness dressed in black with a white clerical collar, an outfit he normally eschews for something more casual. Jon Cortina is a Jesuit priest from the Basque country of Spain who has lived in El Salvador for decades, and while he is both ascetic and passionate, he is an engineer rather than a theologian. His strong, gray eyebrows hover just above his glasses, giving him a scholarly look.

"That has been a big argument many times in El Salvador," Cortina says in his excellent though not perfect English. "I would say no. I mean, all of us, when we talk, no matter whether we say A or B, our speech has political components." Romero's sermons had political content such as denouncing injustices, but there is a distinction. "He was ethical," Cortina continues. "He was a man that was fully ethical and not political. The problem is that in El Salvador, one problem we have is that we are more politically minded and we are not ethically minded. Romero was ethically minded. To tell the truth hurts, and he told the truth, clearly. And that's what the *campesinos* say, 'Always, he was a man who told the truth, no matter what.'"

"What effect did his [views] have on the rich and on the military?"

"Well, not much, because they killed him."[1]

SAN SALVADOR—FEBRUARY 2004

Only a month after discovering that the getaway driver, Amado Garay, is hiding in the United States, we are back in El Salvador for a trip crucial to expanding the case beyond the lone defendant, Álvaro Saravia. Almudena Bernabeu's previous visit cemented some important relationships and opened doors, but it did not immediately lead to the insider interviews we need for evidence against the death squad financiers. The task is difficult because while Salvadorans have a long history of denouncing the oligarchs as a group, naming names has proven dangerous. In 1994, following the declassification of U.S. government documents for the Truth Commission, a former guerrilla commander went to jail for a month on defamation charges for claiming that specific oligarchs had funded the death squads.

One of our first appointments is in an upscale San Salvador neighborhood, its ceramic-roofed houses hidden behind tropical trees and ten-foot walls. From the outside, our destination looks indistinguishable from the neighboring homes. A receptionist buzzes us through the front gate, and we climb a tall set of stairs to reach the first building of what turns out to be a compound with impeccable landscaping. Entering the office, I notice large burlap coffee bags—from our host's company, no doubt—proudly hung on the wall. A woman directs us to a sofa and brings us coffee. Almudena and I sip slowly as we wait for what seems like an hour. We speculate whether the delay is an intentional slight or simply the norm for a busy person.

The man we are here to see has been front and center for the ARENA party's most dramatic political battles. His name also appeared on the list of people suspected of involvement in death squads that U.S. State Department officials gave to the FBI in 1983.

Long after we finish our coffee, he finally arrives. Dressed casually but maintaining a distinguished air, he directs us to a conference room. His manner is neither welcoming nor sinister. Sensing no use in small talk, Almudena explains that we are in El Salvador to investigate the murder of Archbishop Romero. Though our host listens patiently to the pitch, his response begins with a well-worn assessment of who was responsible for the crime. Monseñor Romero could have been killed by the Right or the Left, he says. He adds that the leftist guerrillas might also have killed the Jesuit priests in 1989, conveniently ignoring the testimony of the Salvadoran Army soldiers who already confessed to that crime.[2]

His answer irritates me even as I recognize that his story is consistent with someone of his political background. Attributing an "unsolvable" murder to the "chaos" that gripped the country is a tired tactic. Later, reading Joan Didion's book *Salvador,* I find a passage of striking similarity that quotes the comments of another right-wing figure twenty-two years earlier: "'We don't really know who killed [Romero], do we? It could have been the right . . .' He drew the words out, *cantabile*. 'Or . . . it could have been the left. We have to ask ourselves, who gained? Think about it, Joan.'"[3]

Following the same playbook, our host doesn't give an inch about Romero's assassination. After proclaiming himself "a rabid anti-Communist," he embarks on a pointless debate with Almudena about whether Stalin or Hitler killed more people.

The meeting is not without some value, though. He doesn't whitewash the excesses of El Salvador's top anti-Communist, Roberto D'Aubuisson. Rather than exonerate the ARENA founder, our host distances himself. Yes, D'Aubuisson did have "parallel" organizations involved in crimes, and there was financing of D'Aubuisson's activities, he says, but it was done on an individual level. There was no coordination.

Our host says he had nothing to do with it.

SAN SALVADOR—FEBRUARY 1980

On February 24, exactly one month before Romero was killed, the Sunday gospel was about Jesus rejecting the devil's temptations. In his homily, Romero tied the gospel to the violent reality of El Salvador. He denounced the recent bombing of the archdiocese's radio tower as "an attempt to silence the prophetic and pastoral voice of the archdiocese precisely because it is trying to be the voice of the voiceless." The roots of the violence were clear to Romero. "The authors of this attack want to prevent people from knowing the truth. . . . They do not want people to unite and cry out: 'Enough! Put an end to the exploitation and domination by the Salvadoran oligarchy!'"

For Romero, the wealthy families were undoubtedly to blame for the country's ills: "In the final analysis, those responsible are members of the oligarchy, which at this moment is desperately and blindly trying to repress the people. The dynamiting of [the radio station] is only a symbol. What does it mean? The oligarchy, seeing the danger of losing the complete domination that they have . . . are defending their selfish interests, not with arguments, not with popular support, but with the only thing they have—money to buy weapons and pay mercenaries who massacre the people and strangle every legitimate cry for justice and freedom."

In the lead-up to Easter—"a time of conversion"—Romero called on the oligarchs to reform: "I want to extend a brotherly call, a pastoral call to the oligarchy so that they might be converted and live and use their economic power to bring happiness to people rather than cause ruin and disgrace." Pope John Paul II had just urged all Catholics to give up "superfluous wealth" and help the needy. "I hope that this call of the church will not further harden the hearts of the oligarchs but will move them to conversion," said Romero. "Let them share what they are and have. Let them not keep silencing with violence those of us who offer this invitation." Romero announced that he was a target for assassination: "I speak in the first person, because this week I received notice that I am on the list of those who are to be eliminated next week. But let it be known that no one can kill the voice of justice."[4]

SAN SALVADOR—FEBRUARY 2004

As dusk falls, María Julia Hernández, the longtime head of the human rights office for the archdiocese, drives Nico van Aelstyn to an unknown church. They enter a side room, and a woman is there waiting. Dressed in neat, clean clothes with dark, precisely fixed hair, she appears to be a typical middle-aged San Salvador woman. But Nico knows her background is far from normal. She worked for Roberto D'Aubuisson's ARENA party in its early years, and she secretly testified to the Truth Commission about the financing of the death squads.

Nico begins the interview slowly, easing into the difficult topics. Nico's Spanish is limited, but Hernández has insisted that only he—our lead lawyer—can conduct this interview. Despite her own struggles with English, Hernández acts as interpreter. Nico pulls out a copy of the statement the woman gave to the Truth Commission around 1992. The document is long and detailed, sometimes reflecting her direct quotes and other times paraphrasing her evidence. It starts simply, saying she was invited in September 1981 to participate in a new political party, ARENA, and she became close with many of the founders. "I was a trusted person inside the party," she says in the statement. "I was tasked with writing letters for Roberto D'Aubuisson, who trusted me a lot and held me in high esteem."[5] The document lists many people involved in the early days of ARENA, but the portions that interest us concern the ones involved in violence. She says that D'Aubuisson headed the death squad known as the Maximiliano Hernández Martínez Brigade, which we know was named after the general whose soldiers massacred thousands of *campesinos* in the 1932 Matanza. Among the brigade's members, she adds, was "Toño" Cornejo, a close D'Aubuisson associate who, we have just found out, lives in Miami.[6]

"There was a group of army officers who formed part of the death squads," she says, "and although they were not formally affiliated with ARENA nor did they frequent the party headquarters, in conversations with any of the ARENA founders or members of the security team, they spoke of their support and participation." The list is long but includes Colonel Nicolás Carranza, the defendant in our Tennessee lawsuit. It also includes Álvaro Saravia and his coconspirator in Romero's murder, Eduardo Ávila.

"Those who financed all this," the woman said, included Billy Sol, one of our lead suspects. Among others involved in death squad activity, she lists a one-time Sol colleague, Eduardo Lemus O'Byrne.[7] We know that Saravia told the Truth Commission that Lemus O'Byrne hosted a meeting with D'Aubuisson the day after Romero's assassination and may have provided money to pay the assassin.[8] The ARENA witness relates a different, chilling story. "Another time," she says, "I asked [a D'Aubuisson bodyguard] about the rumor that at Quality Meat, owned by the Lemus O'Byrne family, they used power saws to murder people who later appeared chopped up in trash dumps in San Salvador. . . . [The bodyguard], laughing and joking, told me, 'Look, dear, don't worry, to decapitate someone a saw is useful, like a guitar chord, one pull and the head is gone.'"[9]

The final name of note on her list is Alfredo Mena Lagos. A graduate of California's Menlo College, Mena Lagos used to make public appearances with Roberto D'Aubuisson to denounce Communism on behalf of their organization, FAN.[10] His name appeared multiple times in the documents seized with the Saravia Diary, and U.S. government documents contained allegations that he was involved with the death squads at the same time he was meeting with conservative U.S. political contacts in Washington, D.C.[11] A Germanophile, but "not necessarily Nazi," the boats in Mena Lagos's fishing business were named after Nazi-era German generals.[12]

Nico spends almost three hours going through the witness's Truth Commission testimony with her. He is impressed by how controlled and dispassionate she is. She sits still in her chair, completely rigid, without ever shifting. She is like an undercover agent, Nico thinks. Knowing we need sworn testimony for our case, Nico asks her to give a new statement under oath. She agrees.

I am relaxing in my hotel room when the phone rings. I answer hoping that Nico is calling to update me about a successful meeting with the witness. Instead, he instructs me to come quickly to the church; they need someone who can type in Spanish and English. By the time I arrive, it is already late. As I walk in the room, I feel like an outsider intruding on a closed conversation. I greet the witness and find an old computer in the corner of the room. "You'll be typing an affidavit," Nico tells me. "We'll do it in Spanish and later translate it to English for the court." I am ecstatic but try not to smile.

The witness begins dictating to me in deliberate sentences, allowing me to type as she speaks. When we reach the third paragraph, she says, "I am from a conservative and traditional family but personally I took a political option for social change." This doesn't sound like the ARENA party, I think to myself. "In 1978, I began my political life by supporting in different ways people who I later knew were members of the ERP, part of what was later called the FMLN." My hands almost freeze. The ERP was one of the first guerrilla factions.[13] "The assassination of Monseñor Romero had a very strong impact on my life, and I decided to get involved in the revolutionary process, with all the risks that brought. For that reason, when the opportunity to work in support of the formation of the ARENA party presented itself, I mentioned it to my ERP superiors who made me see the importance of working on aspects of gathering internal information from the party. I ended up accepting."

She was a mole inside ARENA. I am stunned. By outward appearance, she looks like someone who just stumbled across some frightening information during her time as an ARENA worker. This was my impression when reading her Truth Commission testimony. Instead, she was a guerrilla who penetrated the inner circle of a fanatically anti-Communist organization. As I continue typing, I think about her value as a witness in our case. While her true identity does not ruin her credibility, if we use her testimony against one of the financiers, his defense lawyers and the ARENA stalwarts will scream that she has a political bias.[14]

"I gained the trust of many people in the ARENA party," she continues. She had their confidence because she knew several from childhood or from being in the same social circles. She was good friends with many of them even as she wanted them held accountable for what they were doing. "In general, they all shared an anti-Communist sentiment, and the majority knew who among them was involved in the death squads. . . . Many of the top leaders of the party spoke with great pride about the activities of the death squads. Based on the trust and friendships I had, I was able to learn from various sources how they were organized and worked in the period before the formation of the ARENA party."

"On many occasions," she says, "working in the ARENA office, I had the opportunity to see the books that contained financial information about the party donors, which were in the accounting department. I knew that many of these people were linked with the previous financial support of the paramilitary groups known as the death squads." ARENA secretary general Mario Redaelli told her that many of the party's funders had supported D'Aubuisson's group during the "clandestine period" after their arrests at Finca San Luis.[15] "They contained only names and monthly amounts. They didn't contain dates or details of their use. From my [professional] experience, I knew that these weren't accounting books but were for internal control of financing," she says.

"One of the biggest financiers who appeared in the books was Guillermo 'Billy' Sol Bang, who made contributions up to 60,000 colones [$12,000] per month." She names others whose donations were recorded. "I am sure about my memory of these names because at that time I memorized the names that I heard and saw in the documents in the ARENA office," she says. "Each night I wrote them down to give to a person with the ERP." She also saw a "black list" of union leaders, teachers, and others who became targets of the death squads.

She heard accounts of the Romero assassination as well. "On one occasion," she says, "I asked Redaelli if it was true that a .22-caliber rifle had been used to kill Monseñor Romero and he told me no, a precise gun and caliber had been used," a special .223-caliber Roberts rifle. "With that type of bullet," she continues, relating Redaelli's information, "it was impossible to stay alive because it created a small entry wound but inside it acted like a type of drill bit that destroyed. If you didn't die from the bullet, you would die drowning from the internal hemorrhaging that it caused." Redaelli said that "in his house, in a place of honor, he had a very valued trophy that he was going to bring me so I could see it since it was exactly the same as what had been used to kill Monseñor Romero. He also offered to give me a bullet of the same caliber used to kill Monseñor Romero so I could make an amulet that was going to give me good luck. Later he gave it to me."[16]

I continue typing as we reach paragraph 12. It is now very late.

The witness asked Redaelli about the shooter. "He told me the person who killed Monseñor Romero was a professional who came into the country, and that he came and went only for that operation," she says.

Redaelli and others told her that after the 1980 arrests at Finca San Luis, many of them had to leave the country and go to Guatemala. The group included Redaelli, D'Aubuisson, Héctor Regalado, and Antonio Cornejo Arango, the man now in Miami. "When they were in Guatemala," she says, "they had many economic problems. . . . Their problems were solved through the contributions of the financiers. They said that the person who contributed most to the activities of the party was Guillermo [Billy] Sol." The amounts provided by the financiers depended on the need.

Her dictation finally stops and I print the affidavit, now totaling nineteen paragraphs. Satisfied with the document, the witness signs her name and hands the pages to me. I can sense how well she understands the burden of possessing such intelligence and the danger of passing it on to us. Even so, her nerves are far steadier than mine. The church is dark and silent as she leaves. Around 2:00 A.M., Nico and I arrive back at our hotel, and we have a quick drink to unwind. As I return to my room, Nico takes the affidavit out of his bag and locks it in his safe.

ELEVEN

"We Don't Have a Clue What the Hell Is Going On"

THE CONTINUING HUNT FOR SARAVIA
AND INSIDER WITNESSES

FRESNO—AUGUST 2004

We present Judge Wanger with a large binder of written declarations from dozens of people who knew Archbishop Romero or were affected by his death. They come from every sector of society, from Salvadoran catechists to Nobel laureates, and they provide a testament to Romero's broad and lasting impact:

> We had the tremendous privilege of being friends with [Romero], serving him, and helping him; and it was always clear that he was the teacher and that we were the disciples, that he was the guide and we were his followers. Monseñor Romero helped me more than anything with being human in a world of death and injustice. (Jon Sobrino: Jesuit priest in El Salvador, professor, and director of the Monseñor Romero Center)

> We were very clear what Monseñor Romero's role was as pastor, how he knew how to play his role of good shepherd and to give his life for his flock. On one occasion when we were going to Apopa, he asked us what we felt when we were talking to him, if we were scared. The response of everyone was "no" and that we felt strengthened by being with him as our pastor. (Joaquín Alonso Álvarez Campos: Catholic priest in El Salvador's Cristo Salvador Zacamil Parish)

> For the previous two years, I had made many journeys to El Salvador, documenting the living conditions of the poor and the human rights abuses inflicted upon them by their government. I knew Monseñor as a man beloved of his people, who kept his door always open for them, walked among them without protection, lived without protection, and sought no refuge from the dangers in which his flock was placed. . . . I also noticed that

Monseñor was, by his presence, calming all of us. A light shone from him. And in seeing this, I realized that I was in the presence, for the first and thus far the last time in my life, of a living saint. In the twenty-four years that have passed, I have only become more confirmed in that opinion. He was a rare soul on earth, and when he died, the world was diminished. (Carolyn Forché: U.S. poet and human rights advocate)

SAN FRANCISCO—FEBRUARY 2004

With one piece of sworn testimony concerning the death squad financiers, we continue the search for Álvaro Saravia, and we press on with gaining access to Amado Garay in witness protection. The Florida investigator recommended by the Mintz Group calls a phone number connected to Inés Olsson, the woman living at Saravia's Modesto address. Speaking in Spanish, the investigator says he has a package to deliver to Saravia. The woman on the other end is forthcoming and, surprisingly, she says Saravia left for El Salvador only two or three weeks ago. Any package for Saravia should be left with his "ex-wife," she says, since they are still in contact. The investigator is certain the "ex-wife" is Inés Olsson. We have trouble processing the news. If the woman is telling the truth, it means Saravia has been in the United States this whole time and only recently left the country. The other implication is that Olsson lied in telling us Saravia departed a while ago and that she didn't know where he was.

The most logical place to turn now is the U.S. government, because our sources might be able to confirm Saravia's departure from the United States. We receive some bewildering answers. Our first source says that government computers show that Saravia "voluntarily permanently departed" from the United States on September 16, 2003, four days after we filed the lawsuit. The source, however, adds the perplexing detail that when Saravia voluntarily departed, he was escorted onto the plane by an officer from the U.S. Department of Homeland Security (DHS). What's more, none of this information was in the government's computer when the source checked the system back in October 2003.

This raises so many questions it is hard to keep them straight. If Saravia wanted to leave the United States, he could have just gone. Why would he go to Homeland Security before departing? Also, an immigrant cannot simply call up DHS and hop on a plane. And why would Saravia have voluntarily left if, as we have been told, his immigration case was closed in 1991 and he is no longer subject to deportation? Did he leave in order to evade the lawsuit? The timing seems to say yes. But how could he risk taking a plane to El Salvador? Given the danger he faces there, it would have been reckless to go through the airport. And why was there no notice of Saravia's exit in the government's computer in October 2003? Why did it appear in the system later? Why did it appear at all? Usually the government does not keep track of departures.

I start to wonder if the FBI or CIA is involved.

Almudena Bernabeu, meanwhile, calls an intelligence source in El Salvador, and her news is even more stunning: the person has found Saravia in Central America. Not only does this source know where Saravia is—in the hands of "powerful" people, the source says—but this person might be able to get a message to him. Nico van Aelstyn immediately connects the dots with Saravia's "voluntary" departure. "That Saravia was found is big," Nico writes our legal team. "That Saravia is being housed by powerful people— apparently powerful enough to spirit him out of the U.S. with DHS grease on very short notice—is huge."

Almudena has already scheduled another phone call with her source. If he is being sincere, we need to get a proposal ready for Saravia. Nico's e-mail outlines the elements. We want Saravia's testimony in as many forms as possible—a sworn affidavit, a videotaped deposition, taking the witness stand at trial—and he will have to identify everyone involved in the Romero assassination. Nico lists the ways in which we hold the upper hand. "Our biggest point of leverage," he writes, "is the one that we never mention, the fact that we found him and the identity and capabilities of our intermediaries." Judge Wanger has scheduled the trial for August and, as Nico says, it will be "a big trial [with] big names and much media coverage in the United States and El Salvador. It will make Saravia look very, very bad." Our basic message to Saravia, says Nico, is that "the August trial is only the first step in a much larger campaign. Work with us now and you have a chance to shape it in a way that may be a little better for you and your friends."

Russell Cohen, as he often does, raises a useful note of caution. Given the timing of the events, he wants to make sure we aren't being used as political pawns. "Maybe I'm being a little paranoid," he writes, "but if news that Saravia's been located gets out, for the FMLN [party] this may be another Pedro Lobo circus—in reverse—on the eve of the election." Pedro Lobo, we know, was emblematic of the depths to which Roberto D'Aubuisson sank in obstructing investigations of the Romero assassination in El Salvador. In

1984, just ahead of the presidential election in which he ran as ARENA's candidate, D'Aubuisson went on television and played a videotape of an alleged defector from the FMLN guerrillas, named Pedro Lobo, confessing his involvement in Romero's murder. Lobo then gave newspaper interviews in which he implicated top FMLN commanders in the plot, a clear attempt by D'Aubuisson to pin the assassination on the insurgents and absolve himself of culpability.[1]

Pedro Lobo was quickly exposed as a hoax. An ex-convict admitted that he had been bribed while in jail and pressured into recording the false "confession."[2] The prisoner even testified that a Salvadoran colonel, in cahoots with Honduran officials, coached him over several months on how to act like an FMLN guerrilla in order to make the video look genuine.[3] Such were the politics of El Salvador that a leading presidential candidate would go on national television and play a fake confession engineered through an elaborate military plan. Now, Russ's point is that just as D'Aubuisson and ARENA tried to pin the Romero assassination on the FMLN before the 1984 elections, we have to be careful that the FMLN is not manufacturing Saravia's reappearance for political advantage during the 2004 campaign.

Calling her intelligence contact every day, Almudena uncovers more details of how Saravia was located. The source's people were investigating "one of Saravia's group"—he won't say the name over the phone—who was allegedly involved in a different murder plot. Through this, they discovered that Saravia had been seen with the target of their inquiry, likely near the border between Guatemala and El Salvador. Almudena tells her contact we want to get a message to Saravia, and he says he will try. Saravia will be very scared, the source cautions, but "there are ways to approach him." Nico raises the point that if the "powerful" people protecting Saravia find out about all the cards we hold against him, they might kill Saravia. Once again, we have to be careful.

With the Salvadoran elections at the end of March 2004, Almudena's intelligence source goes quiet, a silence then prolonged by an unexpected illness. Our U.S.-based contacts have no more information to add about Saravia. Finding him drops to the bottom of our agenda, particularly because his alleged location outside the United States makes his cooperation with us far less likely. We turn our energies to preparing for our trial against him. In late April, though, Almudena's source comes through and again confirms that Saravia is in El Salvador. The source's associate spoke with Saravia and conveyed the message that we want to talk. The associate told Saravia about our forthcoming trial and the negative attention it will generate for him. Saravia was very nervous, he says.

MIAMI, FLORIDA—MAY 2004

On May 3, I meet Bobby Levinson in person. Through his transition from a mysterious ex-FBI agent to an investigator searching for insider witnesses and helping us with the witness protection program, no one from our legal team has seen him in the flesh. I am anxious and unsure about how this encounter will go. We agree on a breakfast meeting and I get to the downtown restaurant early. While I search for a quiet seat among the vinyl booths and floral patterns, I see a man sitting alone with a Palm Pilot in his hands. Levinson beat me here. He stands to greet me, his 250 pounds straightening to a six-foot-four frame. Even somewhat out of shape, he is clearly someone who cannot be intimidated, even by the Russian mafia he once investigated. When he extends a handshake, though, my preconceptions vanish. His mouth, topped by a thick gray mustache, breaks into a sunshiny grin. Whatever his other skills, Levinson's success in the FBI surely was a result of his charm. Within minutes, he seems like a lifelong friend.

Amicable though the introduction is, we turn quickly to work. Levinson provides information he has gathered from several sources about links between Roberto D'Aubuisson, Álvaro Saravia, and Nicaraguan Contra intelligence chief Ricardo Lao. This reinforces what we already know: in 1985, D'Aubuisson's old boss, Roberto Santiváñez, publicly accused D'Aubuisson of paying Lao to arrange Archbishop Romero's assassination. Saravia also testified to the Truth Commission that Lao once received $40,000 from D'Aubuisson's civilian backers, and the Saravia Diary includes notations of Lao's name and payments to Nicaraguans.[4]

While fascinating, Levinson's great work still has not gotten us where we need to be. I know that my mission is to deliver a message about priorities. "We really need you to focus your limited time on the financiers," I tell him.

Levinson already knows this. "I'm trying to figure out strategies to stay on course," he says. He suggests that we could try to get information from Lao about the financiers. Levinson has recently learned that Lao could be in Honduras. "We could use the U.S. embassy to put pressure on the Honduran government to prosecute Lao for one of his contract murders."

"I don't have good contacts at the embassy," I confess.

"Don't worry," he says, "I'll talk to mine."

Levinson doesn't think his primary source has much on the financiers, but Levinson knows a few wealthy Central Americans and he will try to develop leads there. "That would be great," I say, while also telling him we want to track the whereabouts and assets of the suspected financiers, particularly those connected to Miami. Levinson thinks he might be able to get some people to look into this. "E-mail me your three or four key names," he says.

Despite my protests, Levinson refuses to let me pay for breakfast, and he gives me a firm handshake as he says goodbye.[5] Just hours later, he gets in touch on a subject he had not mentioned during breakfast. A source just contacted him to say that Álvaro Saravia is reportedly living in Nicaragua. As if that was not enough, the source said that Ricardo Lao was not in Honduras but Miami.

The revelation about Lao is explosive because if he is in the United States, he is a possible defendant in our lawsuit. The disclosure on Saravia's whereabouts is harder to gauge. We already know he is outside the United States, and we have an avenue to get to him through Almudena's intelligence source. But that person has been in touch with Saravia in El Salvador, not Nicaragua. Perhaps the source's approach caused Saravia to flee, or maybe Levinson's contact is wrong about Saravia's location. I do not know what to think.

"I received an interesting phone call late last night," Almudena e-mails the team six days later. Saravia, her source now says, is not in some remote Central American town but in *San Francisco,* our very own city in the United States. He is allegedly living with a relative and suffering from poor health, including a loss of eyesight. What's more, according to Almudena's source, Saravia wants to talk and has not blinked at the possibility of a negotiation about the lawsuit. The source assures Almudena that Saravia has evidence about the "second part of the case," the death squad financiers. The source will pass Almudena's contact information directly to Saravia.

It seems incomprehensible, in light of the conflicting information we have received, that Saravia can be in California, but if it's true, none of us knows what to do. How much would Saravia have to give us to even discuss settlement of the case? What kind of a deal could we make? Nico van Aelstyn, as always, has great ideas and his reply to Almudena's e-mail is blunt:

> I think it's critical that we communicate strength. Saravia has to understand that we're holding most of the cards and he's got to really deliver us something powerful before we'd even consider these options. He may be able to do

that, but he has to believe that he's got to go the distance with us: give us everything he knows. If I were him, I'd be tempted to treat us as patsies—give us a few low risk tidbits (e.g., stuff about dead folks like Roberto D'Aubuisson) in return for dropping the case against him. . . . I expect him to be arrogant and wiggly. We need to show him—in our tone as much as anything—that we like our current position and will only change it for something really valuable.

Always looking for an edge, Nico concludes, "If he's seriously ill and may be losing his sight, do we want to involve a priest?"

We again contact a U.S. immigration source, the one who originally told us that Saravia had voluntarily departed from the United Sates days after the filing of the case. "He checked to see if there has been any change since his last check," Russ e-mails us. "Apparently there is a new entry in the [immigration] file, dated September 16, 2003, the same day as the prior entry indicating Saravia's departure from the country and his abandoning of his asylum claim. The new entry states that Saravia is 'in the United States and still in the asylum process; and that he is of interest to [Homeland Security] for possible human rights violations in El Salvador.' If anyone can figure out what is going on, please let me know!"

I'm now worried that the CIA is involved, though for what reason I'm not sure. I reply to Russ in exasperation, "I think we should stop guessing and just admit that we don't have a clue what the hell is going on."

TWELVE

"God Forgive Me for What I'm Going to Do"

AN INSIDER GOES ON THE RECORD

FRESNO—AUGUST 2004

"Did you attend Romero's funeral?" I ask Father Walter Guerra, who advised the archbishop on his Sunday homilies, including the final one before his death. I direct Guerra to a black-and-white photo showing a massive gathering of people in a San Salvador plaza. Over 100,000 mourners fill the square in front of the cathedral.[1]

"Yes," Guerra says. "I was one of those, along with six other priests, who got to carry the body of Monseñor Romero from the altar to the main door in front of the plaza." As the cardinal celebrating the mass began preaching, "the first explosion came from the area where the National Palace is," Guerra says. Many believe the Salvadoran military started the shooting. "There was a stream of people coming this way. . . . They couldn't get in because there were steel gates." Then, he says, "explosions started going off and there was a rush of people going everywhere. . . . Many people were on the ground, and they were trampled." Guerra and the other priests "took Monseñor Romero's body, and we put him back into the cathedral. The people knocked down the steel gates and went into the cathedral. There were at least five thousand of us in the cathedral. And those of us, the priests who carried his body, we took him inside and immediately put him in the burial vault, the one that had been prepared, because of the danger that [someone] would want to take Monseñor Romero's body." After almost two hours, "when the situation little by little had calmed down . . . we went out into the main plaza, and we recovered seventeen bodies."[2]

Three months to the day from the start of our trial, Nico's phone rings. "Nico van Aelstyn," he says into the receiver, his voice tired but still authoritative. Silence greets him on the other end but Nico waits. The silence continues a few more seconds, but on a busy day, these are seconds Nico doesn't have. At last, a voice with a Latin American accent comes through the line, saying slowly, "This is Witness 5145."

Nico has no idea what that means. "I'm sorry?" he says.

"I was told to say only that I'm Witness 5145."

The silence returns, but this time it's on Nico's end. Who the hell is this, he thinks. After a few seconds, the fog lifts. *The witness protection program.* A charge goes through Nico, but he knows he has a problem. He isn't sure if the voice belongs to the getaway driver, Amado Garay, or the other man possibly in the program, former military intelligence chief Roberto Santiváñez. He asks a few careful questions, but the man is clearly nervous, even afraid. The last thing Nico wants to do is scare him off. He does his best to gather information without pushing the man too far.

Around 11:00 A.M., an e-mail from Nico comes to my inbox. The subject line shoots through the screen: "I just got off the phone with Antonio Amado Garay." The driver. My heart doubles its pace. "He's now known as Witness Number 5145," Nico writes. "The Witness Protection Program just gave him my name and phone number and encouraged him to call." Nico mentions Garay's location and occupation, two facts we will guard fiercely from that day forward. "He is willing to do whatever we want because he loves this country and wants to help. I have his home phone number. He confirmed that his prior testimony to Judge Zamora in El Salvador and to the Truth Commission is accurate and that the information is still fresh in his memory."

Before I reach the second paragraph, my phone rings. I know it's Russell Cohen, and I know he's going to be ecstatic. Though a seasoned and serious attorney, Russ has the enthusiasm of a child when it comes to the Romero case. I grab the receiver and listen as Russ details Nico's conversation with Garay. He also mentions a complicating factor I haven't yet reached in Nico's message. Garay's son is in jail and though his sentence is ending, he now faces deportation to El Salvador, a country he left when only a child. As if this isn't enough, the removal hearing is tomorrow and he doesn't have a lawyer. Garay, knowing it's a shot in the dark, asked Nico for help. The request presents a thorny issue, because although we are desperate to have Garay as a witness, we can't be seen as giving him a quid pro quo like representing his son in exchange for his testimony. We also can't give him any money for a lawyer. Nico was noncommittal with Garay, but Russ and I agree with Nico that there is nothing wrong with aiding in the search for a lawyer. I start calling immigration offices I know, and when Almudena Bernabeu returns to the office, she takes over and finds someone within hours.

Capitalizing on the momentum, Nico calls Garay that night to tell him about the immigration lawyer and build more trust. Sensing that he has been successful on both fronts, Nico goes for broke and asks Garay to testify. To Nico's surprise, Garay agrees without hesitation. Anxious to keep him close, Nico phones Garay the next night to set a date for the testimony. It will be a deposition, a pretrial procedure that is under oath but not in front of a judge. Garay remains cooperative, consenting to testify in just two weeks' time.

At every opportunity in their conversations, Garay conveys his undying love for the United States, his view apparently unaltered by the fact that the government is trying to deport his son. He even defends the U.S. invasion of Iraq, saying the war was undertaken because the United States wanted to protect the vulnerable. On that point, he seems to conflate our legal team with the feds, telling Nico, "You are all about protecting people." Garay also reveals how the witness protection program works.[3] Whenever he needs to contact his case manager, he calls a specific phone number he knows by heart because he isn't allowed to write it down. Rather than the usual "hello," the receptionist answers with a code and then passes Garay to his manager. It is the manager who told Garay about us, simply instructing Garay to call Nico and provide his witness number. The manager assured Garay we would know who he was, but the manager forgot to tell Nico to expect a call.

Barely giving us a chance to digest the Garay news, investigator Bobby Levinson follows up on his search for our defendant, Álvaro Saravia. At this point, we still don't know if Saravia is in El Salvador, Nicaragua, or California, but Levinson provides evidence for the Nicaragua theory. A source just spoke with a Nicaraguan man who knows Saravia well and said that Saravia is living in the small town of Chinandega, in western Nicaragua, flying crop dusters over rice plantations. The source told Levinson that if we are interested in getting a message to Saravia, he can help. The source also reported that Ricardo Lao is indeed in Miami, possibly even in jail, but another of Levinson's contacts doubted this was true. The second source promised to check the information at an upcoming Florida horse show that will be attended by several death squad "alumni."

Regardless of Lao's location, we will have to figure out what to do about Saravia. For months, we have wanted to speak directly with him, but just when he seemed willing to talk after our previous message, nothing happened. Now, Levinson's source has him in a new place. Should we send another message? With Garay ready to testify, is it even worth the effort? Although Levinson's source is willing to look for Saravia in Nicaragua, he requires payment and a ticket to Central America whereas Almudena's Salvadoran contact is working without charge. We decide to stay with the man in El Salvador, and I tell Levinson to stand down.

Our reluctance to pay for action on Saravia is a cost-saving measure but also an acknowledgment that the information he possesses is decreasing in importance. We have not forgotten that the financiers are the big fish in the case, but the reality is sinking in that we might not be able to get them. We have been investigating for almost a year, and we still are not ready to name one as a defendant. We have only one witness on the record who has provided information on the overall funding of death squads, and our proof about specific payments for the Romero assassination is thinner. While there is evidence that several suspects supported the death squads, we want overwhelming proof before including them in the lawsuit, because doing so will likely bring in skilled defense lawyers and lead to protracted litigation. While we have not given up, with less than three months until the trial against Saravia the financiers remain frustratingly beyond our reach.

Amid the other developments, we begin strategizing for the Garay deposition set to take place in just over a week. "Team, for this one, we need to think of ourselves as G-men, because that's how he's relating to us," Nico writes in an e-mail. "That means that we dress in suits and such on Monday. I think even G-types dress down on the weekends, but when we go to our closets Sunday morning we should ask ourselves, 'What would an FBI agent wear?' And of course we need to be serious and business-like throughout. We all know this, I know, but I just wanted to confirm." The e-mail is typical of Nico, searching for angles and proposing bold ideas, but Russ replies with a note of restraint. "Although I'm happy to wear a suit," Russ writes, "I think we have to be careful about the G-Men stuff. In fact, I think we may want to expressly put on the record that we are not the government, that we have offered him nothing for his testimony, that we have no influence over his immigration or anything else. And have him say he understands that." I agree with Russ's caution, but I like Nico's sentiment that we don't need to act as though he is doing us a favor. We have about ten days to prepare, and Nico will have to get Garay ready, first by phone and then in person. I take the first shot at drafting 150 questions to ask him. If Garay answers them truthfully and convincingly, we might have enough evidence to win the case against Saravia.

In the days leading up to the deposition, Nico speaks with Garay repeatedly, trying to elicit details about the assassination and prepare him for his testimony, but Garay is a difficult witness. Although he is comfortable talking about other topics, he becomes tentative whenever the subject turns to Romero's murder. He often breaks down crying. Garay is also needy and calls Nico constantly, asking for updates on his son even though we are not involved in the immigration case. Garay begs Nico to call his handlers at the witness protection program because they are upset with him about his son's problems. Nico is sympathetic but firmly declines.

Almudena soon joins the conversations and offers Garay a Spanish-speaking alternative, but Garay refuses to talk in his native language, insisting on English. It appears to be a means of expressing his love for the United States; Almudena thinks perhaps it is an attempt to leave El Salvador behind. There is also no doubt that Garay is traumatized. At CJA, we are accustomed to working with torture survivors suffering from post-traumatic stress but Garay, unlike our clients, is not a victim. His distress comes from living with the crimes, including the Romero assassination, in which he was involved. As a result, he shows an incessant need to explain what a virtuous person he has become. He recites for Nico and Almudena the good deeds he is now doing. Garay also emphasizes the distress he felt when he gave secret testimony in 1987 as part of the criminal investigation in El Salvador. Men surrounded him, he says, peppering him with question after question. Under those circumstances, and being the first person to testify on the record in the Romero case, the pressure was overwhelming.

Although Garay struggles with communicating his role in the assassination, he yearns to talk, and the more he says the more relieved he seems. Each time he begins his account, he gets a bit further before bursting into tears. As with most traumatized witnesses, new details emerge every time he tells the story. After countless hours on the phone, Nico and Almudena travel to meet Garay in person. Russ and I want to go, but we realize that four lawyers is too much considering how besieged Garay felt while testifying in 1987. They arrange to meet at a hotel the day before the deposition. In a repeat of Garay's misadventure twenty-four years ago when he got lost driving the getaway car after Romero's murder, he takes several wrong turns to the hotel and arrives very late. Rather than rush to find Almudena and Nico, he takes the time to duck into a restroom and change into a suit.

By the time they begin, the evening has long since given way to night. Nico asks Garay to tell his story one more time as they interrupt him with questions. Garay, agitated, paces around the room, his steps accompanied by fits of crying. As the clock passes midnight, Garay insists he had not known the mission was to kill Archbishop Romero, and he sticks to that story even as Nico and Almudena press him. He grows stronger and more controlled with each recitation until they finally stop for the night.

The next morning, Almudena and Nico arrive on time for the deposition at the law office but Garay gets lost again. Waiting in the conference room with the videographer and court reporter, neither of whom know the topic of the deposition, Nico and Almudena can do nothing but review their notes and force some small talk. The room is equipped, at Garay's request, with several small and large fans. When the star witness finally announces his arrival at reception, Nico steps out to retrieve him. Entering the room and sitting at the large table, Garay hardly seems like a man with earth-shattering information, and he demonstrates no air of confidence. Even in the death squad, he was at the bottom of the chain, the driver for those who actually planned and performed the executions. While they held meetings in houses, he waited outside in the car. Now, after bearing the burden of his own complicity for decades, his life is a mess. Even under protection in the United States, he still has no peace.

"Could you please state for the record your name," Nico begins.[4]

"Yeah. My name is Antonio . . . my name is Amado Antonio Garay, and I'm a witness of what happened in El Salvador." He insists on speaking in English without an interpreter. As he fidgets, Garay talks of the background no one heard when he testified in El Salvador in 1987. He speaks of living in the small city of Quezaltepeque and running a restaurant serving *pupusas,* El Salvador's national food. He laments an ill-fated attempt to become a priest before he was expelled from the seminary. Like all Salvadoran men, he served in the army for a while. He was drafted into the death squad while running the *pupusería.*

"You know, in the news you see, you know, that it was like a war in that place," Garay says. "I didn't give it too much attention, but they start to worry me a little bit." Two policemen in his town, both named Nelson, started harassing him. "In order to have a normal life with the police over there, you aren't their friend, you are always bothered by them, they ask for money all the time. And in order to not be bothered by them you have to be close to them and show them I'm your friend." Garay did his best not to make them mad. "When Nelson Morales asked me if I want to be a driver, you know, 'No, you know, I'm doing okay with my business.' And he said, 'Well, you know, you look like you're slowing down,' because the people, they were scared to go outside at that time because of, you know, the situation the country going through." Garay is portraying himself as both coerced and naïve.[5]

"Did he say to whom you would be a driver?" Nico asks.

"No. Just he say to drive, you know, for some organization."

"Did you know who he meant by that?"

"No."

"Did you know who he worked for?"

"No. I didn't know. Because at that time I was kind of, my brain was like dumbish." Everyone in the conference room is straining to understand him. "And they were carrying their gun like showing up, you know, intimidate everybody. They sit where they want to sit. If somebody is in their seat, they have to move. . . . Nelson García, he was like a little more tough on me. Like, 'You have to work with us. You know, we're not going to ask you anymore.' And I assume they going to kill me if I don't do what they want me to do. And I said, 'Well, okay.' And then one day they picked me up to go with them to the place with Álvaro."

Nico hands him an old photo of Saravia. Garay confirms this is "Álvaro."

"At what point did you start to have a better understanding of the work that Álvaro and the others were doing?" Nico asks.

"Well, because I saw everybody were getting guns, weapons, you know, and the one I used to see regularly was the Uzi." These guns, Garay explains, were different than the simple rifles he had used in the military. They were automatic weapons. "And I start to know, that's why I got the feeling that this was not a good place to be because it was dangerous. But I have to keep going where I was because obligation, like, you have to do it. I have to be there no matter what. And this is the way I start to feel a fear for myself."

The testimony shifts to the men at the heart of the case.

"You heard people talking to each other using military terms, colonel, major, captain?" Nico asks.

"Well, I find out not because they call themselves like this, because when I used to receive orders from Álvaro, he used to tell me, 'We're going to pick up the colonel or D'Aubuisson or captain,' whatever. You know, 'We're going to take the lieutenant to go somewhere.' So terms like this."

"They referred to each other using those titles?"

"Yes."

"How many times do you think you drove Roberto D'Aubuisson?"

"I think maybe like four times, five times." D'Aubuisson treated him well, Garay says, but always as a driver, not as an equal.

"Did they ever invite you in to participate in any of the meetings?"

"No. No."

"So when you would drive them somewhere, they would go into the house, and you would stay with the car?"

"The thing that normally used to happen when I used to drive for Roberto D'Aubuisson, he would grab his 45 millimeter [handgun], he would hand it to me and say, 'Keep it with you,' you know. 'When I come out, give me back.' 'Okay,' you know. And this is, you know, I never get invited to the meeting, never, never, never."

Nico guides Garay to the day of the assassination, but as his testimony becomes more disjointed, Nico tries to elicit the information while keeping him on track. Garay repeats much the same story as in 1987 but with a few new details and some contradictions. Garay recounts that he, Saravia, and the Nelsons drove to the house with the Japanese cashew trees and he waited outside while everyone went in. He remembers being in a boxy red Volkswagen. At some point, a thin man with a black beard got into the car. The man didn't say much but spoke with a Salvadoran accent. Garay thought another car had been there as well. Then Saravia spoke to everyone, saying that the second car would provide protection for Garay's vehicle.

Nico raises the obvious question, "What did you think you were going to do at that point?"

Garay's answer admits far more than he did in 1987. "Of course," he says, "I'm not going to be like I don't know. It was to kill somebody, but I didn't know who it was at that time." They drove to a church, Garay continues. He recalls arriving at a large, black gate.

"Where was the other car?" Nico asks.

"I think it was, like, I think he moved to the side to let us go."

"To go into the church at the black gate?"

"Yes."

"So that other car stayed out in front of the entrance to the church?"

"Yes."

Nico is posing his questions in a leading way. This is not normally permitted, but given Garay's nonlinear testimony, it seems necessary.

"What time of day was it?" Nico asks.

"I'm not sure what time it was. But maybe around seven in the evening."

"A little bit dark?"

"Dark, yes."

"And what was going on at the church when you got there?"

"Well, like a ceremony, the place was giving a ceremony."

"Celebrating mass?"

"Celebrating mass, yes."

"Did you see the people in the church?"

"I saw a lot of people inside of the church, yes." Garay reviews a photo of the Divina Providencia chapel and confirms it is similar to what he saw.

Nico now tries to develop information that Garay prematurely recited earlier in the deposition. Garay said he saw a priest inside the church standing in front of a large crucifix.

"Did you know at this time who that priest was?" Nico asks.

"No."

"You knew that you were going on a job to kill somebody, and you knew it was somebody in the church."

"Yes."

"Did you know anything more?"

"No, just I knew there is going to be a priest."

"You knew it would be a priest?"

"But specific who, no, I didn't know. I didn't know who it was." After the gunshot, Garay remembers, a nun was looking around to see what had happened.[6]

"What did you hear from inside the church?" Nico asks.

"Screaming," Garay says. "A lot of screaming." Garay tells of driving away and getting lost but finding his way back using a walkie-talkie.

Nico tries to find out the reaction of the other men responsible for the murder. "What was the mood?" Nico asks. "Was the shooter proud? Was he bragging?"

"No."

"People were tense?"

"No. He was like, you know, he didn't seem too happy what he did, no. He was dragging, he was. As a matter of fact . . . " Garay begins crying. It seems like an odd place to trigger such emotions.

"It's all right," Nico comforts him. Almudena asks if he needs a break.

"No, it's okay." Garay composes himself. "This guy I remember now, he said, 'God forgive me for what I'm going to do.' I remember something like that, yes."

"The shooter said that?"

"Yes." The point is a profound one for Garay. "I don't know exactly precisely where it was," he says. "But I remember he said something like, 'God forgive me what I'm going to do to kill a priest.'"

As the emotion subsides, Nico leads Garay in another direction.

"Did there come a time after that when Álvaro [Saravia] and Roberto D'Aubuisson met to talk about things?" This was the controversial part of the 1987 testimony because it implicated D'Aubuisson in the plot.

"Well," Garay says, "the only comment before getting to the big room—"

"What big room?" Nico interrupts.

"Like a conference room where everybody meet to talk about what they're going to do."

"When was this?"

"After it happened, like a week later, something like that."

"Some days afterward?" Nico asks. In 1987, Garay testified that it was three days.

"Yes. When Álvaro talk to D'Aubuisson."

"How did you get there?"

"With a car."

"You drove Álvaro there?"

"Yes. I drove with him over there. And he go to the car and say, 'Mission completed.'"

"Álvaro said that to?"

"To D'Aubuisson." Garay is confused on the point. He previously testified it was the shooter who said "mission accomplished" to Saravia, not Saravia who said it to D'Aubuisson.

"And what did D'Aubuisson say?"

"I recall he said, 'Have you done this thing yet?'" In saying *yet,* Garay probably means *already.* In Spanish, the same word is used for both terms.

"And what did Álvaro say to that?"

"I think he said like, 'Well, that's the plan, you know, that you said that we going to do those thing.' Then they went inside with all the people, and we went to another place." Saravia and D'Aubuisson went inside for a meeting while Garay waited outside. The point emphasizes that in spite of Garay's value as a witness, he is not an insider who can tell us what the death squad leaders had to say about Romero's assassination.

Nico shifts to one of the last issues, the 1980 raid at Finca San Luis. It went unmentioned in Garay's 1987 testimony. This time, though, Garay confirms he was there. He says he drove Saravia and D'Aubuisson to the meeting, and he safeguarded D'Aubuisson's gun. In telling the San Luis story, Garay laments being thrust into the death squad life. "Because in that country it's not like United States," he says. "You have any doubt in your mind, you say, 'What we going to do? What's the purpose to have this gun?' You know, 'Why we carry guns?' You have to shut up and do what they tell you to do. Yes, sir. You know, and, unfortunately, this is the way it is. . . . Just shut up. You little guy, you have to be there, don't move from there. Just stay there. And that's the way they intimidate the people." Garay's bitterness is right on the surface. Despite his own culpability, he wants people held accountable. "That's why I'm so glad that you guys have enough courage to do the thing what you're doing. I admire you guys. It's beautiful what you're doing."

After several hours, the deposition ends. The court reporter and videographer pack up their equipment in silence as Garay stands and leaves the conference room. The others, so as to not be seen with him, follow a while later. We do not know if we will ever see Garay again.

THIRTEEN

"There Must Have Been a Thousand Romeros"

FINAL INTERVIEWS AND TRIAL PREPARATION

FRESNO—AUGUST 2004

"You testified earlier about the important role that you saw [Romero] could play as a bridge between the Salvadoran society," Nico van Aelstyn says to Ambassador Robert White on the deposition videotape. "What then in your view was the impact of his killing?"

"Those who killed Monseñor Romero knew perfectly well what they were doing and what they would accomplish," White says. "They destroyed the one figure in El Salvador that could have served as a bridge, as a creative interpreter between all the different sides, and his removal by violence basically sent a signal that no dialogue was warranted, that what the Salvadoran rich and the military were after was total pressure on this burgeoning movement toward democratic change." Romero's murder "not only reinforced the image of a military that was a law unto itself, it also served as a recruiting tool for revolutionaries, because if you can kill an archbishop, you know, you can kill anybody. No one is sacred." Romero's death only strengthened the armed insurrection.

"Do you believe then that the killing and the impunity with which it was conducted contributed to the civil war at that time?"

"Yes, I do."[1]

SAN SALVADOR—JULY 2004

On our last trip to El Salvador before the trial, we meet a witness who confirms Ambassador White's characterization of the mind-set of the people who killed Romero. "I'm going to tell you something [about Romero's murder]. You have to look at the pros and cons," the witness says. "Monseñor started his homilies at eleven. . . . The country was paralyzed at eleven." Each Sunday, as soon as the homily was over, the security forces had to deploy troops to stop soldiers from defecting to the insurgents. "And they didn't go empty-handed," he says. "They took their rifles with them. So, for the [guerrillas] . . . Monseñor Romero was an enormous help." For the military, "he was a horrible problem."

We ask if Romero was enough of a problem that he was considered a military target.

"You have to see it from a political point of view and a military point of view," he says. To show us the military perspective, he does an impression of a Salvadoran commander lamenting the defections by his soldiers. Then he drops his voice to a whisper. "So Monseñor Romero was a military target. Truly. . . . When you see it that way, the [guerrillas] didn't have to kill any soldiers. The soldiers just left." His tone conveys resignation. "So that guy—I say 'that guy,' Monseñor Romero—was bothersome. That's the military aspect. . . . He was bothersome and he exaggerated things a bit. That's *my* point of view."

Listening to him, I am reminded of Saravia's testimony to the Truth Commission that the Romero assassination gave D'Aubuisson's group prestige and made it easier to raise money. It explains why so many people over the years claimed to have played a role. Everyone wanted credit for the murder. "There must have been a thousand Romeros," the witness jokes, "because a thousand of us killed him."

SAN FRANCISCO—JULY 2004

With the trial a month away, the preparation remains vexing because we do not know who all of our witnesses will be. This arises from the unique fact that the "trial" is not technically a trial but a hearing on our application for default judgment. Álvaro Saravia has not made an appearance in the case, so we are asking the judge to grant us a victory based on Saravia's "default" in failing to enter a defense. If this were a criminal prosecution, constitutionally there could not be a trial in Saravia's absence, but because U.S. law allows for only a civil lawsuit, the rules are different. We are permitted to hold a hearing without him. With Saravia in default, we are not, strictly speaking, required to prove his responsibility for the murder. The trial should only be about assessing how much money he has to pay, but we know that judges have great latitude in default cases. We worry that Judge Wanger might still want to look into the facts.

Our evidence against Saravia, still our only named defendant, is strong, especially with Amado Garay's deposition. With the combination of the Saravia Diary, Saravia's 1990 statements to U.S. embassy official Richard Chidester, his testimony before the Truth Commission, and the commission's report finding Saravia responsible, we have plenty as long as the judge admits it all into evidence. Where we have come up short is the death squad financiers. We have spoken with witnesses who have information on them, but securing their testimony has been difficult. Most likely, we will have to continue that part of the investigation after the trial.

Despite ongoing questions, by early August we begin to finalize our witness list. We focus on lining up witnesses to speak to the damages caused by Romero's murder and his enduring significance to El Salvador and the world. We agree on the need to present the living Romero: how he evolved as archbishop, the brave words he preached, the withering pressure he was under. Father Walter Guerra agrees to testify about helping Romero with his homilies, including his final Sunday sermon. Father Bill Wipfler, former director of the Human Rights Office of the U.S. National Council of Churches, will describe his trip to El Salvador that coincided with that final homily. Bishop Thomas Gumbleton, founding president of Pax Christi, says he will be honored to testify. Father Jon Cortina, from the Central American University, who survived the many threats and attacks against the Jesuits in those years, will chronicle his own relationship with Romero and explain the archbishop's theology.

We also secure the participation of Atilio Ramírez Amaya, the judge who investigated Romero's death and survived his own assassination attempt in 1980. María Julia Hernández, once an assistant to Archbishop Romero and then the long-serving director of the archdiocese's human rights office, agrees to testify. Esther Chávez will describe her participation in the Ecclesial Base Communities organized by *campesinos* with the help of people like Romero's Jesuit friend, Rutilio Grande. Naomi Roht-Arriaza, a U.S. law professor, will testify about the illegal nature of El Salvador's Amnesty Law that has enshrined impunity for those like Saravia who are responsible for horrible atrocities. Terry Karl, the Stanford professor and El Salvador expert who has been running a meticulous research operation for months, will teach the court why and how Romero was killed.

We also discuss the getaway driver, Amado Garay. We have recently been in contact with a U.S. witness who has filled in a piece we never had before: how investigators first discovered Garay in the 1980s. Gordon Ellison, a former FBI agent, has a long history in Central America. In 1981, after Ellison left the FBI, the AFL-CIO labor federation hired him to investigate the killing of three land-reform experts, including two U.S. citizens, at the Sheraton Hotel in San Salvador. In the course of that work, Ellison made important military contacts and came to know the official in charge of investigating Romero's murder. "He explained that he spent a great deal of time with Colonel Nelson Iván López y López, the head of the investigative unit in El Salvador," Russell Cohen writes us after speaking with Ellison. In the mid-1980s, the Christian Democratic government, supported and financed by the Reagan administration, created a Special Investigations Unit (SIU) as the centerpiece of reforms to El Salvador's justice system. The SIU's work is what led to Garay's original 1987 testimony and the attempted extradition of Álvaro Saravia from the United States.

"In late 1987," Russ writes, "López y López told Ellison that [the SIU] had received information on Garay's location. Garay was reported to be living just north of San José, Costa Rica, which was where Ellison was living at the time. López y López asked Ellison to help find the place." López y López and his second-in-command traveled to San José. "They then picked up Ellison and together they drove north of town, into a coffee growing area. Together they found the house. A nice, typical, wooden house. They made several passes to check things out." López y López contacted the Costa Rican police for assistance in picking him up. "Garay was reportedly very cooperative."

Russ asked Ellison if the FBI played a role in finding Garay. "He suggested that the FBI was providing some general assistance to the investigative unit," and the Salvadoran polygraph operator received some police training at the FBI National Academy in Quantico, Virginia. "Ellison suspects that [the man] polygraphed Garay, as he polygraphed all suspects and witnesses at that time." This makes sense because we have several public sources stating that Garay passed a lie-detector test.[2]

With these details from Ellison, we discuss whether we should call Garay at trial. We have his video deposition, which is all we ever thought we would get. For the sake of history, though, we come around to the idea that we should try to convince him to testify in open court. No one with firsthand knowledge about Romero's assassination has ever done this. We contact the witness protection program—"the cloak and dagger set," as Nico calls them—to see if in-court testimony is feasible. Would they provide protection for Garay even though this is not a criminal trial? After several phone calls, the answer comes back that the U.S. Marshals can escort Garay to Fresno and provide security at the courthouse, but we would have to pay. We agree to cover the costs.

With the logistics arranged, and our fingers crossed, Nico and Almudena talk to Garay.

FOURTEEN

"Of a Magnitude That Is Hardly Describable"

THE ROMERO ASSASSINATION CASE
GOES TO TRIAL

FRESNO—AUGUST 2004

"Do you see any value in holding accountable in a court of law in the United States those responsible for the killing of Archbishop Romero?" Nico van Aelstyn asks Ambassador Robert White.

"I think it's of great importance," White says, "first as a way of demonstrating what a free, democratic society with a strong system of justice can bring out. Secondly, I regard it, in a sense, something of atonement because we did collaborate with violence and the death squads." He is referring to the U.S. government. "In fact, in many ways we encouraged this violence and certainly did very little to stop it. And so I think that a country that demonstrates and has a capacity to look back and make judgments about what it did wrong in the past, I think that there's no way that you can open up a new future unless you recognize what went wrong in the past."[1]

SAN SALVADOR—AUGUST 2004

Two days before the start of our trial, *La Prensa Gráfica*, one of El Salvador's largest papers, runs the first of a ten-part series about the life of Roberto D'Aubuisson. To all of us on the legal team, the timing seems deliberate. "Why Roberto D'Aubuisson? Why now?" the author writes in the first article. "Because now is the time to open doors to memory, because somehow it has to start, and because the indisputable weight of this personality upon the Salvadoran reality cannot be ignored. Today begins a series of entries about the life of Roberto D'Aubuisson, his family, his political beginnings, his days in darkness and light. Beyond the myths, this is his story."[2]

Another article the same day leads with an exclusive interview. "Twenty-five years ago we began this fight, sure that we wouldn't make it out alive," says Fernando "El Negro" Sagrera, the man whom the Truth Commission named as one of Álvaro Saravia's coconspirators in the Romero assassination. "It was hard. They persecuted us and defamed us unspeakably. For twenty-five years I've stayed silent. This is the first and last time I will tell this story: the story of my friend, of the man and great leader who was Roberto D'Aubuisson, the story of ARENA." Sagrera tells his tale with great force, complete with denials of links to the death squads. "It was a labor without respite, day and night, without money or a support structure. At that level, the guerrillas, the government, a group of traitorous officers, and even the *gringos* already had us in their sights. We were bankrupt idealists."[3]

Sagrera's story provides the public-relations counterpoint to our imminent trial.

FRESNO—AUGUST 24, 2004

There are few moments in real-life trials that provide the theatrics of a *Perry Mason* episode. When there are lawyers on both sides defending their clients' interests, virtually everything is known. Evidence has been exchanged, witnesses cross-examined, and briefs written. The system is actually designed to bring all the evidence to the surface. Almost nothing remains under wraps. This lawsuit is different because we do not face opposing counsel, and our defendant is on the run. All communications in the case have been between the judge and our legal team, and the only information available to the public is what we decided to release. Even when we sent the media a list of the people who would testify at trial, we omitted the name of the most valuable witness. On this first morning of trial, everyone in the Fresno courtroom is in the dark about the prized testimony they will soon hear.

Nico van Aelstyn is already on his feet. "There are a couple of housekeeping items we would like to address before getting into the proceeding today," he tells Judge Wanger as the audience shifts in their seats, eager for the real trial to start.[4]

"Just to tell you what we plan to do," Nico continues, "I would provide an opening statement this morning, and then we will have three witnesses today. The Reverend Canon William L. Wipfler will testify first. Bishop Thomas Gumbleton will testify following the Reverend Wipfler." Nico's tone is conversational and dry, giving no hint that something important is on the way. "In the afternoon, we expect the testimony of Amado Antonio Garay." Synchronized gasps rise behind me, dissolving into murmured exchanges as people absorb that the getaway driver will testify in court. Almudena Bernabeu, at last unburdened of her great secret, turns like the Cheshire cat and winks at friends in the audience.

After a few other preliminary issues, Nico moves to the opening statement. His voice changes, the tone hushed, as he becomes less a lawyer and more an actor beginning a soliloquy:

> On the quiet leafy grounds of a hospital for terminal cancer patients in San Salvador, there is a chapel. It is shortly after 6:00 P.M. on March 24, 1980, a warm evening, and the doors to the chapel are open. From outside, you can hear the words of the service, a commemoration of the occasion of the first anniversary of the death of Sara de Pinto. Monseñor, as he was known then and still known today, the archbishop of San Salvador, Óscar Arnulfo Romero, was celebrating a mass. Monseñor stands at the altar facing the congregation and reciting the holy words that he has so many times before, though, as always, adapting them a little to the circumstances of that service. The bread and the wine are brought forward to the altar. At that moment, a car pulls up in the open drive in front of the chapel. The driver bends forward in his seat to inspect something on the floor of the car. Monseñor lifts the chalice, raising it in his arms over his head in offering.

The technician hits "play" on his computer. Romero's voice enters the courtroom, and his translated words appear on the large screen above. "This Eucharist is precisely an act of faith. In Christian faith, we know that at this moment, the consecrated bread becomes the body of Christ, who offered himself for the world's redemption, and in this chalice, the wine transforms into the blood that became the price of salvation." This is a central part of the mass. "Let this immolated body and this blood sacrificed for mankind nourish us and dedicate our bodies and our blood to the suffering and pain just like Christ, who did so not for himself but to offer concepts of justice and peace to his people. Let us unite closely in faith and hope in this moment of prayer for Doña Sarita and ourselves—"

A boom explodes from the speakers as confused murmurs grow to shrieks of panic. In just seconds, silence mercifully intervenes as the recording cuts off, sparing us the screams that surely continued in the church. Nico stands motionless as though contemplating the moment. Like Walter Cronkite announcing the murder of John F. Kennedy, he says, "Monseñor is dead."

The horrifying photos of the subsequent moments in the chapel come to the screen. In black and white, nuns and congregants scramble to Romero's aid as blood pours from his mouth and nose. They try to hold up his head. They rush him to a car, their bodies in motion but their faces showing it is already too late.

With the terror of the assassination now established, Nico leads the judge through the details of the lawsuit. He describes Saravia's role and D'Aubuisson's supervision. "Yet in almost twenty-five years," he says, "not a single person has been held accountable for this crime, not in El Salvador nor anywhere else. In fact, some of those behind this killing rose to the highest positions of power in that country and their influence is still being felt today." Nico concludes by returning to Romero's significance:

> Finally, this case can help to establish one of the most important preconditions for societal reconciliation: the channeling of vengeance into the rule of law through the creation of historical record and the establishment of historical truth. Is this claiming too much in this proceeding, here in a courtroom in Fresno, California? No. We are not dealing with just one of the more than seventy-five thousand civilians that were murdered during this terrible period of violence in El Salvador. We are dealing with the one case that has come to represent them all. Monseñor is that important.

Around lunchtime, the U.S. Marshals arrive with our key witness, Amado Garay, sneaking him through a back entrance. Garay's face is scruffy; the Marshals told him not to shave in order to provide a bit of disguise. The protections appear not to have helped his psyche, because he looks petrified.

We had been unsure if Garay would testify in court. The video deposition had been difficult enough, but out of what seemed to be a sense of duty, Garay said yes when we asked him to come to Fresno. Now, as Almudena and Nico chat with him during the lunch break, Garay tells them something they have never heard before. He confesses that he was the getaway driver for about twenty assassinations in El Salvador. While unsurprised by the fact, Nico and Almudena tell Garay he will have to mention this on the stand.

Though choppy and emotional, Garay's testimony seems fine to me. He largely repeats what he said in his 1987 testimony and his recent deposition, with a few new details and a couple of inconsistencies. He recalls how the two National Policemen named Nelson forced him to become a driver for Saravia and D'Aubuisson. The men in the group carried a lot of weapons, Garay says as he labels it a death squad. He testifies that Saravia considered priests to be their biggest enemy.[5]

Garay again recounts the day of Romero's murder. He drove Saravia to a house with Japanese cashew trees and then switched cars and got behind the wheel of a Volkswagen. Saravia came out of the house with a tall bearded man. Saravia told the man, "It's better to shoot in the head because maybe he have a bulletproof vest. You have to be sure he get killed." Garay drove the bearded man to a location with a large gate.

"Inside the gate was like a long path," Garay testifies. "And [the bearded man] said, 'Go to the gate.' I start to go. He said, 'Stop in front of the church.' . . . And when I stopped in the front door to the church, he say, 'Look like you are fixing something in the car.'" While Garay was bent over pretending to repair something, he heard an explosion behind him. The bearded man said, "Relax. Just go slow and get out."

Judge Wanger asks Garay for details. "When you heard the explosion in the car, did you turn to see what the noise was?"

"No," Garay answers. "Because I kind of figured out. Besides, I saw this guy get into the car with a big rifle. I assumed they were going to do something like that."

The judge is an ex-marine and wants to know what kind of gun it was. Garay is not sure.

"It was a long weapon with a mirror, like a telescope."

"Telescopic sight?"

"Yes, sir."

Judge Wanger makes us nervous by jumping in to ask Garay questions. We realize that our fears are coming true. Rather than simply accept the facts as we allege them—something normally done in cases where the defendant does not appear—the judge wants to analyze the evidence and make us prove Saravia's responsibility for the murder through witness testimony. The problem is that beyond Garay, most of our witnesses are going to testify about Romero's life, not his death.

Throughout his testimony, Garay refers to Romero simply as "the priest." This, I know, was a common nomenclature among the death squads. There was no sense that they were attacking the archbishop, one of the most influential figures in the country and a holy man known around the world. Instead, they belittled him as "that priest," a mere member of a group with which they were at war. I remember the man in San Salvador describing Romero as a "military target." I sense that Garay is not intentionally following that model but he is stuck in the vernacular in which he had once been immersed.

"Did you ever learn who the victim of the shooting was?" Judge Wanger asks him.

"No, sir," Garay says.

"You don't know who the person was who was shot?"

"No, sir."

"But you think it was a priest?"

"Yes, after the shooting, I find out that he was not just a priest, he was Monseñor."

Someone with no background in Latin America would not have found the answer profound, but the Salvadorans in the courtroom sense its significance. Although every bishop in El Salvador is referred to with the respected title of "Monseñor," the label is always attached to a surname. There are Monseñor Rivera, Monseñor Chávez, Monseñor Sáenz Lacalle. But if the last name is ever omitted, the speaker is referring to just one person. In El Salvador, there is only one "Monseñor."

"Did you ever learn his name?" Judge Wanger asks.

Garay thinks for a moment. He hesitates, drawing out the syllables, "Mon . . . se . . . ñor . . . "

He is searching.

"Famous name . . . famous . . . famous . . . "

I am shocked he can't remember the name. Garay has never shown any malice toward the archbishop and in fact, he said our cause was a righteous one. His lapse in memory, though, speaks volumes about the low regard his compatriots had for the Catholic Church. As Garay struggles for the answer, people in the audience are becoming agitated. A few whisper the name.

"Monseñor . . . "

The buzz in the crowd grows louder.

"I don't remember right now his name," Garay says, but his face shows he is still thinking. Neither Nico nor Judge Wanger says a word. Embarrassed, I slump in my chair.

Garay looks up in triumph.

"Óscar Romero. Monseñor Romero."

Our second day centers on the testimony of Atilio Ramírez Amaya, the judge who investigated Archbishop Romero's death in 1980 before fleeing when attackers tried to kill him. Ramírez Amaya's account helps us build our factual case, tying the Salvadoran military to Romero's murder and its cover-up.

"Would you consider the investigation of Monseñor's murder to be normal?" I ask Ramírez Amaya.

"No, no," he says with conviction.

"Did the National Police arrive first at the scene, as they normally would do?"

"No, they did not arrive."

"Did the National Police take fingerprints at the crime scene, like they would normally do?"

"No, they did not take fingerprints."

We go through the list of everything they should have done.

"Were the National Police involved in security at the autopsy, as they would normally be?"

"No, no. They did none of these things."

"And did the National Police investigate the attempted murder against you, as they would normally do?"

"No, they did not." In fact, when detectives arrived at his house after the attack, they threatened him. "They said, 'Don't you worry. Those were just amateurs. They are just learning. If we had come, in less than five minutes we would have taken care of everything.'"[6]

After court ends for the day, the focus suddenly shifts to our own security concerns. Our coworker Sonia Estival, who is responsible for transporting witnesses, tells us that a large SUV with tinted windows followed her to the airport. The car tracked Sonia closely and refused to pass even when she slowed down. After she stopped for an ambulance, Sonia continued waiting on the shoulder but the SUV did not go around.

We are unnerved listening to Sonia's story when we hear that some personal items have disappeared from the hotel. The laptop of Professor Terry Karl's student assistant, an important CD still in its drive, has vanished. A member of our team also noticed suspicious people in the hotel who seem to be watching us. To top it off, we learn that one of our witnesses received veiled threats before leaving El Salvador. In just one night, the fear that has permeated Central America for decades has seeped into the case in Fresno. We meet as a team and decide to tell the judge the next morning.

FRESNO—AUGUST 26, 2004

The day starts with a meeting in Judge Wanger's chambers. Sonia tells the judge about being followed the day before. We inform him of the laptop's disappearance and our other concerns. The judge treats the situation seriously and orders the U.S. Marshals to provide security for the rest of the trial. Marshals will accompany Sonia, one car in front of her and one in back, wherever she and the witnesses drive. They will stand guard as we enter and exit the courthouse each day. While the Marshals begin making those arrangements, we return to the courtroom.

We move to Professor Karl's expert testimony, and she delivers a history lesson on El Salvador. The fact that the gallery is not full matters little because Karl's audience is Judge Wanger. She gives the context for the assassination of Archbishop Romero and its aftermath, detailing the roles of the oligarchy, the security forces, the junta, Liberation Theology, D'Aubuisson, Saravia, and others. She interprets the testimony that has preceded hers and sets up the witnesses still to come.

In the afternoon, Jon Cortina describes his surprising role in a key event the night of Romero's murder. Cortina, the Jesuit priest from Spain's Basque country, once worked with Salvadoran *campesinos* in the community where Father Rutilio Grande was murdered. He interacted frequently with Romero, so we have called Cortina to testify about Romero's life and theology, but last night he told us a stunning story about the assassination. We hope it will add an important piece to our factual case.

"How did you find out about Monseñor Romero's assassination?" I ask him.

"I was at the university, and they phoned me," Cortina says. "It's one of those things, you get the information and you do not know what to do." Cortina and others went to the Policlínica, the hospital where Romero's body was examined. At the Policlínica, Cortina learned that many of the eyewitnesses to Romero's murder suspected the shooter was a news photographer, Eulalio Pérez, who had been sitting in the back of the church. Their hypothesis was that Pérez rigged his cameras to fire a bullet. Some of them actually detained Pérez, and they were still holding him at the church.

"I said I know something about photography and I could maybe go there and see whether the camera has been prepared to fire a bullet," Cortina testifies. "I went there with a priest ... because I was afraid to go by myself. The [church] was just crowded with soldiers and policemen and all sorts of people." This is an important point because Judge Ramírez Amaya has already testified that when he arrived a few hours later, no police came to assist him with the investigation of the crime scene.

"The photographer was brought down. I saw the cameras. I told [the other priest], 'Well, this cannot be because of the cameras.'" There was nothing strange about them at all. "Then the photographer said, 'Well, then, take me with you.'" They went to the newspaper's offices. "We developed all the pictures [taken] at the moment of Monseñor Romero's killing."[7] The photos became some of the most famous in Salvadoran history.

FRESNO—AUGUST 27, 2004

Francisco Acosta, who founded a university named after Archbishop Romero, testifies that he lost seventy-two relatives during the civil war. "One day," he says, "we turn on the TV, and Major Roberto D'Aubuisson was speaking there." It was February 1980. "He said that my brother, Jorge Alberto Acosta, the first one in the family, was the biggest subversive of the northern region of El Salvador."[8]

"How did you feel when you heard that?" Russell Cohen asks him.

"Really bad," Acosta says, "because we knew that once Roberto D'Aubuisson say something, something would happen for sure. So I was really uncomfortable.... Sure enough, three days later, four in the morning, about twenty-eight soldiers and men in civilian clothes came to his house on the slope of the volcano and surrounded his house, and they started to shoot at him.... Well, none of the bullets went through him and not through his baby either." Though the family later found a number of casings, somehow the bullets missed them. "He escaped through the hills, and like two miles away, he fell down.... Around five in the morning, some workers on the way to work found him there and went to my house to say what happened.... I brought him to my house in San Salvador. It was really tough. Because in front was living somebody from the army, and they are all the time checking who was where and doing what. And we said he can't be here because that would be a real problem for us, for our safety." Acosta contacted several people for help, but they all turned him away. Everyone was scared.

"So my last attempt," he says, "I went to Bishop Romero's office, and I brought [my brother] there, and I said, 'Monseñor Romero, what should I do? All the possibilities are closed. What should I do?' And Monseñor Romero told me, 'Look, I understand. Leave him here at the seminary.' His office was in the seminary. And he said, 'Leave him here. We will take care of him.'" Acosta's brother stayed there three weeks. "He finally found a way to go to the Mexican embassy, and my brother asked for political asylum at the Mexican embassy and was provided the political asylum." It was just one example of many in which Romero's intervention saved someone's life.

In the afternoon, we return to Terry Karl's testimony, which has come in segments scattered throughout the trial. She builds on Francisco Acosta's account about Death Squad TV. "I had never seen anything like this before," Karl says.

> I turned on the television in El Salvador, this was in 1983, and there was a program on the history of rock and roll. . . . Since it was a state of siege, I couldn't go out, and I was stuck in my room, and I was watching this program. . . . The program stopped, faded off the screen and instead, what was clearly a homemade video came on, and a man said, "Me llamo Santiago Hernández." My name is Santiago Hernández. You could see him from the chest up. He said, "Soy comunista." I'm a Communist. He proceeded to say that he had fallen into the hands of the people's justice and that he awaited the fate of the people's justice. He confessed on television that he was a Communist. Three other people confessed on television that they were Communists. The next day I went with some reporters to a house and I saw all four of those people dead. And Santiago Hernández, who was the first person to talk, had written across his chest, "por ser comunista," for being a Communist.

"What was extraordinary to me," Karl says, "is that this was actually on television. At that point, I was, frankly, so shocked by something like this and having seen it on television, I then started investigating how this could have happened." She talked to intelligence officials at foreign embassies. "They showed me, inside their embassies, death squad confessions. They also showed me some of the denunciations by Roberto D'Aubuisson. I then went to the U.S. embassy and asked the same question, and I was shown by members of the embassy their recorded copies of D'Aubuisson denouncing people on television."

"Did Roberto D'Aubuisson denounce Monseñor Romero on television as well?" Nico asks.

"Yes, he did. He said right before Archbishop Romero died, that the archbishop had one last chance to change his ways."[9]

Hearing Karl's testimony, I suspect that Judge Wanger now understands what the rest of us have already known. Archbishop Romero, even in the face of overt, personal danger did not change his ways. Had he done so, he would have abandoned his people, the voiceless of El Salvador, leaving his flock unprotected against the wolves. When Romero gave his life in their defense, his monumental stature only increased through his martyrdom. As our fourth day of the trial comes to an end, I hope we have convinced the judge on this point but I have no way to know. Judge Wanger, true to his nature, reveals nothing. We will have one week off before we reconvene for a final day of testimony next Friday. At the end of that session, we will finally learn what the judge thinks of the case.

NEW YORK—AUGUST 31, 2004

During the intervening week, an op-ed by Guatemala's Nobel laureate Rigoberta Menchú appears in the *New York Times*. "This case," she writes, "is being watched closely throughout Central America, where fragile new democracies suffer the lingering effects of unpunished wartime crimes. The failure to bring human rights violators to justice encourages more violence. . . . The lack of arrests in the Romero murder was a signal that Salvadoran armed forces and paramilitary groups enjoyed impunity for their crimes, quickening the country's descent into a brutal 12-year civil war that left more than 75,000 civilians dead."

Menchú raises a point we have mentioned in the trial though only as background. It can't be our central focus because our case is against Saravia, but it is the elephant in the room, particularly a U.S. courtroom. "The Saravia trial, while an inspiring exercise in American law, does raise disturbing questions about United States policy," she writes. "How did Mr. Saravia come to live in California in the first place? Declassified State Department and Central Intelligence Agency documents reveal that the government was aware of Mr. Saravia's alleged involvement in the Romero assassination as early as May 1980. The trial also represents an opportunity to examine, albeit obliquely, the responsibility of the Salvadoran government and its closest ally, the United States, in the events that led to the deaths of tens of thousands of Salvadoran civilians."

She concludes with a point previously raised by Ambassador Robert White: "It is a sort of redemption, then, that the first trial in this murder is taking place in an American court. Let us hope that justice will be served at last in the case of Óscar Romero, and that it will inspire the governments of the United States, El Salvador and other nations to prosecute the many human rights abusers who live openly among us."

FRESNO—SEPTEMBER 3, 2004

The courtroom gallery is full on our last day, and many in attendance are from California's Salvadoran community. Salvadorans in the United States have followed the case closely. Some who live close to Fresno, and others from farther away, have come to the trial. Others who joined us for the previous week are now gone. Several of our witnesses from El Salvador returned home, as did the New York–based member of our legal team, Patty Blum.

Professor Terry Karl finishes her marathon testimony by discussing the raid at Finca San Luis, the Saravia Diary, the consolidation of power by extremists in the military, Roberto D'Aubuisson's political career, and Saravia's confessions to the U.S. government and Truth Commission. She also speaks to the damages in the case, the impact of Monseñor Romero's death. "I think that the killing of Archbishop Romero was one of the most important events provoking a civil war in El Salvador," she says. "[He was a] bridge person, somebody who could try to build consensus within the moderate right, the center, and the moderate left and could in fact have avoided a civil war in El Salvador."[10] The ensuing conflict, we know too well, cost tens of thousands of civilian lives, most of them from guns, bullets, and bombs deployed by Salvadoran soldiers but supplied by the United States.

Nico van Aelstyn continues the point in his closing argument. "The killing of Archbishop Romero," he says, "was not brutal in a bloody way, as so many other atrocities in El Salvador were. A sniper's bullet is almost benign compared with the tales of torture and mutilation that emanated from that stricken land. Yet Archbishop Romero's killing was exceptionally brutal due to the powerful symbolism of the deed."[11] Nico turns to the support for Romero around the world, as shown in the declarations we have submitted.

Three Nobel Peace Prize laureates from the Americas, as some examples, provided declarations. . . . And here in the United States, we have heard from two members of Congress. . . . And from Europe, we have heard from priests and academics, and we have learned of Romero's place among the ten modern martyrs that grace the entrance to Westminster Abbey in London.

Just yesterday we heard from one more voice and one more continent. Archbishop Desmond Tutu of South Africa, who also was awarded the Nobel Peace Prize in 1984 for his nonviolent opposition to the Apartheid regime, submitted a declaration. I would like to read a few paragraphs from it as I touch on this. Archbishop Tutu wrote:

> I never had the privilege of meeting Archbishop Oscar Romero, but I certainly knew of him and his efforts to speak out against the human rights abuses committed by the then government of El Salvador.
>
> I felt we were partners together in similar situations, speaking the word of God to encourage our people who were battered, beaten and oppressed by governments whose role should have been to nurture, protect, and uplift their citizens.
>
> In 1980, when Oscar Romero was assassinated, I was general secretary of the South African Council of Churches. It was a great shock to us, even though we knew that many of his clergy had been attacked, killed, or been disappeared. We never believed that a man with such passion and compassion would be attacked and shot.
>
> His assassination in public with his people was reminiscent of the assassination of another great man, Mahatma Gandhi. Such a brutal act demonstrated the arrogance of the perpetrators, their total disrespect for life and confidence in their impunity.
>
> This confidence stands on the support they enjoyed from a foreign nation, the most powerful in the world. It is this collaboration that allowed those in power in El Salvador to ignore their people and seek their own political ends. Such powerful alliances served the interests of the few and have led to the misery and suffering of millions in many developing countries. Tragically, El Salvador has been such a victim.
>
> Oscar Romero was a true martyr. He died for his faith and for what that says about caring, sharing, love, and freedom. He is a role model and an example of what it means to live out one's faith at whatever cost. He is one of those great men to be remembered and revered for his defense of human rights and belief that this is a moral universe. Evil and oppression do not have the last word. They will be overcome by their glorious opposites, love and freedom. This case is evidence that this is so.
>
> The purpose is not retribution, but to seek the truth, and to restore the moral balance. This case is a message to those who would hold on to power and profit and who turned the military might of their country on their own people to crush them. The voice of the people cannot be silenced forever. Righteousness will prevail. It is the truth that will ultimately make us free.

As I listen to the poetic words, I keep my head down, fighting back tears. I sense everyone in the courtroom is doing the same. Nico makes his final appeal. "There is a practice in Latin American countries of pronouncing the presence of the departed, 'Monseñor Romero. *Presente.*' Monseñor Romero is present among us," Nico explains. "By achieving justice here today, we can help to ensure the resurrection of the living Romero, the one who stood bravely, yet humbly, in defense of human rights, who spoke truth to power out of a deep and abiding love for the dignity of all human beings. And such an act of justice might itself be one of redemption, of resurrection. Let us act then to achieve justice. For Monseñor Romero and all those for whom he still gives a voice. Monseñor Romero. *Presente.*"

Judge Wanger has remained stoic during Nico's emotional speech. "All right," he says, "I'm going to provide a partial oral statement of decision." I look at my watch—it is late in the afternoon and the air conditioning will soon be shut off. Like everyone else, I expect the judge to be quick with his remarks. As a team, we have no idea how he is going to rule. We expect to be victorious, something that should be a sure thing with no defense lawyers opposing us, but Judge Wanger has given nothing away. We prepared for a trial mostly about the impact of Romero's death—the damages—but with Amado Garay's testimony and Terry Karl's analysis, the judge has shown a strong interest in the underlying facts. If he is going to analyze whether we have proven Saravia's involvement in the assassination, the result is still far from clear.

"There are two concerns in approaching a case that involves issues that go beyond the law," Judge Wanger begins. "And in some ways, the law is inadequate, and it does not have a voice to recognize the kinds of concerns that have been presented through the testimony of witnesses who actually lived and experienced and know what this case concerns." He goes through the law, as he must, and finally he gives a hint about where he is heading:

The evidence shows that there was a consistent and unabating regime that was in control of the country of El Salvador. . . . It functioned as a militarily controlled government that engaged in systematic and continuous violations of human rights that were effectuated for the purposes of perpetuating the concentration of land and wealth in an oligarchy. . . . Those rights were not enjoyed because of a repressive regime which utilized actively and continuously the means and methods of murder, torture, kidnapping, and other physical and psychological weapons to create a state of fear, intimidation, coercion, and repression. And it was the position and the role of the decedent in this case, Archbishop Romero, [to be] a voice that stood for independence and that would not be intimidated nor silenced in the light of what he knew was a threat to his very existence. He predicted his own death. He knew he would be killed, and he was killed by the forces that had proved continuously that they were ready, willing, able and continued to engage in that conduct.

This is a good start, but potential pitfalls remain as the judge moves to the first legal issue, the statute of limitations, the rule requiring that cases be filed within a reasonable time after the events occurred. This lawsuit has come decades after the murder. "Here, of course, nothing could have been more public and more known to the world than the assassination of the archbishop of the nation of El Salvador," he says. "So why is the case brought twenty-three years later?" My stomach turns a few flips. "It must be shown that extraordinary circumstances exist where you know you have legal rights [but] extraordinary circumstances such as the unavailability due to war . . . prevent your access to a court." He summarizes the proof we presented to show that this case is indeed extraordinary: there has never been a full judicial inquiry into Romero's murder, the man assigned to investigate it in El Salvador suffered his own assassination attempt, and the ARENA party obstructed all efforts at justice. Judge Wanger seems to be in agreement with us. "The evidence shows that the [Salvadoran] government, including the court system, especially the Supreme Court . . . did everything in their power to abdicate their judicial function, to ignore, to distort," he says. "They fabricated evidence." He implies that bringing the lawsuit in California before 2003 simply was not possible. We are safe on that issue.

The hour in Fresno is now well past five. What I had expected to be a quick ruling has grown loquacious, and the air conditioning has clearly been turned off because the temperature is rising. Judge Wanger turns to whether there is enough proof to show that Saravia is responsible for Romero's assassination. He goes through Garay's testimony in detail and, in contrast to the Salvadoran Supreme Court, Judge Wanger believes the getaway driver is credible. Regarding Saravia:

> [The] evidence and the documents support a finding that to be liable for the wrongful killing of another being, you don't have to pull the trigger, you don't have to be present. You can plan, you can facilitate, you can aid, abet. And here the obtaining of a trusted, reliable, and competent driver, the payment of the assassin, the reporting to the mastermind, D'Aubuisson, all are what the law calls "overt acts," where two or more persons agree to engage in conduct which is unlawful. The law recognizes that . . . even though you

don't commit it yourself, even if you are not present, even if you don't see it, you are . . . as accountable and responsible as the person who pulls the trigger.

At long last, he seems to be reaching the moment we have waited for. "And here the defendant Saravia, I find, has been proved by a preponderance of the evidence to be a coconspirator, an aider and abettor, to be vicariously and actually liable, in law and fact, for the murder of the archbishop."

Though couched in legal language, the judge has just said we won.

"And in this case," Judge Wanger continues, "the damage is multifaceted and it is of a magnitude that is hardly describable." That phrase, "of a magnitude that is hardly describable," echoes in my mind. "The law can provide only dollars," he says. "It cannot restore. It can't build monuments, it can't hold services. It can only say to the defendant, 'You are liable for what you have done, and for that, you must pay.' And the only thing that we can in a civil court require that the defendant pay is money." This has always been the downfall of our only option: a civil lawsuit under a limited U.S. law. "Every witness and counsel has eloquently stated better than I can state the value of the archbishop of El Salvador, Monseñor Romero, [and] what he meant to his country and to the world. And so here the compensation that is awarded cannot measure that. You can't account for such an individual."

Judge Wanger is reaching his final ruling. "In this case," he says, "the court finds that the appropriate measure of damages . . . to compensate the plaintiff for the loss of the decedent is $2,500,000. Because there is a moral element, and to punish and to set an example . . . the sum of $7,500,000 in punitive damages is awarded to the plaintiff." It's a judgment of $10 million.

The judge looks at Nico. "Is there anything further?"

Nico jumps up. "No, Your Honor. We have nothing further, thank you."

"All right," the judge says. "We will stand in recess."

We rise to our feet as Judge Wanger marches down the stairs and out the door. For a moment, no one makes a sound. I start to cry as we finally turn to each other and start hugging. While I wipe the tears from my cheeks, someone in the audience shouts, "¡Monseñor Romero!"

A chorus responds, "¡Presente!"

"¡Monseñor Romero!"

"¡Presente!"

"¡Monseñor Romero!"

"¡Presente!"

FIFTEEN

"The Fleas Always Stick to the Skinniest Dog"

THE VERDICT'S IMPACT ON SARAVIA

TEGUCIGALPA, HONDURAS—OCTOBER 2006

"You aren't with the government, are you?" the man asks me, two years after our trial has ended. He is nervous but not skittish, scared but in control. He has good reason for his question because I am wearing a suit, trying to look as official as possible, and he has spotted my laptop wired to my iPod, a microphone attached at the end. We are hoping but not expecting that he will let us record our session, but really the equipment is there to show him that we are serious. Along with Almudena Bernabeu, we occupy a small suite in one of Honduras's ritzier hotels perched atop a hill overlooking the capital city. The surroundings providing a contrast to the life our subject is now living.

We waited an agonizing hour for him in the lobby, more nervous with each passing minute that he had decided to call off the meeting. When he finally arrived, another person was with him, someone we didn't know and hadn't expected. This only increased our anxiety. We all tried to act like it was a normal encounter, shaking hands and talking about the long drive they had just made, but the small talk could only last so long. He dismissed the other man, telling him to return later in the day. As we rode the elevator up to the suite, I was struck by how thin he was. I almost hadn't recognized him, dozens of pounds lighter than in his photo, though the reddish hair was still a giveaway. He tells us the weight loss is a result of stress.

He was already prepared to meet Almudena, who by now is semifamous as the Spanish lawyer making waves in El Salvador, but I am the tall *gringo* with the recording device, so I am the one who concerns him. Almudena told him I would be here, but he still wants to make sure I am not with the FBI or, worse, the CIA. I assure him I am only a nonprofit lawyer. With our guest now placated, Almudena begins to explain the details of the verdict we won against him two years ago.

SAN FRANCISCO—MAY 2005

Eight months after our trial, investigator Bobby Levinson contacts me with an intriguing lead. Levinson's best source made contact with a Nicaraguan man who reported that he had recently been in Managua, Nicaragua, and was surprised when he walked into a restaurant there and saw Álvaro Saravia. He learned that a mutual friend was allowing Saravia to stay in his Managua home. Saravia seemed settled in Nicaragua, where he was living under a pseudonym.

As I read Levinson's e-mail, I think, here we go again. Even with the trial long over, we are still stuck in a game of Where in the World Is Álvaro Saravia. The only thing that makes this different, at least, is that it was a direct sighting.

Our reaction to Levinson's news is moderate interest matched by exhaustion. Given previous reports of Saravia's location, we are skeptical, although the idea that he is hiding in Nicaragua is not far-fetched. Even if true, is there anything for us to do almost a year after our trial? "Outing him is really the only option that I can think of—trying him in the press to make his life uncomfortable," Nico van Aelstyn writes the legal team. "I don't think we have anything to discuss with him. We have little or no leverage with him now. I don't think he has much to say about the financiers anyway."[1] Capturing the way we all feel, Nico writes that we could out Saravia "to make his life unpleasant and to keep the story in the news." We take steps to examine whether legal action can be taken in Nicaragua, but the research reveals few good options, and the logistics prove difficult. Busy with other cases, we let the matter drop.

In November, a Tennessee jury finds Colonel Nicolás Carranza, El Salvador's vice-minister of defense in 1980, responsible for torture and crimes against humanity committed by the Salvadoran security forces. Our case against Carranza does not concern Romero's murder, even though the colonel was in power when Romero was killed and some think that Carranza was involved. The Tennessee trial, focusing on other Salvadorans who were tortured or whose families were murdered, takes all our energy in late 2005 and allows no time for further investigation of Romero's death. But no matter how much we ignore it, the Romero case keeps coming back to us.

In February 2006, Almudena receives an e-mail from Gerardo Reyes, an award-winning reporter with Miami's *El Nuevo Herald* newspaper. The subject line reads, "URGENT." "I am in a Central American town that I cannot identify," Reyes writes. "Since yesterday I have been speaking with ex-captain Saravia." According to Reyes, Saravia contacted him out of the blue and offered to speak without holding anything back ("with his pants off," as the phrase goes in Spanish) about the Romero assassination. Reyes went to visit him but Saravia changed course, saying he needed help with his economic and security situation. When Reyes countered that he would not pay a source, Saravia pitched the idea that Reyes write a book about Saravia's involvement in Romero's murder. Faced with Reyes's refusal to be his lackey, Saravia gave him only enough to write an article that hinted at what Saravia knew. Saravia was showing himself to be strategic, planting clues here and there with the hope that eventually his payday would come. He even asked Reyes what would happen if he decided to cooperate with us, the lawyers in the lawsuit against him.

On March 24, 2006, the anniversary of Romero's assassination, *El Nuevo Herald* runs Reyes's article, followed two days later by a partial transcript of the interview. In the story, Saravia reveals only a few details while promising he will come clean in a book. "I must tell the truth," Saravia says. "I'm not going to tell lies, regardless of the consequences." Saravia claims he is willing to ask forgiveness from the current archbishop of San Salvador. "That's a moral obligation I have, as a human being, to society, the church and myself." I am struck by the oddity of Saravia feeling an obligation to the Catholic Church even as he admits to Reyes that his group saw "the face of the enemy" in Romero. The present archbishop, for his part, seems very pleased with Saravia's statements. "God always forgives when there is true repentance and a desire to make amends," Archbishop Fernando Sáenz Lacalle says. "How good it is that someone who bears so heavy a load on his conscience can lay it down and find peace and God's friendship."[2]

If we can believe Saravia's words, he reveals what he was doing at the time we filed the lawsuit in 2003, claiming he left the United States after a dispute with a female friend. Though he does not use her name, this provides some possible confirmation about his relationship with Inés Olsson, the woman he lived with in Modesto. Saravia says he crossed the border into Mexico and traveled to Honduras, where he sold cheese in the streets until he saved enough money to open a bar. One Sunday in September 2004, Saravia opened a newspaper and saw an article reporting that he had been ordered by a court in California to pay $10 million for his role in the assassination of Archbishop Romero. The news shattered Saravia's somewhat tranquil existence and he closed the bar, left Tegucigalpa, and went to live on an empty beach. "Although he doesn't admit it," writes Reyes, "it is clear he feels besieged by a phenomenon he senses in the air: the closing-in of a quiet legion of exhumers of injustices devoted to hunting torturers, human rights violators, and war criminals to the ends of the earth."

Saravia admits to knowing the identity of the shooter and others involved, but he refuses to disclose the information without protection. He prefers, it seems, to put it all in a book. "People will realize where my participation ended and how I was accused of things for which I was not responsible," he insists. "I didn't run the operation." Rather, he says, certain people provided financing for the assassination while others were paid to participate To make his point, Saravia tells a story about being in a bookstore where he overheard a nun saying she was looking for a book on the death of Archbishop Romero. Without revealing his identity, Saravia asked the nun about her interest in the topic. She responded that she was very happy because Álvaro Saravia, the man who assassinated Romero, was now in jail for crimes against humanity. He felt the need to correct her, noting that Álvaro Saravia was not the one who had pulled the trigger, and he was not in prison. As Saravia left the bookstore, he thought to himself that he was sick and tired of people thinking he was the shooter. "Of course," he says, "since I'm the only one out in public, the fleas always stick to the skinniest dog." Even through his bitterness, though, Saravia shows he is not lacking in self-importance. "If I speak," he says, "El Salvador will tremble."

Though Saravia's interview makes news—a leading Jesuit in El Salvador calls it "a miracle from Monseñor Romero himself"—everything calms down after a few days. Neither Salvadoran nor Nicaraguan authorities take action. Bobby Levinson continues to send us updates from his sources about Saravia's movements in Central America, but we move on to other things. Saravia, for his part, fails to deliver on the empty threats he made in the pages of *El Nuevo Herald*. I doubt very much that he is drafting a tell-all book. Instead, like a prairie dog, he is poking his head out of his hole to check the wind. I assume he will now retreat below the surface.

That is why I am so stunned, two months later, when Saravia leaves a message on Almudena's voice mail.

Saravia does not say why he is calling us. Is it desperation? Curiosity? Intimidation? Cruelty? Whatever his justification, the moment feels eerily similar to the surprise two years ago when Nico answered his phone to hear Amado Garay say, "This is Witness 5145." We decide to return Saravia's call but emphasize that he is the one who owes a duty to us, not the other way around. We have a $10 million verdict against him, so we have all the leverage. That afternoon, while I listen silently on speakerphone, Almudena dials Saravia. From the start, their tone is respectful, with Almudena calling him "Don Álvaro" and his reciprocating with the formal "Señora Almudena." Saravia seems under control, and as they get past the pleasantries, he says that, contrary to all other reports, he is living in Honduras, north of Tegucigalpa. It is clear he wants to be rid of the judgment; it is like a weight around his ankle dragging him toward the bottom of a lake. I sense that he mistakenly believes the civil case could lead to his arrest, and although we can't misrepresent to him what the verdict means, it is to our advantage for him to link the two in his mind.

"I can give you the person who is responsible for the crime," Saravia says calmly but with some urgency. "He's the only one who can satisfy the judgment." Almudena counters that the lawsuit is in Saravia's name so only he can make the verdict go away. The call feels like the beginning of a long conversation, perhaps even a negotiation. Even if he does not fully understand the process, Saravia seems to be trying to settle the case. He promises to phone again in a week.

In time, a relationship with Saravia evolves. He does not have consistent access to a phone so the discussions require some effort, but he and Almudena speak regularly. They develop a bizarre rapport. Though she despises him and everything he has done, she recognizes that he isn't stupid and has a good sense of humor. Despite some light moments, though, he continues to insist, often in a demanding tone, that we do something to make the judgment go away. Almudena, with all the patience she can muster, reminds Saravia that we have no reason to help him, and after a few months their discussions reach a stalemate as his unrelenting attitude persists. Just as she is about to break off communication, Saravia adopts a more humble stance, admitting that he has almost no friends and wants to leave Honduras. He is afraid of going back to El Salvador, and he seems to be running out of options. He asks that we send him, in writing, everything we want from him, including questions to be answered and steps to be taken. He will set up an e-mail account where we can send the list.

We take a few weeks to prepare the long and complicated list. If we are going to contemplate negotiations about settling the case—a stage we have not reached but are maybe starting to approach—we will need extensive information from Saravia about Romero's assassination and the death squads, especially the financiers. As we finalize the draft, we know that follow-up on a positive response can't be done over the phone, so Almudena and I consult our schedules and envision a trip to Honduras. Two more weeks pass before Saravia sends a reply. "Señora Almudena," he writes, "I received the list of questions. I read them thoroughly and I don't have any problem in answering them. October 17 or whatever you indicate is fine for me and has been confirmed with sufficient time for me to be in Tegucigalpa one day ahead and for me to make the necessary preparations for the trip." Despite Saravia's willingness, he still pushes back. "My personal situation is not so comfortable, as you know," he says, "so I ask you if it is not a problem to send me some allowance for my trip." Almudena tells him no.

TEGUCIGALPA—OCTOBER 2006

As I assure Saravia that I am not a U.S. government agent, we sit down at the kitchen table of our Tegucigalpa suite. The curtains on the windows are drawn shut and the door is locked from the inside. Saravia's manner is cordial if not pleasant, and he responds well to Almudena's attempt to lighten the mood as we share a few tempered laughs. I am struck again by his red hair, now even more pronounced against his gaunt face. He is frighteningly thin compared to the old black-and-white photo we have memorized.

For our part, this will not be a negotiation but a conversation to see how far Saravia will go. Under no circumstances are Almudena and I going to give a hint of willingness to settle the case unless Saravia gives us concrete answers to our questions. He has to show his good faith before we show ours, and we are prepared to walk away with nothing. We are impressed, though, by Saravia's intelligence and sophistication. He certainly is not the stupid drunk some have portrayed, and his manner of speech shows a certain level of education. He is knowledgeable about the lawsuit and CJA's other cases, including the Tennessee trial against Colonel Carranza, and he sounds like he has spoken with a lawyer. Saravia now knows the verdict against him is civil rather than criminal in nature and can't land him in jail, but he remains obsessed with the idea that the judgment has reinforced a perception that he was the actual assassin. He repeats the story about the nun in the bookstore who mistakenly asserted he was the shooter. "I'm not responsible," he protests, saying that the notoriety has made it impossible for him to live freely. "That judgment is a death sentence for me," he says.

To my mind, his point is both perceptive and naïve. The case undoubtedly cements the fact of Saravia's participation in the murder, and even he no longer denies that he had a role. But in obsessing over the notion that Salvadorans mistakenly think he was the shooter, he implies that he is less culpable because he did not pull the trigger. This distinction, frankly, is ludicrous, but his bitterness at being the scapegoat, so evident in his interview with Gerardo Reyes, colors almost everything he says.

Saravia tells us of his aborted attempts to improve his security, but he pleads that access to money is his only avenue to safety. Some cash would allow him to live and travel where he wants without fear of reprisal. He brings up his interest in writing a book and hints that he wants our help. "We won't give you money," Almudena reminds him, and he doesn't push the issue. It becomes clear that Saravia contacted us because he perceives that we are the people best placed to arrange for his safety. He understands that we want to expose the full truth about the murder plot, and he possesses the information to make that happen. Saravia also feels spurned by the Catholic Church, telling us he spoke personally with San Salvador's archbishop but the archbishop refused to talk about the assassination. I am stunned to hear this if it is true, because the archbishop made public statements that the lawsuit would aid Romero's beatification, and he even expressed a willingness to forgive Saravia. I hope Saravia is lying about the whole episode.

We steer him toward our list of questions, and he again declares his willingness to talk but not now, not until he is safe. He says he will testify, but only once his security is ensured. Even so, he partially engages us on some details of his life in El Salvador at the time Romero was killed. There is no doubt, for example, that Saravia and his companions were engaged in violence. He refers to his group as a "death squad" and consistently talks about Roberto D'Aubuisson as its leader, but he also tries to distance D'Aubuisson from the group's activities. Saravia expresses his disgust with the fact that every time a violent act occurred in El Salvador, D'Aubuisson was blamed for it. "What evidence do you have that D'Aubuisson was involved in violence?" he asks us, conveniently forgetting his own repeated testimony about the issue. "If D'Aubuisson was as important as everyone says, I would have been a government minister."

Saravia tells us the Romero assassination was not a sophisticated plot or the product of a specific order from D'Aubuisson. He claims he had not thought that killing Romero was an important objective, but his compatriots Negro Sagrera and Eduardo Ávila were fired up about it that day. They took the lead on the operation, he says. I have the impression Saravia is implying that a decision to murder Romero was made by others—probably higher-ups—but that no details or plans were provided. His group simply knew that Romero was to be killed and they decided to do it. To reinforce the point, Saravia insists that the Operation Piña page captured along with his diary has nothing to do with the Romero assassination. "*Piña* means a grenade," he scoffs.

While I don't know whether to believe Saravia on this point, I can't reject his assertion out of hand. Many consider Operation Piña to be the smoking gun implicating Saravia and D'Aubuisson in Romero's murder. The skeptic in me, though, has often wondered if it is too convenient. A document in D'Aubuisson's handwriting with the precise details of Romero's murder is seized from D'Aubuisson's attaché case along with a book bearing Saravia's name only two months after Romero died? Why did D'Aubuisson hold on to it? Why did he need to write it down in the first place? Even now, after spending years thinking about it, I am unsure what to think.

Saravia does not hide his bitterness against El Salvador's rich and power-ful. "We were set up," he says, implying that the oligarchs who wanted Romero killed used the death squad to do their dirty work. The fact that Saravia and the others were arrested at Finca San Luis in 1980 showed that they had been mere pawns in a bloody game. Saravia says many of the wealthy Salvadorans on our list of suspected financiers gave support to D'Aubuisson. Alfredo Mena Lagos helped D'Aubuisson a lot, he says. Saravia himself some-times lived at Mena Lagos's house.

Saravia tells us a bit about the shooter. Without revealing the name, Saravia says he was an old marksman from the National Guard. Saravia insists he did not know the man's name at the time of the assassination, but a few years later, when Saravia was working for businessman Roberto Daglio, the shooter showed up at Saravia's office. "What are you doing here?" Saravia scolded him.[3]

I find the dialogue exhilarating but frustrating as we get only hazy glimpses of the bigger picture. Distinguishing truth from half-truth and half-truth from fiction is difficult, and whenever we push for details beyond the wisps of information Saravia lets slip, he retreats to his position that he can't say more without protection. He continues to feel us out, calculating whether he can trust us. He knows we have kept our word in coming to meet him and we have not pulled any surprises, but he still is not comfortable giving us the full story. After several hours, we have gone as far as we can. Saravia wants protection, in the form of financial help, but we won't entertain any negotiations unless he answers all our questions. Despite his crushing circumstances and obvious interest in telling his side of the story, Saravia holds firm. Almudena and I stay true to our position that we are prepared to walk away with nothing. With a long pause in the conversation, we reach an implicit understanding that the meeting is over. We tell Saravia he should call us if he wants to take any further steps.

Leaving my untouched computer on the table, we follow Saravia back to the deserted lobby. Though I have no sympathy for his lot in life, I can't avoid the fact that he looks pathetic, his shrunken frame shouting his current despair. As he turns to leave, I think about a question Almudena posed when he was telling us how fanatical the members of his group had been. "Why did you do it?" she asked. "Why did you kill Monseñor Romero?" Saravia, despite his many words, never answered the question. He could not seem to find a justification for what they had done.

The next morning, Almudena's cell phone rings. "Señora Almudena," Saravia says as she answers and presses the phone to her ear to hear the choppy words on the other end. "You're right," he says. "We should do this the legal way. I'll do it however you want." Almudena looks at me in astonishment, but as she begins speaking, Saravia's phone starts to cut out. She yells into the receiver but he can't hear, and the line goes dead. We wait for Saravia to call back but the minutes pass with nothing more. Almudena tries dialing him a few times but she can't get through. Her phone doesn't ring again, and we return home to the United States empty-handed.

Epilogue

To this day, Álvaro Saravia remains the only person held responsible by a court of law for the murder of Óscar Romero, and his penalty is nothing more than a dollar figure he has never paid. This lamentable reality is less an indication of the significance of the lawsuit we brought and more an indictment of the tight lid that impunity has imposed whenever efforts to seek accountability have bubbled up in El Salvador. The Amnesty Law passed in 1993, five days after the Truth Commission named Saravia, Roberto D'Aubuisson, and others as the men who killed Romero, endured for twenty-three years, surviving ARENA's departure from political power and the ascension of the former guerrilla party, the FMLN, to a second consecutive presidential term. But in July 2016, the Constitutional Chamber of El Salvador's Supreme Court, a body more independent of outside influence than the one that threw out the arrest warrant against Saravia in 1988, ruled the Amnesty Law unconstitutional. One of the judges who voted to scrap the amnesty was previously a lawyer in the archdiocese's human rights office who investigated the abuses that Monseñor Romero denounced from his pulpit.

As this book goes to print, the likelihood that Romero's killers will someday sit in the dock of a San Salvador criminal court is uncertain. Even with the removal of the Amnesty Law, it remains to be seen if the Salvadoran government will demonstrate the political will necessary to fully prosecute Romero's murder. But other Latin American countries with similarly dark pasts have recently shown that once a ray of light emerges, demands for accountability grow and authorities find the courage or political astuteness to act. Perhaps now the decades of labor by so many in El

Salvador and elsewhere, publicly and clandestinely, to bring justice to their slain archbishop will pay off. If criminal charges never come, Salvadorans will have to comfort themselves with the knowledge that the Vatican, after two decades of its own internal political struggles, has beatified Archbishop Romero and will soon place him in the exalted pantheon of Catholic saints.

In the days after Almudena Bernabeu and I return from Honduras in 2006, our hope that Saravia's dropped phone call on the final day of our trip might provide a glimmer of promise is dampened by Saravia's silence. Less than three weeks later, we are stunned to read an article in *Diario Co Latino.* "On Wednesday afternoon," the story begins, "a man who identified himself as Captain Álvaro Rafael Saravia, linked to the assassination of Archbishop Óscar Arnulfo Romero, contacted *Diario Co Latino* to give an interview." Saravia, it appears, had a change of heart about our usefulness and went back to peddling his sad story to the media. "Captain Saravia swears that the trial left him practically in the street, as he closed his business, and he had to move and stay far away from everyone," the article says. Saravia's latest interview shows his familiar pattern, as he admits to some things, denies others, and contradicts himself on certain points. Diverging from what he told us and *El Nuevo Herald,* Saravia denies having a direct link to the Romero assassination and calls the judgment against him "unjust." "If I had testified," he boasts, "if I had been present at the hearing, if I could have defended myself with all the means that I have, it would not have come to that resolution. Maybe today is a little late to talk but I know that the federal judges in the United States are open to any negotiation."[1]

In the article, Saravia is still threatening to publish a tell-all book. "Who Monseñor Romero was, who Roberto D'Aubuisson was, who Captain Álvaro Rafael Saravia was," he says, "this is part of the first chapter of my book." Saravia claims his manuscript will come out on March 24, the anniversary of Romero's assassination. The thought makes me sick. Whether any of this is true, his three forays into storytelling in 2006—to *Diario Co Latino, El Nuevo Herald,* and us—never lead to any comprehensive account of Romero's murder. Saravia's desperation results in some enlightening disclosures, but he apparently has not reached the personal depths necessary to tell everything he knows. He still leaks only glimpses of fact that, despite their importance, remain overshadowed by misdirection and undisclosed details. Saravia's final appearance in *Diario Co Latino,* the worst of the bunch, is full of obfuscation as he manipulates the truth the same way he claims the oligarchs manipulated him.

I leave CJA in the summer of 2007 to pursue other endeavors and start writing this book. Saravia, to my temporary relief, returns underground, but his silence does not last. In 2008, two years after his last interview, Almudena e-mails me from CJA with a familiar challenge: "Guess who left a message on my answering machine today?" Saravia is back, and just as before, Almudena engages Saravia in a series of discussions that takes months to hash out. Saravia, it is now clear, has no intention of writing a book, but he is still seeking money and protection in exchange for his story. Once again, he promises to tell everything to a journalist, as though we haven't heard that before.

This time, however, a reporter is also looking for Saravia. Carlos Dada, founder of the groundbreaking *El Faro* online newspaper, came to know Professor Terry Karl while taking courses at Stanford, and he has launched his own search for Saravia. Karl connects Dada with Almudena, and when Saravia calls in 2008, Almudena puts Dada and Saravia together. Over the next year, Dada secretly meets with Saravia eight or nine times, and Saravia goes back on the record, even posing for photographs.[2]

In March 2010, just days before the thirtieth anniversary of Romero's assassination, *El Faro* publishes the story. Dada's writing, which will later win well-deserved awards and accolades, tells as much of Saravia's story as we are ever likely to get. Although some details about the financiers are incomplete and repeat what we have heard before, his disclosures are probably the best anyone can expect.[3] The story, however, begins with a disappointingly familiar comment from Saravia as he reads a piece Dada authored many years before.

"You wrote this, right?" Saravia asks.

"Yes," Dada replies.

"Well it's wrong."

"Why?"

"It says here, 'Several years after murdering Archbishop Romero.' And I didn't kill him."

"Who killed him then?"

"Someone else."

That "someone else" is the trump card Saravia has held firmly in his hand for thirty years, the lottery ticket he hopes will someday deliver him from misery. "You have to descend into hell to find Saravia," Dada writes in describing a Saravia even frailer than the thin man we encountered in Honduras four years ago. Saravia's condition, it appears, has deteriorated further as he endures a friendless existence in poverty and total exile. It is quite a contrast from his early days. "Saravia was crazy," an extremist member of the ARENA party anonymously tells Dada. "He would see that you had a toothache and ask you what happened. So you'd say a dentist had messed you up, and the next day, the dentist would be dead." An ARENA founder, Ricardo Valdivieso, labels Saravia a "psychopath," a word that, whether true or merely useful in making Saravia a scapegoat, once attached to ARENA's hero, Roberto D'Aubuisson.[4] For his part, Saravia remains bitter and defiant in his current desolation. "Thirty years have gone by and it's still the same shit," he says. "I don't have anything to hide anymore. For what? How could I be any more screwed than I am now? Nothing! I get the feeling that there's a conspiracy and that they really don't want to know who in the hell killed Romero."

Given the opportunity to say who killed Romero, however, Saravia demurs.

"A foreigner?" Dada asks him.

"No. An *indio,* one of our own," Saravia says. "He's still out there somewhere."[5]

"You didn't fire the gun, but you participated."

"Thirty years and this is going to persecute me until I die. Of course I participated. That's why we're here talking."

"And why is it you want to talk now?" Dada asks.

"Because of my children," Saravia says. "Even they look at me as if I'm Hitler."

Saravia recites a version of the assassination similar to those he has offered previously but with more detail, and Dada finds corroboration that has not existed before—a new witness who confirms that he, Saravia, and Negro Sagrera sat in a car outside the church gate during Archbishop Romero's murder. Gabriel "Bibi" Montenegro, speaking for the first time in thirty years, tells Dada that the three of them, all armed, drove to the Camino Real hotel and then the Divina Providencia church in Montenegro's white Dodge Lancer. With Montenegro high on drugs and alcohol, they waited out in the street as the assassin shot Romero.[6]

Negro Sagrera, for his part, unconvincingly denies any involvement. "Hasn't it ever happened to you," he asks Dada, "that when you don't have anything to do with something you use the expression 'I don't give a shit because I don't have anything to do with that?'" About Saravia, Sagrera adds, "That guy's a demented alcoholic."

Saravia tells Dada, just as he told the Truth Commission, about a meeting a few days after the assassination at the house of poultry scion Eduardo Lemus O'Byrne. Saravia says Lemus O'Byrne provided the money to pay the shooter, but when Dada interviews Lemus O'Byrne, he denies any role. "They were a couple of heavies," Lemus O'Byrne says about Saravia and Sagrera. "I never had anything to do with them. I defend principles, but they had become warlords and mafiosos." About the reunion at his house, he says, "I do not recall that meeting. That meeting never happened." Lemus O'Byrne, though, does not follow the usual playbook of defending Roberto D'Aubuisson. Though a founder of ARENA, he broke with D'Aubuisson early over a mysterious plane crash that killed his brother-in-law. Shortly after the accident, D'Aubuisson married the brother-in-law's widow, and Lemus O'Byrne blames D'Aubuisson for the death, even alleging that when a friend started investigating the crash, the "D'Aubuisson, Sagrera, and Saravia group tried to kill him." At that point, Lemus O'Byrne claims he flexed his muscle. "I said to [D'Aubuisson]," he tells Dada, "You don't mess with me because I will bust your ass."

This exchange, if it happened, explains why Saravia is so bitter. Although Saravia refuses to accept culpability for Romero's death, he is not wrong that others are responsible. The only people who would have dared to threaten Roberto D'Aubuisson in the way Lemus O'Byrne claims he did were those above D'Aubuisson in the Salvadoran social hierarchy, the men and women who held court in Miami boardrooms and condos or behind wire-topped fences in San Salvador, funding and directing the death squads. They are the ones that Saravia, a former member of those death squads, now so thoroughly despises. Asked by Dada what should be done to the others responsible for Archbishop Romero's murder—a list on which Saravia clearly includes some of the oligarchs—Saravia responds in a decidedly non-Romero manner, "They should squeeze their balls like they used to and let's see if they don't sing!"

Until he emerges again from his purgatory of resentment and desolation, these are the enduring words of Álvaro Saravia. A Cold Warrior in what was once a very hot Salvadoran war, he performed the dirty work of the oligarchs and his military superiors. For a time, Saravia had all the money and liquor he could consume. Now destitute and desperate, he remains the only man ever judged for killing Archbishop Romero, the only man who spent time in jail, the only man now in hiding because of his guilt. His situation is pathetic, the result of many bad acts and at least some measure of bad luck. But even though he would never admit it, Saravia is in many ways blessed. Despite aiding in the most notorious murder in his country's history, he never faced justice there, benefitting from obfuscation by the Salvadoran Right and a lack of political will from the Left. He still has not paid a cent of the $10 million judgment against him, and most fortunately for someone who has spoken out several times, he is still alive (as far as we know). His survival, though it may be attributable to chance or indifference, is probably due to the fact that, of all the beans he has spilled, he has not spilled the most valuable ones. Despite his many threats, Saravia has yet to make El Salvador tremble.

A coffee shop in Ottawa, Canada—where I have done much of the writing of this book—is part of a local chain that serves fair-trade coffee. Near the front window of the cafe hangs a painting that I assume is displayed to show the types of people the company supports. The subject is a Latin American man of at least partially indigenous descent. He could be from any one of many countries, and though his skin is darker than that of most Salvadorans, he could just as easily be from El Salvador. His dress reflects that of a poor farmer—worn burgundy pants, a sweater covered by a light jacket, a round hat with a wide brim. One of his dirty sandals is firmly planted atop a bag of coffee beans. His head is tilted back proudly, a confident grin beaming from his face. I have never doubted that the painter wanted to express that the man's gratification sprang from the knowledge that *his* coffee, not that of a wealthy landowner in a bygone era, is what was being consumed in that Canadian cafe.

I have often thought of that painting as I write about Óscar Romero and the men who killed him. The *campesino* in the painting represents the people Romero gave his life defending, the voiceless to whom Romero gave a voice. More than anything else, the coffee beans picked by exploited and impoverished Salvadoran workers generated the massive inequalities and repression that Romero confronted. Those *campesinos,* Romero often said, were his flock, and he was their shepherd. Without them, there was no reason for Romero to die. Without them, there are no statues of Romero and no highways and airports bearing his name. There are no visits by popes and presidents to his tomb. Without them, Romero would not have died a martyr or be headed down the path to sainthood.

Romero's beatification in May 2015—the last step before being named a saint in the near future—comes thirty-five years after his assassination precipitated El Salvador's disastrous civil war. Tens of thousands died in horrific ways during the conflict, most of them *campesinos* killed by the Salvadoran military. Even after the war ended, right-wing Salvadoran governments spent two decades ignoring or undermining Romero's memory while a petition for his sainthood languished in the Vatican due to his controversial legacy. Only a confluence of events, including the rise of Francis to the papacy and the election of left-leaning governments in El Salvador, has liberated Romero's cause. While this has brought a broader acceptance of Romero as a historic figure, many of his followers feel Romero's public image has been distorted and sanitized, the more revolutionary lessons he preached erased as Romero becomes an icon acceptable to all sectors of society.

At the 2015 mass to finally beatify Romero, Archbishop Vincenzo Paglia, the official who successfully steered Romero's cause through the Vatican, speaks to the hundreds of thousands gathered in San Salvador. Few *campesinos* or poorer Salvadorans are permitted in the areas near the stage, but Roberto D'Aubuisson's son, a politician like his father, attends the ceremony.[7] Archbishop Paglia reminds the crowd of how Romero would have judged the scene. "He is happy for this day but he is not happy about his beatification. He did not need it," Paglia says. "Romero is happy because he sees us together. This was the dream he had for the country and the church. It is for them that he gave his own life." But "from heaven," Romero "urges us not waste this, not to let it burn out. This means that now starts a new time for El Salvador, and for anyone who loves the church and the poor. This is how we pick up Romero's legacy." Romero called on everyone to be martyrs, Paglia says, "to give our lives for the gospel, for others, and for the poor. Yes, dear friends, this beatification asks us all to be martyrs, to give our life for others, for a world of peace and love as did Monseñor Romero."[8]

Paglia's call reflects some of Romero's final words on earth. "Let us all do what we can. We can all do something, at least have a sense of understanding," Romero said in his final homily, moments before being shot. "We know that no one can go on forever, but those who have put into their work a sense of great faith, of love of God, of hope among human beings, find it all now results in the splendors of a crown that is the certain reward for those who work in this way, spreading truth, justice, love, and goodness on earth." We must make the ultimate sacrifice, Romero said, "not for ourselves, but to bring about justice and peace for our people."[9]

Afterword

Benjamín Cuéllar

Today's El Salvador is not what Blessed Archbishop Romero dreamed yesterday even if through him "God passed through El Salvador." This is one of the most brilliant and memorable phrases of another Salvadoran martyr, Ignacio Ellacuría, the Jesuit murdered with his colleagues and two women in 1989. God certainly walked hand in hand the length and breadth of the small country with Romero. And because of his transcendence, the legacy of this good shepherd transcended borders to become the most universal among any of us born in this land. But it is a land that continues to be soaked in blood, with the majority of its people still suffering from exclusion and inequality. As a result, people still flee El Salvador, regardless of the risks, to find safety in other lands that they do not enjoy in their own.[1]

Romero's dream was of a country that had, and could find, a way out. That is how he said it from his Sunday pulpit: "Many times here in El Salvador I have been asked: What can we do? Is there no way out of the situation in El Salvador? And I, full of hope and faith, not only a divine faith but a human faith, believing in the people, say: Yes, there is a way out, but . . . Don't close the exits!"[2]

"How can we," Monseñor Romero said in sharing the thoughts of the Latin American bishops who met in Puebla in 1979 in their third episcopal conference, "contribute to the well-being of our Latin American communities when some still maintain their privileges at any price, and others feel disheartened while still others promote processes for their survival and the affirmation of their rights? . . . What can we offer you?" The answer referred to the disabled person "who at the doors of the Jerusalem temple begged for alms and when Peter and John entered to pray, the poor beggar kept looking at them . . . and Peter said these words, 'We have no gold or silver to give you.'

That's what the bishops also said. 'We don't have gold or silver to give you, but we give you what we have. In the name of Jesus of Nazareth, stand up and walk.'"[3]

Ellacuría, for his part, maintained that only in a utopian and hopeful way "can one believe and have the spiritual strength to try, along with all the poor and oppressed people of the world, to reverse history, subvert it, and move it in a different direction."[4] The last two points together should have provided the way out for El Salvador: people standing up and deciding to walk, making headway toward changing history and moving toward the achievement of the common good. The Salvadoran people did it during the second half of the 1970s but then stopped. The penultimate time that they took to the streets and flooded the capital's downtown in huge numbers was January 22, 1980; the last time, seventy-eight days later, was during the funeral of Monseñor Romero, Sunday the 30th of March.

On the first occasion, the Coordinadora Revolucionaria de Masas, a coalition of popular organizations formed in January 1980, organized the demonstration and the people came knowing that murderous bullets would be fired at them. But despite that and other enormous difficulties, it happened. There was no funding, but there was imagination. There were no social media, but there was passion. In the end, there was mass organization. In those days, Héctor Dada was a member of the Revolutionary Government Junta. He considered that expression of the masses—he called it a popular celebration— "the largest ever seen in Central America."[5] It has been said there were 250,000 participants. "No one had seen anything like it . . . and I, honestly, thought that the demonstrators were going to try to take the presidential palace."[6] It happened then, in the El Salvador of 1980, and it was something tremendous.

Three months after that rally, and after it was throttled by the state's criminal gunfire, Dada "felt like someone shot him in the chest" when he learned they had murdered Romero. That deplorable execution was the warning that, going forward, no one would be safe if they questioned the regime. They killed the highest dignitary in the country's Catholic Church; how would they not be ready to kill students, teachers, *campesinos,* workers, religious people, and others? The assassination also represented the cruel and prophetic death of any possible political and peaceful solution to the conflict. The war drums began beating more loudly.

The organized people—those who stood up to walk the path toward liberation from their social ills, the same as those of the masses—had no options other than to die at the hands of the government forces, to kill as members of the insurgent forces, or to flee the situation to save their lives. Thus, the light started to go out on the struggle, from below and inside, as a result of state repression and the militarization of the social movement. Those who were active, exercising their rights of citizenship, took a gamble on their highest interests, the promises of a triumphant and liberating revolution that would come after the defeat of the enemy on the battlefield.

Thus, all the quiet avenues to peace closed and a furious explosion came down on the country. It started with the first big insurgent offensive launched on Saturday, January 10, 1981. The hostilities, between a government army that was hit hard by a guerrilla force that gained greater strength with the passing years, lasted eleven years and a few days.

Before and throughout the war, the support of the White House and the Pentagon was 100 percent decisive in propping up the regime's armed forces. In that context, Monseñor Romero wrote his famous letter to President Jimmy Carter and read it during his homily on February 17, 1980. He told the U.S. president that if he truly wanted to "defend human rights," he should stop the military aid that was about to be sent to the Salvadoran government, and Carter should guarantee that his administration would not intervene directly or indirectly in the Salvadoran conflict.

"Your government's contribution," he said, "instead of favoring greater justice and peace in El Salvador, will undoubtedly sharpen the injustice and repression inflicted on the people, whose struggle has been for respect of their most basic human rights." Carter was succeeded by the visceral anti-Communist Ronald Reagan, with an "ideology" recorded in the "Santa Fe I Document," drawn up by a special committee and disseminated in May 1980. Its authors and the then candidate for president saw "internal subversion" and "external aggression" as being indistinguishable in Central America.

This group of "hawks" was convinced that the "propaganda" in the "general and specialized media" in Central America inspired forces that were "explicitly hostile" to the United States. They also blindly believed that in this strategic region central to Washington's interests, it was a mistake to assume that it was possible to "easily impose U.S. style democratic alternatives to authoritarian governments." They likewise called for dismantling the "human rights policy" promoted by Carter and replacing it with "a non-interventionist policy of political and ethical realism."

As the "third element" of their "hemispheric security system," they sought to reactivate their "traditional military ties within this hemisphere by offering military training and assistance to the armed forces of the Americas with particular emphasis on the younger officers and non-commissioned officers." They also proposed providing "technical and psychological assistance to all countries" of the hemisphere—though clearly not Cuba, Nicaragua, and Grenada—"in the struggle against terrorism, regardless of the source."[7]

This was the regional policy that Reagan would introduce to the White House beginning on January 20, 1981. As a result, after Romero's death, the five existing guerrilla groups—which later merged on October 10, 1980, into the FMLN—sped up the course of events. Among other actions, they dismantled and militarized the existing powerful social movement but without the necessary resources—primarily weapons—to carry out a war against a government army that the United States, notwithstanding Carter, had never abandoned.

The unified insurgency wanted to take power before January 20, 1981, that is, before Reagan took over. As a result, it launched its incipient armed forces on an adventure, with the beginning of the offensive ten days before the change of government in the United States. The FMLN did not achieve its elusive objective, but it grew and grew until it dealt its opponents significant military defeats, forcing them to sit down and reach an agreement ending the war in 1992.

There was no military victory for either side. For the FMLN, with negotiations and the agreements reached through them, it was a political victory achieved through the construction of a power base capable of making the Salvadoran government accept the process and sit down to talk with the FMLN's political representatives as "equals." It was a power base created from, in addition to military force, the combination of popular sentiment against the war and international solidarity that repudiated the grave human rights violations committed by the Salvadoran regime.

In addition, the intervention of the United Nations and the Organization of American States, as well as the UN secretary-general's group of friendly countries made up of Spain, Colombia, Venezuela, and Mexico, was decisive. Just as big was the role of external actors in the process to end the war in El Salvador. The United States and Soviet Union must be added to this list.

The day on which the combatants agreed to lay down their weapons, in the downtown of the Salvadoran capital they exuberantly celebrated the end of hostilities. The celebration was sold to the people and the world as a display of national joy over the arrival of peace. It was, however, more a particular and clear harbinger of all the bad that would later be sold to Salvadoran society. There were in fact two versions of the celebration: the official one, with ARENA at the head, in one camp; the other by the FMLN, in the other camp. They found themselves separated by a block of buildings between them.

Nobody, or almost nobody, at the time saw this as a harbinger. It was impossible to think that those two parties would be a reflection of what was to come. Amid the widespread euphoria inside and outside the country, it was difficult to foresee what would become the political reality in the coming years: one of polarization resulting in permanent division, though without falling into the political violence of the past. The parties that signed the peace accords therefore achieved something important but nothing at all decisive in terms of advancing resolutely on the path toward peace.

The end of the war via the political route and in the quickest time possible was the first step of the peace process agreed to in Geneva in April 1990, and it was the most obvious step in the short term. But there was a medium and long term on the horizon. Three other components had to be formulated: democratizing the country, unconditional respect for human rights, and societal reunification. There was nothing to lose, and yet this nothing was lost in favor of those who controlled the process and caused the country to miss out on the opportunity to change course.

Why? Because the masses went back to getting the short end of the political stick, and now they are summoned only when there are elections. The "insurgents," having reached an agreement and returned to being rivals inside a system that had previously been unattainable, decided to move their eternal struggle from the trenches to the voting booths. They told—or more accurately, mandated—the people to remain hopeful. The Salvadoran people do not have to worry or get involved in changing the country; the parties that previously fought to the death—whether that fight was clean or dirty— would bestow on them democracy and would respect human rights. Those promises never became reality because ARENA, as well as the FMLN, whether as the government or the opposition, obstructed and continue to obstruct a true and necessary national unity focused on solving the most serious national problems.

From the end of the war until today, these two parties have dedicated themselves to tearing society in two and keeping the population—beaten down by hunger, violence, corruption, and impunity—from being the principal protagonist and the decisive factor in overcoming the status quo. The rhetoric and practices of these two absolutist and all-powerful parties in El Salvador—which are still determined to undermine popular participation in decisions that affect people's daily lives—are the same as the rhetoric of George W. Bush: you're either with us or against us. And so it is not possible, nor will it become so, to overcome these ills that make life untenable for people and instead forecast that death is always possible, be it slow or violent.

Regarding a slow death, the Salvadoran government reports that according to "measurements of multidimensional poverty, of all Salvadoran households 35.2 percent are multidimensionally poor. This equates to approximately 606,000 households and about 2.6 million people."[8] Concerning violent death, El Salvador ended 2015 with 6,653 murders (out of a population of over six million). In 2014, there were 3,921. The rate of violent death per 100,000 citizens increased between 2014 and 2015 by nearly 50, from 68.3 to 115.8.[9] Of the number officially recorded at the end of 2015, 1,012 people between the ages of zero and nineteen were murdered.[10] The University Institute on Public Opinion evaluated the situation in the country during 2015. Only 3.6 percent of people surveyed responded that crime had decreased during 2014; 14 percent said it was the same; and 82.5 percent said it had increased.[11]

"Looking at the statistics, one can see it is not a situation we would hope for or wish on children," says Nadine Perrault, who represents UNICEF in El Salvador.[12] Her counterpart in El Salvador's Human Rights Ombudsman's office, Ana Margarita de Guardado, says, "To be young at this time is like feeling a constant danger right at your back. It's not being able to get out, being trapped. . . . The youth of this country have no hope because an adolescent who wakes up each day without knowing if he or she will stay alive is a sign of a country in crisis."[13]

This is the reality in El Salvador. It is nothing less than a hell from which people have to escape in search of paradise beyond its borders, regardless of the dangers to be faced on the way through purgatory. And in that reality, there are no signs, even far off in the distance, that something is going to change. It is clear that nothing will happen as long as the familiar political machines—the party founded by the person accused of Romero's death and the old guerrilla army, with its own "sins" that are not as talked about but are also serious—continue to be the only options. They will continue, election after election, to attack each other and promote themselves as the only solution without actually being a solution. Meanwhile, must the masses continue suffering? Are there no exits providing liberation from exclusion and inequality, from violence and insecurity? One has to come back to saying, full of hope and faith, yes there are. But they have to be opened!

In his homily on January 6, 1980, Romero provided the key, still relevant today, in the following terms:

> Therefore, I call on all those who make up this enormous multitude, who find themselves between the two extremes, to seek their place in order to participate in the common political work of our nation. Seek your vocation, and in the light of the Word of God, reflect. Now is the time when the people have to use their ingenuity and carry out new initiatives. It is not necessary to use established means. Rather there are other approaches where Christian inspiration can lead our deeply Christian people. In this, I am speaking about what [the 1968 bishops' conference at] Medellín called for: the awakening of the people and the need for organization and participation of the people so that they do not remain passive spectators, but rather become the architects of their own destiny.

The people, who came out to form a sea of humanity in the streets of San Salvador when they said goodbye to their shepherd on Sunday, March 30, 1980, actually did return to do so again. Thirty-five years later, on May 23, 2015, at the beatification mass for Monseñor Romero, the Salvadoran good shepherd began to perform his most important miracle, but now it remains to be finished. That day, he brought the people together in an act of justice from the Vatican, and now what remains is to bring together the masses to demand the justice that is owed them on every level: the banishment of hunger and violence, of corruption and impunity. May they go out into the streets, organized and participating actively as protagonists on the road to justice that has been bargained away by the forces of ill. We still must build a force of good: one that comes from the people. Because while Romero's people continue to suffer, our blessed martyr, who is with us every day, will also continue to suffer.

ACKNOWLEDGMENTS

This book has taken ten years to complete, and during that time numerous people have supported me in countless ways. Every person who was kind enough to ask, "How's the book coming along?" helped sustain me through the process.

My deepest gratitude goes first to everyone involved in our investigation and lawsuit. Nico van Aelstyn, Patty Blum, Almudena Bernabeu, and Russell Cohen, among many others, made up a legal team worthy of the immense challenge of putting Monseñor Romero's case before a court. The prominence of Terry Karl and the late Robert White in this story demonstrates their profound importance to the case and the broader fight for justice in El Salvador. Once I decided to write a book about our experiences, everyone on the team gave me continuous encouragement, help, and feedback, even though the endeavor took far longer than I imagined. I particularly thank Patty Blum, who reviewed several versions of the manuscript and deserves significant credit for helping me shape the published version.

I have the greatest admiration for everyone who has fought in myriad ways for justice in El Salvador, specifically for Monseñor Romero. This includes our client—the plaintiff in the lawsuit against Álvaro Saravia—who remains anonymous. Sadly, because El Salvador remains such a violent place, I cannot mention some of the people whose efforts were so vital not only to our case but also to the groundbreaking work that came before and continues to this day. Whatever our lawsuit accomplished, we stood on the shoulders of many investigators, journalists, lawyers, activists, and others who have labored in the face of danger to expose the truth about Romero's assassination and seek accountability for those responsible. Among those I have been able to name, I want to thank Paulino Espinoza and Guayo Quijano for the many ways in which they helped us and for their friendship throughout the case. Unfortunately, several of those who testified at trial are no longer with us, but they, like all the witnesses whose testimony is quoted, brought to the witness stand intelligence, grace, and courage. My gratitude also goes to Benjamín Cuéllar, a tremendous human rights advocate, for writing the eloquent and sobering afterword. Gene Palumbo has been a good friend and a great resource during my return trips to El Salvador to complete the manuscript.

Many people, past and present, affiliated with the Center for Justice & Accountability contributed to the case and this project. I am indebted to Sandy Coliver, who gave me my start in this field almost fifteen years ago and has provided mentorship, contacts, and encouragement in my career and with this book. Félix Kury was an invaluable resource and friend throughout, and he, Nora Sotelo-Kury, and Casimiro Sotelo provided tremendous help with translations. As described in the book, the Mintz Group carried out incredible pro bono work on the case. Bobby Levinson also put together a significant and skillful pro bono investigation. May he come home soon.

In 2007, I decided to take a year off from work to begin writing. I asked for donations to support my efforts and the response was overwhelming. I thank each and every person who supported me financially in getting the project off the ground. Others who were helpful in different ways during those early days include Elizabeth Vincenty, Rob and Caroline McKnight, Chris McKenna, Milly Marmur, Mark Tauber, Demián Oksenendler, Alyson Cabrera, Damian Spieckerman, Tanny Karunakar-Spieckerman, Mary Alinder, Sherry Unruh, and David Oliver. As the project developed, Victor Wishna and François Larocque provided insightful feedback on the manuscript. Thanks to Carlos Dada and Craig Pyes for taking the time to discuss important factual details. Leigh Matthews created a great new website for the launch of the book.

It is a privilege to publish the book with the University of California Press. I truly appreciate Kate Marshall's enthusiasm, guidance, and patience as we have moved this from a developing manuscript to a publishable book. My thanks also to Kate Hoffman, Bradley Depew, Ryan Furtkamp, Zuha Khan, and everyone else at UC Press. I appreciate the significant time and discerning comments provided by all the peer reviewers, on both the manuscript and the proposal. Julie Van Pelt was a pleasure to work with on the copyediting.

My sister, Jen, and brother-in-law, Matt, have helped and sustained me in more ways than they know. I have loved sharing the journey with them. My mother, Lou, and my father, Jim, gave me the spirit of adventure and the moral compass that led me to the field of human rights, and their support every step of the way has been extraordinary. I am honored to share with my dad the title of lawyer and with my mom the distinction of author. My wife, Gen, has been my companion, advisor, editor, researcher, calming presence, and source of strength at every turn. I never imagined when I started this adventure a decade ago in a different country that I would get to share it with someone so understanding and generous.

NOTES

PREFACE

1. María López Vigil, *Memories in Mosaic* (Washington, D.C.: EPICA, 2000), 401. The description of the events on March 24, 1980, is based on witness statements to Salvadoran authorities and U.S. lawyers, media accounts, and excerpts from López Vigil, *Memories in Mosaic*.

2. Óscar Romero, homily, March 24, 1980, www.romerotrust.org.uk /homilies-and-writings/homilies. All cited Romero homilies can be found at this location.

3. "AP Was There: Salvadoran Archbishop Assassinated in 1980," Associated Press, February 3, 2015. See also Jorge Pinto, *El grito del más pequeño* (Mexico: Editorial Comete, 1985), 281. A man named Napoleón Martínez, who arrived late to the mass and claimed to see vehicles protecting the area outside the church, was later abducted and never seen again. Pinto, *El grito,* 281–82; Declaration of Roberto Antonio Martínez Monterrosa to the Investigations Unit of the Executive Unit of the Commission to Investigate Criminal Acts, April 6, 1987.

INTRODUCTION

1. Óscar Romero, homily, March 23, 1980.

2. Due to the ongoing danger, several people in El Salvador who helped us immensely during the investigation are not named in this book. They are either omitted altogether or referred to anonymously. This should not be interpreted as diminishing their roles. Some of them have spent decades carrying out courageous work in human rights, journalism, or other fields, and their prudence has kept them safe. Often they made the connections for us and set up meetings with key witnesses. They guided us in putting together a case that could be tried in the United States.

1. "INFORMATIONAL GOULASH"

1. All quotations in this section are from the testimony of Atilio Ramírez Amaya, trial transcript in *Doe v. Saravia,* No. CIV-F-03–6249 OWW (E.D. Cal., August 25, 2004), 204–40. On occasion, particularly with trial testimony, I have slightly altered quotations to improve flow when such changes do not affect the substance of what the speaker said. For witnesses who testified in Spanish, the court transcripts reflect only the English translation, provided in real time by court interpreters; I have slightly altered such quotations when the phrasing of the in-court translations was awkward or "word for word" rather than capturing the true meaning the witness intended in Spanish.

2. "FBI investiga asesinato de Mons. Oscar Romero," *EFE,* March 28, 1980; CIA document, "Background on Assassination of Archbishop Romero," May 28, 1987. All references to CIA, State Department, and FBI documents are to the declassified versions, all in author's possession.

3. CIA document, untitled, March 25, 1980.

4. Police report by Major José Francisco Samayoa to Major Miguel Antonio Méndez, May 12, 1980, in author's possession. See also CIA document, "Arrest of Rightist Coup Plotters," May 8, 1980; and Craig Pyes, "Salvadoran Rightists: The Deadly Patriots," *Albuquerque Journal,* December 1983, 18–19.

5. State Department document, "Breakfast Meeting with Military Members of JRG on Aftermath of D'Aubuisson's Arrest," May 9, 1980.

6. Though the planner is usually referred to as the Saravia Diary, it is not a diary in the normal sense of that word in English. It is a day planner or datebook with space for the user to write daily appointments. "Saravia Diary" daily planner, trial exhibit in *Doe v. Saravia,* No. CIV-F-03–6249 OWW (E.D. Cal. 2004).

7. Testimony of Terry Karl, trial transcript in *Doe v. Saravia,* No. CIV-F-03–6249 OWW (E.D. Cal., September 3, 2004), 649–50.

8. Carlos Dada, "Así matamos a monseñor Romero," *El Faro,* March 22, 2010, www.elfaro.net/es/201003/noticias/1403. *El Faro* first reported the connection in 2010, based on a source with insider knowledge. An earlier U.S. State Department cable, however, stated that the seafood company, Mariscos Tazumal, was founded in 1982, two years after the documents were seized at Finca San Luis. State Department document, "The Saravia Extradition and the D'Aubuisson Mafia," October 3, 1988. The cable did not provide a source for the founding date, so the information might not be correct.

9. Testimony of Karl, in *Doe v. Saravia,* September 3, 2004, 650.

10. On the document, the word is actually written "PINA," but it has generally been presumed to be *piña.* A witness later told me that PINA was an acronym and the word should have never been read as *piña.*

11. Ibid., 651–52.

12. Robert White, interview with author, 2008.

13. Testimony of Robert White, deposition transcript in *Doe v. Saravia,* No. CIV-F-03–6249 OWW (E.D. Cal., July 22, 2004), 36.

14. For comparison to McCarthy, see Pyes, "Salvadoran Rightists," 7.

15. Eliot Brenner, "Washington News," United Press International, February 6, 1984.

16. Stephen Kinzer, "Ex-aide in Salvador Accuses Colleagues on Death Squads," *New York Times,* March 3, 1984.

17. CIA document, "El Salvador: The Role of Roberto D'Aubuisson," March 4, 1981.

18. Roberto Morozzo della Rocca, *Oscar Romero: Prophet of Hope* (London: Darton, Longman and Todd, 2015), 210.

19. Dada, "Así matamos"; testimony of Karl, in *Doe v. Saravia,* September 3, 2004, 652.

20. State Department, "Breakfast Meeting."

21. Craig Pyes, "Who Killed Archbishop Romero?" *Nation,* October 13, 1984.

22. Robert White, communication with author, 2008; Raymond Bonner, "The Diplomat and the Killer," *Atlantic,* February 11, 2016, www.theatlantic.com/international/archive/2016/02/el-salvador-churchwomen-murders/460320.

23. Bonner, "The Diplomat"; State Department document, "Conversation with National Guard Officer," November 19, 1980.

24. State Department, "Conversation."

25. Pyes, "Who Killed Archbishop Romero?"

26. State Department, "Conversation."

27. Pyes, "Who Killed Archbishop Romero?"

28. State Department, "Conversation."

29. Bonner, "The Diplomat."

30. State Department, "Conversation."

31. Pyes, "Who Killed Archbishop Romero?"

32. Ibid.

33. For further details about the murder of the churchwomen, see chapter 5.

34. State Department document, "Security Officer Comments on Sheraton Murders, Other Rightist Violence," April 23, 1981.

35. Killer repeated that he gave the bullets to the shooter. He said "emphatically" that the weapon was not a .22 caliber but rather a 9 millimeter. State Department, "Security Officer Comments." A year later, Killer said the bullet was also a 9 millimeter. State Department document, "Majano Documents, D'Aubuisson and the Murder of Romero," May 24, 1982. However, investigating judge Ramírez Amaya and others were clear that the bullet was a .22 or .223. This could have affected Killer's credibility on the Romero assassination, though in 1985, the embassy found a second source on the meeting that mentioned drawing lots. An embassy cable described a source's report that a D'Aubuisson associate, Captain Eduardo Ávila, said in 1982, "I was drinking with D'Aubuisson, [National Guard lieutenant Rodolfo] López Sibrián and others. We drew matches to see who got the honor of killing Romero." State Department document, "Activities of Captain Avila," April 17, 1985. A later cable stated that Ávila told a source (presumably the same one) about the planning meeting with D'Aubuisson. The embassy judged this source to be credible, saying the information "fully supports" Killer's story. State Department

document, "Entry of Roberto D'Aubuisson into the U.S.," August 2, 1985. The cable did not mention Killer's presumably erroneous insistence that a 9-millimeter bullet killed Romero rather than a .22 caliber.

36. State Department document, "Rightist Doings," August 14, 1981.

37. State Department document, "Assassination of Archbishop Romero," December 21, 1981.

38. Testimony of Robert White, U.S. Congress, Senate Committee on Foreign Relations, *The Situation in El Salvador: Hearing before the Committee on Foreign Relations,* 97th Congress, April 9, 1981, 117.

39. State Department document, "Mexican Columnist on D'Aubuisson Diary," May 17, 1982.

40. State Department, "Majano Documents."

41. According to a May 1982 U.S. embassy cable, Captain Eduardo Ávila confessed his role in the assassination to a U.S. acquaintance, though he had overdosed on valium when he made the disclosure. Pyes, "Who Killed Archbishop Romero?"; "Salvadoran Officer Linked to Deaths," Associated Press, May 19, 1983; FBI document, "Unknown Subjects: Furnishing Funds and Weapons to Salvadoran Death Squads in El Salvador," May 15, 1984, 82.

42. Testimony of Robert White, U.S. Congress, House of Representatives, Committee on Foreign Affairs, *The Situation in El Salvador: Hearing before the Subcommittees on Human Rights and International Organizations and on Western Hemisphere Affairs,* 98th Congress, February 6, 1984, 42. See also "Ex-envoy Charges D'Aubuisson Coverup," *Facts on File World News Digest,* February 10, 1984.

43. "Ex-envoy Charges," *Facts on File.* The State Department also claimed that Killer had died, but White's sources in El Salvador reported that Killer was alive. Pyes, "Who Killed Archbishop Romero?" Killer was allegedly killed later, in the early 1990s. Bonner, "The Diplomat."

44. Judge Atilio Ramírez Amaya later insisted to us that the shooter got out of the car to fire the gun. Another witness agreed, because the bullet entered Romero's body with a flat trajectory that was impossible if the shot had come from inside the car.

45. The above narration is from the declaration of Amado Antonio Garay to the Investigations Unit of the Executive Unit of the Commission to Investigate Criminal Acts, November 19, 1987; and the declaration of Amado Antonio Garay to the Fourth Criminal Court, November 20, 1987, both in author's possession.

46. Confidential source, interview with legal team, 2003.

47. Ibid. See also Judge Alberto Zamora Pérez, *acta* memorializing activity with Amado Antonio Garay, November 21, 1987, in author's possession.

2. "IN VIOLATION OF THE LAW OF NATIONS"

1. Dada, "Así matamos."

2. Metzi Rosales Martel and Christian Guevara Guadrón, "¿Quién es Álvaro Saravia?" *La Prensa Gráfica,* March 20, 2005.

3. Ibid.; "Capitán Álvaro Rafael Saravia dice: 'D'Aubuisson cayó en una trampa,'" *Diario Co Latino,* November 6, 2006.

4. Dada, "Así matamos."

5. Testimony of White, in *Doe v. Saravia,* July 22, 2004, 34–35.

6. Beth J. Stephens et al., *International Human Rights Litigation in U.S. Courts,* 2nd rev. ed. (Leiden, Netherlands: Martinus Nijhoff, 2008), 8.

7. Ibid., 5, 134.

8. Ibid., 1.

9. Ibid., 9.

10. Ibid., 75–77.

11. Ibid., 311. In 2013, the U.S. Supreme Court significantly curtailed the scope of the ATS by ruling that there is a presumption that the statute does not apply to conduct outside the United States. *Kiobel v. Royal Dutch Petroleum Co.,* 569 U.S. 12, 133 S. Ct. 1659 (2013).

12. The first and only criminal case for torture came in 2006 when the Bush administration successfully prosecuted Chucky Taylor, a U.S. citizen and the son of Liberian warlord and president Charles Taylor, for committing and overseeing torture in Liberia. *U.S. v. Belfast,* 611 F.3d 783 (11th Cir. 2010).

13. The International Criminal Court only has jurisdiction when crimes are committed in or by the nationals of countries that ratified the treaty that created the court or through a resolution by the United Nations Security Council.

14. Nicholas P. Weiss, "Somebody Else's Problem: How the United States and Canada Violate International Law and Fail to Ensure the Prosecution of War Criminals," *Case Western Reserve Journal of International Law* 45 (2012): 593–95.

15. This is not unusual. For example, an Ethiopian torturer found employment at the same Atlanta hotel where one of his victims worked. Andrew Rice, "The Long Interrogation," *New York Times,* June 4, 2006.

16. See Carolyn Patty Blum, "The Settlement of *American Baptist Churches v. Thornburgh:* Landmark Victory for Central American Asylum-Seekers," *International Journal of Refugee Law* 3, no. 2 (1991): 347–56.

17. The survivors' trial was not the first time the Generals stood accused in the West Palm Beach courthouse. Two years before, García and Vides Casanova defended themselves against charges that they were responsible for the 1980 rape and murder of the four U.S. churchwomen, the crime about which the U.S. embassy's source, Killer, provided critical information. In fact, the decades-long search for justice in the churchwomen's case was the reason the Generals were discovered in the United States. In 1998, during a trip to El Salvador, attorneys at the Lawyers Committee for Human Rights (now Human Rights First) learned that García and Vides Casanova were living in Florida, and the churchwomen's families filed a civil lawsuit against them in a U.S. court. The case failed at trial, however, with a jury finding that the plaintiffs did not prove that García and Vides Casanova had "command responsibility" for the murders committed by their subordinates. *Ford v. Garcia,* 289 F.3d 1283 (11th Cir. 2002). The plaintiffs' loss reinforced that being on the "right" side of a human rights case was no guarantee of victory and indicated that a successful

lawsuit would require better evidence about a commander's practical ability to control subordinates. The torture survivors' subsequent trial addressed that issue, relying heavily on the Lawyers Committee's extensive research. In 2015 and 2016, the U.S. government deported Vides Casanova and García to El Salvador, a result of long-standing efforts by CJA and many of the people involved in the civil lawsuits.

18. From this point forward, I use first names to refer to my colleagues on the legal team in the Romero case in order to convey the close-knit nature of our relationship.

3. "THE ENEMY COMES FROM OUR PEOPLE"

1. Testimony of White, in *Doe v. Saravia,* July 22, 2004, 18.

2. State Department document, "Preliminary Assessment of Situation in El Salvador," March 19, 1980.

3. Michael McClintock, *The American Connection: State Terror and Popular Resistance in El Salvador* (London: Zed Books, 1987), 90–91; Raymond Bonner, *Weakness and Deceit: U.S. Policy and El Salvador* (New York: Times Books, 1984), 20.

4. McClintock, *American Connection,* 94.

5. Bonner, *Weakness and Deceit,* 21.

6. McClintock, *American Connection,* 95–96.

7. Bonner, *Weakness and Deceit,* 22.

8. Jeffery M. Paige, *Coffee and Power: Revolution and the Rise of Democracy in Central America.* (Cambridge, MA: Harvard University Press, 1998), 14.

9. Juanita Darling, "Book Reveals Identities of El Salvador's Richest Families," *Los Angeles Times,* August 21, 1998.

10. Bonner, *Weakness and Deceit,* 22; McClintock, *American Connection,* 96; Paige, *Coffee and Power,* 107.

11. Paige, *Coffee and Power,* 107–8.

12. Bonner, *Weakness and Deceit,* 16. See also McClintock, *American Connection,* 101.

13. McClintock, *American Connection,* 104–6; Paige, *Coffee and Power,* 109.

14. Paige, *Coffee and Power,* 117; Walter La Feber, *Inevitable Revolutions: The United States in Central America,* 2nd ed. (New York: W. W. Norton, 1993), 74.

15. McClintock, *American Connection,* 107–11.

16. Paige, *Coffee and Power,* 121–22.

17. McClintock, *American Connection,* 114–15.

18. Ibid., 110–11; Paige, *Coffee and Power,* 103; William Stanley, *The Protection Racket State: Elite Politics, Military Extortion, and Civil War in El Salvador* (Philadelphia: Temple University Press, 1996), 51.

19. McClintock, *American Connection,* 101.

20. Bonner, *Weakness and Deceit,* 23.

21. Paige, *Coffee and Power,* 103; McClintock, *American Connection,* 113.

22. Paige, *Coffee and Power*, 103. See also McClintock, *American Connection*, 113.

23. McClintock, *American Connection*, 115.

24. Thomas P. Anderson, *Matanza: El Salvador's Communist Revolt of 1932* (Lincoln: University of Nebraska Press, 1971), quoted in Bonner, *Weakness and Deceit*, 23.

25. McClintock, *American Connection*, 4.

26. Paige, *Coffee and Power*, 120.

27. Anderson, *Matanza*, quoted in Bonner, *Weakness and Deceit*, 23–24.

28. Paige, *Coffee and Power*, 22; testimony of Karl, in *Doe v. Saravia*, August 26, 2004, 292.

29. Paige, *Coffee and Power*, 22.

30. Testimony of Karl, in *Doe v. Saravia*, August 25, 2004, 242–48.

31. "Ex-envoy Charges," *Facts on File*.

32. Testimony of Karl, in *Doe v. Saravia*, August 26, 2004, 309–10.

33. McClintock, *American Connection*, 12.

34. Ibid., 13.

35. Ibid., 13, 19–27.

36. Ibid., 22–23 (emphasis in original).

37. Ibid., 24.

38. All quotations in this paragraph are from Allan Nairn, "Behind the Death Squads," *Progressive*, May 1984, 20–28.

39. Tommie Sue Montgomery, *Revolution in El Salvador: Origins and Evolution* (Boulder, CO: Westview Press, 1982), 120.

40. Paul Heath Hoeffel, "The Eclipse of the Oligarchs," *New York Times*, September 6, 1981.

41. Luis Escalante Arce, "Salvadoran Reacts to Ambassador White's Accusation," publisher and date unknown, in author's possession.

42. Nairn, "Behind the Death Squads."

43. Christopher Dickey, "The Truth about the Death Squads," *New Republic*, December 26, 1983, 18; Craig Pyes and Laurie Becklund, "Inside Dope in El Salvador," *New Republic*, April 15, 1985, 19.

44. Testimony of Karl, in *Doe v. Saravia*, August 26, 2004, 326.

45. State Department document, "Restraining the Right: Major D'Aubuisson," February 20, 1980; Laurie Becklund, "Salvador Death Squads: Deadly Other War," *Los Angeles Times*, December 18, 1983.

46. Pyes, "Salvadoran Rightists," 6.

47. Testimony of Karl, in *Doe v. Saravia*, August 26, 2004, 327.

48. Ibid., 293–94.

49. Stanley, *Protection Racket State*, 138–40.

50. Testimony of Karl, in *Doe v. Saravia*, August 26, 2004, 343–44.

51. Stanley, *Protection Racket State*, 150. See also Comisión de la Verdad para El Salvador, *De la locura a la esperanza: La guerra de 12 años en El Salvador* (San Salvador: Naciones Unidas, 1993), 141–42; and CIA document, untitled, March 10, 1984.

52. Pyes, "Salvadoran Rightists," 7.

53. Dada, "Así matamos."

54. Ibid.; testimony of Álvaro Saravia to the Truth Commission, "Report on the Death Squads in the Files of the El Salvador Truth Commission," n.d., in author's possession.

55. Stanley, *Protection Racket State,* 150, 164, 190.

56. Ibid., 163, 189; Dickey, "Truth about Death Squads"; State Department document, "PDC Leader Assassinated," February 23, 1980. According to the memoir of one of the oligarchs, Guillermo Sol Bang, "In one of those meetings of the Broad National Front, at the beginning of 1980, I met a thin but muscular guy. . . . He gave us a well-documented presentation about the Communists' strategy to take power in El Salvador. He detailed the level of Marxist infiltration in the universities, churches, unions, political parties and even the armed forces. He had been an intelligence officer." Sol continued, "He had copies of documents and videos that he put at our disposal so that together we could develop a strategy to fight back. That officer . . . was Major Roberto D'Aubuisson." Marvin Galeas, *Sol y acero: La vida de Don Guillermo Sol Bang* (San Salvador: Editorial Cinco, 2011), "La Guerra" chapter. Another oligarch, Orlando de Sola, told a similar story about a meeting with D'Aubuisson in November 1979. Geovani Galeas, "El exilio del ingeniero González," *La Prensa Gráfica,* August 29, 2004.

57. Testimony of White, in *Doe v. Saravia,* July 22, 2004, 33.

58. Stanley, *Protection Racket State,* 190; Galeas, "El exilio del ingeniero."

59. Testimony of Karl, in *Doe v. Saravia,* August 27, 2004, 549–50.

60. Testimony of Karl, in *Doe v. Saravia,* August 26, 2004, 349–50.

61. Ibid., 331–33. See also Bonner, *Weakness and Deceit,* 310.

62. Stanley, *Protection Racket State,* 128.

63. Bonner, *Weakness and Deceit,* 146.

64. Ibid., 181–82.

65. Stanley, *Protection Racket State,* 179–80; State Department, "Preliminary Assessment."

66. Jerald A. Combs, *The History of American Foreign Policy,* vol. 2, *From 1895,* 3rd ed. (Armonk, NY: M. E. Sharpe, 2008), 293.

67. Bonner, *Weakness and Deceit,* 183.

68. Ibid., 181. White's ambassadorship was not universally supported. North Carolina's conservative senator Jesse Helms, a D'Aubuisson supporter, considered White a "leftist" and a "dangerous ideologue," despite White's condemnation of the armed leftists in El Salvador. Helms delayed White's confirmation for more than a month. Thomas A. Sancton, Bernard Diederich and Roberto Suro, "The Land of the Smoking Gun," *Time,* August 18, 1980.

69. State Department document, "D'Aubuisson Attacks PDC and USG," March 3, 1980.

70. State Department document, "Reaction in Guatemala to Salvadoran Agrarian Reform Measures," March 12, 1980. Others at the press conference, including Alfredo Mena Lagos, Alfonso Salaverría, and Juan Wright, later appeared on a list

of people suspected of involvement in death squads that U.S. State Department officials gave to the FBI. See FBI document, "Furnishing of Funds and Weapons to Salvadoran Death Squads," December 9, 1983.

71. State Department document, "Draft Manifesto of Major D'Aubuisson for Use in Aborted Rightwing Coup," May 8, 1980.

72. State Department, "Preliminary Assessment."

4. "THE DOOR OF HISTORY"

1. Testimony of William Wipfler, trial transcript in *Doe v. Saravia*, No. CIV-F-03–6249 OWW (E.D. Cal., August 24, 2004), 37–42.

2. Thomas M. Kelly, *When the Gospel Grows Feet: Rutilio Grande, SJ, and the Church of El Salvador: An Ecclesiology in Context* (Collegeville, MN: Liturgical Press, 2013), 215; Inter-American Commission on Human Rights, *Report on the Situation of Human Rights in El Salvador*, November 17, 1978, www.cidh.org/countryrep/ElSalvador78eng/TOC.htm.

3. Kelly, *Gospel Grows Feet*, 169; James R. Brockman, *Romero: A Life* (Maryknoll, NY: Orbis Books, 2005), 9.

4. Rodolfo Cardenal, *Rutilio Grande, mártir de la evangelización rural en El Salvador* (San Salvador: UCA Editores, 1978), quoted in Brockman, *Romero*, 9.

5. Kelly, *Gospel Grows Feet*, 6–15.

6. Ibid., 14.

7. Ibid., 7, 23–24, 32, 71.

8. Ibid., 50.

9. Ibid., 61.

10. Ibid., 65.

11. López Vigil, *Memories in Mosaic*, 21, 29; Brockman, *Romero*, 40.

12. López Vigil, *Memories in Mosaic*, 22–27; Roberto Morozzo della Rocca, *Primero Dios: Vida de Monseñor Romero* (Buenos Aires: Edhasa, 2010), 84.

13. Morozzo della Rocca, *Primero Dios*, 76.

14. Kelly, *Gospel Grows Feet*, 57.

15. Ibid., 67.

16. Second Vatican Council, *Gaudium et Spes: Pastoral Constitution on the Church in the Modern World*, 1965, para. 43, quoted in Kelly, *Gospel Grows Feet*, 67.

17. Ibid., para. 63, quoted in Kelly, *Gospel Grows Feet*, 71–72.

18. Ibid., para. 66, quoted in Kelly, *Gospel Grows Feet*, 72.

19. Gustavo Gutiérrez, *A Theology of Liberation: History, Politics, and Salvation* (Maryknoll, NY: Orbis Books, 2004), xxv.

20. Kelly, *Gospel Grows Feet*, 76.

21. Pope Paul VI, *Populorum Progressio: Encyclical of Pope Paul VI on the Development of Peoples*, March 26, 1967, para. 24, http://w2.vatican.va/content/paul-vi/en/encyclicals/documents/hf_p-vi_enc_26031967_populorum.html.

22. Kelly, *Gospel Grows Feet*, 78, 80.

23. Segunda Conferencia General del Episcopado Latinoamericano, "Introducción," in *Documentos finales de Medellín,* September 1968, para. 4, www.ensayistas .org/critica/liberacion/medellin/medellin2.htm.

24. Kelly, *Gospel Grows Feet,* 87–89.

25. Segunda Conferencia General del Episcopado Latinoamericano, "Pobreza de la Iglesia," in *Documentos finales de Medellín,* paras. 2, 12, www.ensayistas.org /critica/liberacion/medellin/medellin16.htm.

26. Ibid., para. 10.

27. Penny Lernoux, *Cry of the People* (New York: Doubleday, 1980), 37, quoted in Montgomery, *Revolution in El Salvador,* 99.

28. Brockman, *Romero,* 45. See also Morozzo della Rocca, *Primero Dios,* 85–90, 123.

29. Rutilio Grande, "Violencia y situación social," *Estudios Centroamericanos* 262 (1970): 369, quoted in Kelly, *Gospel Grows Feet,* 116.

30. Ibid., 370, quoted in Kelly, *Gospel Grows Feet,* 118.

31. Kelly, *Gospel Grows Feet,* 119.

32. Gustavo Gutiérrez, *Theology of Liberation,* xiii.

33. See Paulo Freire, *Pedagogy of the Oppressed,* trans. Myra Bergman Ramos (New York: Continuum Press, 2006), 85, cited in Kelly, *Gospel Grows Feet,* 142.

34. Empowerment of the *campesino* population was also the focus of an organization that preexisted Grande's arrival in Aguilares, the Christian Federation of Salvadoran Campesinos (FECCAS). Likewise, before Grande came to Aguilares, a young priest, José Inocencio Alas, had begun similar efforts in a nearby community. In 1970, Alas was abducted, beaten, and left naked near a cliff in the first direct attack by government forces on a Catholic priest. Montgomery, *Revolution in El Salvador,* 98.

35. López Vigil, *Memories in Mosaic,* 91.

36. Montgomery, *Revolution in El Salvador,* 106; Kelly, *Gospel Grows Feet,* 199.

37. Montgomery, *Revolution in El Salvador,* 106.

38. Brockman, *Romero,* 48.

39. Ibid., 49.

40. Ibid., 54.

41. Ibid., 56–58.

42. Ibid., 4.

43. Rutilio Grande, homily, February 13, 1977, www.uca.edu.sv/publica/cartas /ci371.html.

44. Brockman, *Romero,* 4; testimony of Jon Cortina, trial transcript in *Doe v. Saravia,* No. CIV-F-03–6249 OWW (E.D. Cal., August 26, 2004), 376.

45. Montgomery, *Revolution in El Salvador,* 110.

46. Ibid., 109.

47. Testimony of Cortina, in *Doe v. Saravia,* August 26, 2004, 375. See also Brockman, *Romero,* 8.

48. Brockman, *Romero,* 9; López Vigil, *Memories in Mosaic,* 101–3.

49. Brockman, *Romero,* 160; testimony of Cortina, in *Doe v. Saravia,* August 26, 2004, 386–88; Morozzo della Rocca, *Oscar Romero,* 77.

50. Kelly, *Gospel Grows Feet*, 216. See also Brockman, *Romero*, 10–11.

51. Brockman, *Romero*, 14–16.

52. López Vigil, *Memories in Mosaic*, 117–18.

53. Montgomery, *Revolution in El Salvador*, 114.

54. Brockman, *Romero*, 29.

55. Montgomery, *Revolution in El Salvador*, 109; Bonner, *Weakness and Deceit*, 66.

56. McClintock, *American Connection*, 185–86. See also Brockman, *Romero*, 65.

57. Brockman, *Romero*, 197.

58. Montgomery, *Revolution in El Salvador*, 166; testimony of Karl, in *Doe v. Saravia*, August 26, 2004, 336, 354, 359.

59. McClintock, *American Connection*, 180; Brockman, *Romero*, 64–67.

60. McClintock, *American Connection*, 178; Brockman, *Romero*, 64–67, 71, 99.

61. Brockman, *Romero*, 100, photo insert.

62. Despite the absurdity of such headlines, the issue of whether Romero himself was motivated by theology or politics has long been debated. Most who knew him well say that he was not political and that his commentary about conditions in El Salvador was based on his reading of church doctrine. Testimony of Cortina, in *Doe v. Saravia*, August 26, 2004, 390; Brockman, *Romero*, 190–92. As part of the beatification process, the Vatican concluded that Romero's theology was in line with orthodox Catholic principles. Andrew Buncombe, "Pope Francis Recognises El Salvador's Slain Archbishop Oscar Romero as Martyr and Opens the Way for Beatification," *Independent*, February 4, 2015.

63. Karl, in *Doe v. Saravia*, August 26, 2004, 353–56.

64. Brockman, *Romero*, 31; López Vigil, *Memories in Mosaic*, 169.

65. Brockman, *Romero*, 31–32.

66. López Vigil, *Memories in Mosaic*, 170–71.

67. Roberto Valencia, "Beto Cuéllar, el abogado," *El Faro*, March 30, 2015, www.elfaro.net/es/201503/noticias/16761/Beto-Cuéllar-el-abogado.htm. After Romero's assassination, Socorro Jurídico faced increased danger and eventually closed when Cuéllar and others fled El Salvador. The archdiocese opened a new human rights office, Tutela Legal, in 1982 that continued the precarious task of investigating abuses.

68. Brockman, *Romero*, 145–46; Morozzo della Rocca, *Oscar Romero*, 173–74.

69. Letter from "La Falange" to Óscar Romero, May 30, 1979, in author's possession.

70. Brockman, *Romero*, 27.

71. Ibid., 196.

72. Ibid., 200. Some of the officers sought Romero's advice about their plans before the coup happened. Stanley, *Protection Racket State*, 130, 133, 141.

73. Brockman, *Romero*, 215; López Vigil, *Memories in Mosaic*, 331–36.

74. Brockman, *Romero*, 214, 217. García visited Romero to complain, but Romero continued to believe that García was "a figure who weakens the credibility of this process of change in the country." Diary entry, January 10, 1980, in *Mons. Óscar A. Romero: Su diario* (San Salvador: Imprenta Criterio, 2000), 353.

75. Óscar Romero, homily, February 24, 1980.

76. Óscar Romero, homily, February 17, 1980.

77. Óscar Romero, homily, February 10, 1980.

78. Óscar Romero, homily, February 17, 1980.

79. López Vigil, *Memories in Mosaic,* 365.

80. Stanley, *Protection Racket State,* 197.

81. Ibid.

82. Óscar Romero, homily, February 17, 1980. See also Brockman, *Romero,* 227; and López Vigil, *Memories in Mosaic,* 374.

83. López Vigil, *Memories in Mosaic,* 374.

84. Linda Cooper and James Hodge, "Archbishop Oscar Romero, El Salvador's Most Trusted News Source," *National Catholic Reporter,* March 21, 2015, http://ncronline.org/news/global/archbishop-oscar-romero-el-salvadors-most-trusted-news-source.

85. Stanley, *Protection Racket State,* 194–96.

86. Nairn, "Behind the Death Squads." See also Morozzo della Rocca, *Oscar Romero,* 210.

87. State Department, "Preliminary Assessment."

88. Óscar Romero, homily, February 24, 1980.

89. Óscar Romero, homily, March 9, 1980.

90. Morozzo della Rocca, *Oscar Romero,* 208–11.

91. Perhaps the most famous quote attributed to Romero concerned the contemplation of his own death, but a leading Romero biographer concluded that the quote is apocryphal, invented by a journalist. The day after Romero's murder, the journalist wrote that Romero had said, "I have often been threatened with death. But I must say that as a Christian, I do not believe in death without resurrection. If they kill me I will rise again in the Salvadoran people." Morozzo della Rocca, *Oscar Romero,* 137–38.

92. Police report by José Ramón Campos Figueroa to the Chief of the Police Investigations Unit, March 14, 1986, in author's possession; report by Cruz Argueta Hurtado to the Chief of the Investigations Unit of the Executive Unit of the Commission to Investigate Criminal Acts, June 3, 1987, in author's possession. See also Morozzo della Rocca, *Oscar Romero,* 210.

93. Brockman, *Romero,* 239.

94. Testimony of Walter Guerra, trial transcript in *Doe v. Saravia,* No. CIV-F-03–6249 OWW (E.D. Cal., August 27, 2004), 513–14.

95. All quotations in this section are from the testimony of Wipfler, in *Doe v. Saravia,* August 24, 2004, 53–70.

5. "A BED TO DROP DEAD IN"

1. Trial transcript in *Doe v. Saravia,* August 24, 2004, 7–10.

2. Throughout the remainder of this book, quotations pertaining to our investigation and lawsuit come from discussions or other communications between the

person quoted and one or more members of our investigative or legal team, unless otherwise specified. Individual citations are not provided.

3. Blair Craddock. "Local Link to Assassination," *Modesto Bee,* September 18, 2003.

4. Testimony of Karl, in *Doe v. Saravia,* August 27, 2004, 582–84.

5. State Department document, "Millionaires' Murder Inc.?," January 6, 1981.

6. As a result of the cable, the FBI launched an investigation but reported being unable to find sufficient evidence of death squad financing. FBI, "Unknown Subjects." An FBI memo stated that on January 15, 1981, shortly after the "Millionaires' Murder Inc.?" cable, the FBI interviewed the Salvadoran lawyer who was the source of the information on the Miami Six. The lawyer told the FBI he had no direct knowledge of the six being involved in death squads and he did not believe they were capable of such activity. FBI document, "Viera Altamirano, Luis Escalante, Arturo Muyshondt, Julio Salaverria, Juan Ricardo Salaverria, Roberto Edgardo Daglio, Roberto D'Aubuisson," March 11, 1981. It is possible that the "Millionaires' Murder Inc.?" cable was wrong, but it is also possible that the source got cold feet when questioned by the FBI. Later, in 1983, U.S. embassy officials, including Carl Gettinger, went to the FBI with a list of twenty-nine suspects. FBI, "Furnishing of Funds." The FBI launched another inquiry that included interviews of several key people but did not result in any charges.

7. Salaverría's name is in documents captured with the Saravia Diary. He was openly supportive of D'Aubuisson and appeared at press conferences with him in 1980. Hoeffel, "Eclipse of the Oligarchs"; State Department, "Reaction in Guatemala." Salaverría was on the list of people suspected of involvement in death squads that State Department officials gave to the FBI in 1983. FBI, "Furnishing of Funds."

8. Margot Hornblower, "The Exiles," *Washington Post,* March 22, 1981.

9. Ibid. Orlando de Sola was on the list of people suspected of involvement in death squads that State Department officials gave to the FBI in 1983. FBI, "Furnishing of Funds." He has denied involvement in the death squads. Daniel Valencia and Carlos Martínez, "Plática con Orlando de Sola: 'No soy escuadronero, ni un mercantilista aprovechado,'" *El Faro,* July 10, 2009, http://archivo.elfaro.net/Secciones/platicas/20090710/Platicas1_20090710.asp.

10. Saravia Diary. A witness told the Truth Commission that Simán was a death squad financier. Testimony of confidential source to the Truth Commission, "Report on the Death Squads in the Files of the El Salvador Truth Commission," n.d., in author's possession.

11. Saravia Diary; Pyes and Becklund, "Inside Dope," 15–18; Laurie Becklund, "Illicit Money Figure Linked to D'Aubuisson," *Los Angeles Times,* February 19, 1985. Guirola's family owned Finca San Luis. Saravia and another witness told the Truth Commission that Guirola was involved in death squads.

12. Saravia Diary; testimony of confidential sources to the Truth Commission, in "Report on the Death Squads"; Geovani Galeas, "Escuadrones, la leyenda negra," *La Prensa Gráfica,* October 3, 2004. Llovera implicated himself and other D'Aubuisson associates in the kidnapping ring. State Department document, "Update on Kidnap-Ring Case," May 21, 1986.

13. "Violenta huida de White de la residencia a la embajada de EUA," *Diario el Mundo,* May 12, 1980; Galeas, "El exilio del ingeniero."

14. Galeas, "El exilio del ingeniero"; testimony of Saravia, in "Report on the Death Squads."

15. Pyes, "Salvadoran Rightists," 10–11. See also Jack Anderson, "Guatemalan Tinderbox," *Washington Post,* February 22, 1981; and transcript of *The Houses Are Full of Smoke,* directed by Allan Frankovich (New York: Mystic Fire Video, 1989), 106–7.

16. Pyes, "Salvadoran Rightists," 10.

17. Ibid., 5, 10, 42.

18. Ibid., 8; Galeas, "El exilio del ingeniero."

19. Pyes, "Salvadoran Rightists," 38, 40; Geovani Galeas, "La fundación de una bandera," *La Prensa Gráfica,* September 5, 2004; Galeas, *Sol y acero,* annex titled "Discurso . . . Armando Calderón Sol." As Professor Karl said in our trial against Álvaro Saravia, "There had been a sense among some members of the Republican Party that the problem in El Salvador, conservative versus liberal versus Communist insurgency, could be understood somehow like [in the United States], that somebody like D'Aubuisson was kind of like . . . an especially conservative Republican." Testimony of Karl, in *Doe v. Saravia,* August 26, 2004, 308.

20. State Department document, "D'Aubuission [sic] Press Guidance," July 3, 1980; State Department document, "D'Aubuisson Press Conference in Washington," July 2, 1980.

21. Bonner, *Weakness and Deceit,* 74. See also testimony of Robert White, trial transcript in *Ford v. Garcia,* 99–8359-CIV-HURLEY (S.D. Fla., October 12, 2000), 583.

22. Lawyers Committee for Human Rights, *El Salvador: Human Rights Dismissed* (New York: Lawyers Committee for Human Rights, 1990), 63–64; Comisión de la Verdad, *De la locura,* 60–65.

23. Bonner, *Weakness and Deceit,* 222.

24. Testimony of White, in *Ford v. Garcia,* October 12, 2000, 578.

25. Bonner, *Weakness and Deceit,* 236–38, 309, 324–34.

26. "Ex-Salvador Ambassador, Critic of US Foreign Policy, Dies," Associated Press, January 19, 2015.

27. Bonner, "The Diplomat."

28. Bonner, *Weakness and Deceit,* 77.

29. Anthony Lewis, "Abroad at Home; Showing His Colors," *New York Times,* March 29, 1981. Slight variations of the quotation appear in Bonner, *Weakness and Deceit,* 75, and William P. Ford, "Film Preserves Haig's Words on Murders," *New York Times,* April 12, 1993. Jeane Kirkpatrick, later Reagan's United Nations ambassador, said the churchwomen "were political activists on behalf of the [guerrillas]." Bonner, "The Diplomat."

30. Ford, "Film Preserves Haig's Words."

31. Bonner, *Weakness and Deceit,* 256.

32. See Pyes, "Salvadoran Rightists," 42–43; Bonner, *Weakness and Deceit,* 255–63; Robert G. Kaiser, "White Paper on El Salvador Is Faulty," *Washington Post,* June 9, 1981.

33. Bonner, *Weakness and Deceit,* 234.

34. Ibid., 11–12, 138, 240, 270.

35. Ibid., 322.

36. Margaret Popkin, *Peace without Justice: Obstacles to Building the Rule of Law in El Salvador* (University Park: Pennsylvania State University Press, 2000), 49.

37. Bonner, *Weakness and Deceit,* 344.

38. Ibid., 340.

39. Ibid., 293.

40. Politicians on the Left did not participate in the elections. Many of the best candidates had been murdered, and others surely would have died had they campaigned openly. Ibid., 297–99; McClintock, *American Connection,* 294. The guerrillas boycotted and, in some cases, attempted to obstruct the elections. Bonner, *Weakness and Deceit,* 299.

41. Bonner, *Weakness and Deceit,* 310–11.

42. Testimony of Karl, in *Doe v. Saravia,* September 3, 2004, 678–79; Bonner, *Weakness and Deceit,* 310–11.

43. Bonner, *Weakness and Deceit,* 313.

44. Ibid., 309; McClintock, *American Connection,* 296.

45. Comisión de la Verdad, *De la locura,* 142–43; Stanley, *Protection Racket State,* 228.

6. "ARENA'S ACHILLES' HEEL"

1. Testimony of Karl, in *Doe v. Saravia,* September 3, 2004, 648–52. During our investigation, two witnesses confirmed that the papers seized at Finca San Luis belonged to D'Aubuisson.

2. Jessica Ávalos, "Fallo pone fin a litigio con Enel Tribunal sobresee a ocho acusados en caso CEL-Enel," *La Prensa Gráfica,* July 4, 2015.

3. Galeas, *Sol y acero.*

4. Ibid.

5. Becklund, "Salvador Death Squads."

6. Pyes, "Salvadoran Rightists," 6.

7. Interview of Rodolfo López Sibrián, September 12, 1993, republished in *Los escuadrones de la muerte en El Salvador* (San Salvador: Editorial Jaraguá, 1994), 269–70. D'Aubuisson publicly supported López Sibrián when he was accused of abuses. William M. LeoGrande, *Our Own Backyard: The United States in Central America, 1977–1992* (Chapel Hill: University of North Carolina Press, 1998), 177; Bonner, *Weakness and Deceit,* 47.

8. FBI, "Furnishing of Funds."

9. Comisión de la Verdad, *De la locura,* 142–43; Stanley, *Protection Racket State,* 228.

10. Americas Watch, *El Salvador's Decade of Terror: Human Rights since the Assassination of Archbishop Romero* (New Haven, CT: Yale University Press, 1991), 92.

11. CIA document, "Allegation by Chief of the Nationalist Republican Alliance (ARENA) Paramilitary Unit That a National Guard Officer Assassinated Archbishop Oscar Arnulfo Romero in 1980," April 22, 1983.

12. Celerino Castillo III and Dave Harmon, *Powderburns: Cocaine, Contras and the Drug War* (Oakville, ON: Mosaic, 1994).

13. Douglas Farah, "Death Squad Began as Scout Troop," *Washington Post,* August 29, 1988; Elisabeth Jean Wood, *Insurgent Collective Action and Civil War in El Salvador* (Cambridge: Cambridge University Press, 2003), 87; Comisión de la Verdad, *De la locura,* 142–43.

14. Wood, *Insurgent Collective Action,* 88; testimony of Saravia, in "Report on the Death Squads."

15. Comisión de la Verdad, *De la locura,* 137.

16. "El gobierno acusa al doctor Antonio Regalado de haber asesinado Monseñor Arnulfo Romero," *Diario Latino,* February 7, 1989.

17. Comisión de la Verdad, *De la locura,* 142–43; testimony of confidential sources to the Truth Commission, in "Report on the Death Squads." Many accused the Christian Democrats of pressuring Garay for political purposes. Although I later came to agree that they used Garay's testimony for partisan reasons, it is interesting that Garay's selection of Regalado's mug shot in February 1988 came just one month before legislative elections. Report by Velarmides Castillo Medrano to the Chief of the Executive Unit of the Commission to Investigate Criminal Acts, February 2, 1988, in author's possession. The Christian Democrats appear not to have publicized the identification of Regalado at that time, as might have been expected. They waited until February 1989, before the presidential election and only after the Salvadoran Supreme Court, in an equally political decision, dismissed Garay's testimony as "not fully credible." Comisión de la Verdad, *De la locura,* 137. ARENA won the presidential election anyway.

18. Comisión de la Verdad, *De la locura,* 137; declaration of Julio Alfredo Samayoa to the Fourth Criminal Court, February 21, 1989, in author's possession.

19. Comisión de la Verdad, *De la locura,* 137.

20. State Department document, "Romero Case Becomes Campaign Issue," March 2, 1989.

7. BABY ROBBERS, MAD BOMBERS, AND
OTHER ASSORTED CRIMINALS

1. State Department document, "FBI Participation in Interrogation of Alvaro Saravia," n.d.; testimony of Karl, in *Doe v. Saravia,* September 3, 2004, 677.

2. Dada, "Así matamos"; testimony of Saravia, in "Report on the Death Squads."

3. Dada, "Así matamos."

4. Testimony of Saravia, in "Report on the Death Squads"; Declaration of Francisco René Molina Quiroa to the Investigations Unit of the Executive Unit of the Commission to Investigate Criminal Acts, August 26, 1988, in author's possession.

5. State Department, "Millionaires' Murder Inc.?" The FBI interviewed Daglio in 1981 in Miami. He denied the allegations and said he had only limited contact with D'Aubuisson. FBI, "Viera Altamirano." Daglio was also on the list of people suspected of involvement in death squads that State Department officials gave to the FBI in 1983. FBI, "Furnishing of Funds."

6. Declaration of Molina Quiroa to Investigations Unit.

7. Rosales Martel and Guevara Guadrón, "¿Quién es Álvaro Saravia?"; State Department document, "Update on Legal Office Cases," February 23, 1990; *Saravia y Ciudad Real vrs. Juzgado Cuarto de lo Penal de San Salvador* (Sala de lo Constitucional de la Corte Suprema de Justicia, October 4, 1994) (No. 5-S-94).

8. Confidential sources, interviews with legal team, 2003.

9. Immigration and Naturalization Service, "Warrant of Arrest for Alien: Alvaro Rafael Saravia-Marino," October 22, 2004, in author's possession; Alfonso Chardy and Elisabeth Donovan, "Torture Suspects Find Haven in U.S.," *Miami Herald,* August 1, 2001.

10. State Department document, "Romero Assassination," August 14, 1992. *Negro* is the Spanish word for "black" but is sometimes used as a crude nickname for someone with darker, though not black, skin. The term does not have the same connotation as the word *negro* in English.

11. Ibid.; State Department document, "El Salvador: Movement on Romero Case," November 4, 1987.

12. State Department, "Movement on Romero Case."

13. Ibid.; State Department, "Romero Assassination"; "Tramitan extradición de acusado en caso Romero," *El Diario de Hoy,* November 25, 1987; "Saravia fue detenido en Miami," *Diario Latino,* November 25, 1987.

14. State Department, "Movement on Romero Case."

15. Testimony of Saravia, in "Report on the Death Squads."

16. State Department, "Romero Assassination"; State Department, "Saravia Extradition"; State Department document, "GOES Meeting with State/Justice Dept. Officials on Romero and Zona Rosa Cases," December 5, 1987.

17. State Department, "Saravia Extradition."

18. State Department document, "Personnel Support for Human Rights Actions," November 5, 1988.

19. State Department document, "Your Telephone Conversation with Ambassador Walker," n.d.

20. State Department document, "ARENA Courts PCN for Second Round," April 3, 1984; Richard Chidester, interview with author, 2008.

21. Brockman, *Romero,* 121–22.

22. Ibid., 121.

23. Ibid., 123.

24. "D'Aubuisson entrega recurso a corte hoy," *El Mundo,* November 25, 1987.

25. Salvadoran Supreme Court of Justice, Constitutional Chamber, judgment regarding Alvaro Saravia's habeas corpus petition, December 19, 1988, in author's possession.

26. Regarding delays in the Miami case, see State Department document, "Extradition: Saravia to El Salvador," July 20, 1988.

27. State Department, "Saravia Extradition."

28. State Department document, "D'Aubuisson Admits Involvement in Efforts to Block Saravia Extradition," January 25, 1989.

29. "Certification of Extraditability and Order of Commitment," *In re: Extradition of Alvaro Rafael Saravia,* No. 87–3598-CIV-EXTRADITION-JOHNSON (S.D. Fla., September 27, 1988), 8–9.

30. Salvadoran Supreme Court of Justice, judgment regarding Alvaro Saravia's habeas corpus petition; Comisión de la Verdad, *De la locura,* 137.

31. Lindsey Gruson, "U.S. Warns Salvador on Rights Cases," *New York Times,* January 7, 1989. See also testimony of Karl, in *Doe v. Saravia,* August 27, 2004, 595.

32. State Department, "D'Aubuisson Admits Involvement."

33. State Department document, "USG Response to Deterioration in Human Rights Situation in El Salvador," January 7, 1989.

34. State Department document, "Revised Materials for VP Quayle's Meetings in El Salvador," February 3, 1989.

35. State Department document, "Saravia Revelations," May 17, 1990.

36. Chidester, interview with author.

37. Garay, in his 1987 testimony, placed the house in the San Benito neighborhood. Escalón and San Benito are wealthy neighborhoods next to each other in San Salvador.

38. State Department, "Saravia Revelations." One of our sources said that Ávila was allegedly responsible for the attempt to kill Archbishop Romero on March 9, 1980, with the dynamite that never detonated. Ávila previously admitted his role in Romero's murder. See chapter 1.

39. Ibid.; State Department document, "Discussions with D'Aubuisson Accomplice," n.d.

40. State Department, "Saravia Revelations"; Chidester, interview with author.

41. State Department, "FBI Participation in Interrogation."

42. Chidester, interview with author.

43. Richard Severo, "Roberto d'Aubuisson, 48, Far-Rightist in Salvador," *New York Times,* February 21, 1992.

44. Comisión de la Verdad, *De la locura,* 137–38. The conclusion about Alejandro Cáceres is supported by the Saravia Diary and Amado Garay's testimony. An entry in the diary, made under March 13 but among a list of items that appear to correspond to other dates in March, seems to refer to March 24. It reads, "24 III 80 Almuerzo en casa de Alex ₡70.00" (24 III 80 Lunch in Alex's house 70.00 colones).

Cáceres owned the house with the Japanese cashew trees mentioned by Garay in his testimony. Dada, "Así matamos"; Zamora Pérez, *acta;* declaration of María Ines Rosales Martínez de Nieto to the Investigations Unit of the Executive Unit of the Commission to Investigate Criminal Acts, August 23, 1988, in author's possession; declaration of Roberto Girón Flores to the Fourth Criminal Court, February 10, 1989, in author's possession.

45. Comisión de la Verdad, *De la locura,* 138.

46. Inter-American Commission on Human Rights, *Monsignor Oscar Arnulfo Romero and Galdámez v. El Salvador,* Case 11.481, Report No. 37/00, OEA /Ser.L/V/II.106 Doc. 3, April 13, 2000, para. 17, http://cidh.org/annualrep/99eng /Merits/ElSalvador11.481.htm.

47. Ibid., para. 18. It remains unclear whether Saravia even knew about this step—because he did not officially file a request for amnesty until later in 1993. Efren Lemus, "La farsa de la investigación del asesinato de monseñor Romero," *El Faro,* May 23, 2015, www.elfaro.net/es/201505/noticias/16994/La-farsa-de-la-investi-gación-del-asesinato-de-monseñor-Romero.htm.

8. "YOU'RE MAKING A LOT OF NOISE"

1. Testimony of Karl, in *Doe v. Saravia,* September 3, 2004, 699–700.

2. The source for information in this section is the testimony of Saravia, in "Report on the Death Squads," supplemented by other sources as indicated. The Truth Commission transcripts contain both verbatim quotations and paraphrasing of what Saravia said.

3. Among them were Salaverria, Daglio, Wright, Cornejo, Argueta, Lemus O'Byrne, Regalado Duenas, Regalado Mathies, Mena Lagos, and De Sola. In some sources, Lemus O'Byrne's name is spelled *Obirne.* To avoid confusion, I have changed all references from *Obirne* to *O'Byrne.*

4. Saravia repeated several details he had already told Richard Chidester. He clarified that the "son of a former president" who found the shooter was indeed Mario Molina. Molina "loaned" the shooter—a bodyguard for ex-president Molina who was still on active duty in the National Guard—for the Romero operation. Saravia claimed that neither he nor D'Aubuisson ever knew the name of the shooter, although ARENA founder, Jorge "Chivo" Velado, later employed the man as a driver and bodyguard. Saravia himself later saw the assassin, by then clean-shaven with short hair, driving with Velado, and Velado identified him as Romero's assassin. Velado later denied these allegations, saying, "I didn't know this Saravia and I never went around with anyone, ever. I have nothing to say about any of that." Dada, "Así matamos." According to a note in the transcript of Saravia's Truth Commission testimony, Héctor Regalado told the commission that someone inside the ARENA party had taken the shooter into his employ.

5. See also Dada, "Así matamos"; Ismael Moreno, "End of ARENA and Future of the FMLN," *Revista Envio,* November 1987. Saravia also said that while Garay

and the shooter were at the chapel in the Volkswagen, Negro Sagrera and a man named Bibi Montenegro were in a second vehicle nearby to monitor how the operation went.

6. See also Dada, "Así matamos."

7. Saravia said that D'Aubuisson assigned disposal of the car to Negro Sagrera. See also Dada, "Así matamos." If true, this point—in combination with the assertions Saravia made to Chidester—is particularly important in terms of D'Aubuisson's involvement. Amado Garay's 1987 testimony gave the impression that D'Aubuisson and Saravia had not spoken about the assassination until three days later, when Saravia met D'Aubuisson at a castle-like house. (Saravia told the commission that the house belonged to Roberto Daglio, his old boss at the Atarraya seafood company.)

8. Saravia said he gave the money to Walter Musa. See also Dada, "Así matamos." The U.S. embassy's source, "Killer," named Musa as the shooter.

9. See also Comisión de la Verdad, *De la locura,* 142. The name "Guayo Lemus" also appears on the piece of stationery seized with the Saravia Diary that shows the same logo as the Operation Piña page. Both Mathies Regalado and Lemus O'Byrne appeared on the list of suspected death squad financiers that State Department officials gave to the FBI in 1983. FBI, "Furnishing of Funds."

10. Bonner, *Weakness and Deceit,* 138.

11. Ibid.

12. Stanley, *Protection Racket State,* 228.

13. Bonner, *Weakness and Deceit,* 273, 278–79.

14. Testimony of Terry Karl, trial transcript in *Chavez v. Carranza,* No. 03–2932-Ml/P (W.D. Tenn., November 7, 2005), 1084–91.

15. Pyes, "Salvadoran Rightists," 40.

16. Nairn, "Behind the Death Squads."

17. Pyes, "Salvadoran Rightists," 2–4, 38, 40.

18. Testimony of Karl, in *Doe v. Saravia,* September 3, 2004, 679–80.

19. John Maclean, "Salvadoran Death Plot Bared," *Chicago Tribune,* February 3, 1984.

20. Testimony of Robert White, in U.S. House of Representatives, *Situation in El Salvador,* 42.

21. White named "Enrique Viera Altamirano." The embassy's source said "Viera Altamirano," but the cable indicated in a subsequent sentence that "N. Viera Altamirano is a principal figure" in the financing of death squads. State Department, "Millionaires' Murder Inc.?" Napoleón Viera Altamirano was the founding publisher of *El Diario de Hoy* but he passed away in 1977. His son, Enrique Altamirano Madríz, took over the paper. "Nuestro Fundador: Napoleón Viera Altamirano," *El Diario de Hoy,* n.d., http://archivo.elsalvador.com/conozcanos/nota1.asp; "Historia de El Diario de Hoy: 69 años haciendo historia," *El Diario de Hoy,* n.d., http://archivo.elsalvador.com/conozcanos/nota2.asp. Enrique Altamirano was on the list of people suspected of involvement in death squads that State Department officials gave to the FBI in 1983. FBI, "Furnishing of Funds."

22. "Salvadoran Rebuts Charge of Death-Squad Link," Associated Press, February 7, 1984; "Ex-envoy Charges," *Facts on File.* When the FBI interviewed Daglio later, he denied involvement in death squad activity. FBI, "Unknown Subjects."

23. Dada, "Así matamos."

24. *Muyshondt v. White,* No. 84–863 (D.D.C. 1985).

25. Declaration of Garay to Investigations Unit; testimony of Álvaro Saravia, in "Report on the Death Squads."

26. FBI, "Unknown Subjects."

27. Testimony of confidential source to the Truth Commission, in "Report on the Death Squads."

28. Kinzer, "Ex-aide in Salvador." García and Carranza both relocated to the United States and became defendants in CJA lawsuits. As discussed in chapter 2, García and another top official, Carlos Vides Casanova, were found liable for the torture of three Salvadoran civilians. Many years later, the United States deported them to El Salvador. In 2005, a jury in Tennessee held Carranza responsible for crimes against humanity, including the torture and murder of several Salvadoran civilians. All three men defended themselves in part by referencing their close cooperation with the U.S. government during the 1980s.

29. Ibid.

30. Ibid.

31. See Philip Taubman, "Salvadoran Was Paid for Accusations," *New York Times,* March 21, 1984.

32. Philip Taubman, "Top Salvador Police Official Said to Be a C.I.A. Informant," *New York Times,* March 22, 1984.

33. Ibid.; Bonner, *Weakness and Deceit,* 366 (for quotations). While Carranza publicly denied being a CIA informant, he spoke openly about working with the United States on intelligence matters. Carranza told journalist Allan Nairn that Salvadoran security officers and U.S. officials shared information, including surveillance reports. Nairn, "Behind the Death Squads."

34. Robert J. McCartney, "Salvadoran Police Chief Denies Link to CIA, Tells of Death Squad Probe," *Washington Post,* March 23, 1984. Two decades later, Colonel Carranza, under oath in CJA's Tennessee lawsuit against him, admitted that he was a paid informant for the U.S. government. Testimony of Nicolás Carranza, trial transcript in *Chavez v. Carranza,* No. 03–2932-Ml/P (W.D. Tenn., November 10, 2005), 1470–72. At trial, former U.S. ambassador Robert White testified that he knew about the CIA's ties to Carranza and requested that the CIA station chief take Carranza off the payroll, but the CIA refused. Testimony of Robert White, trial transcript in *Chavez v. Carranza,* No. 03–2932-Ml/P (W.D. Tenn., November 1, 2005), 364–66.

35. McCartney, "Salvadoran Police Chief Denies."

36. "Salvador Envoy Ousted in Death Squad Report," *New York Times,* April 1, 1984. Colonel Carranza actually named the source during a press conference. McCartney, "Salvadoran Police Chief Denies."

37. Comisión de la Verdad, *De la locura,* 19n16, 141; State Department document, "Bio on Apparent Source for NYT Death Squad Article," March 12, 1984.

38. A CIA informant alleged that Santivañez worked with D'Aubuisson to recruit Álvaro Saravia for death squad operations. The source also claimed that Santivañez was given the rifle used in the Romero assassination and tasked with disposing of the evidence. CIA document, untitled, March 10, 1984.

39. Don Oberdorfer, "Wealthy Exiles Implicated in Salvadoran Bishop's Death; Ex-intelligence Chief Levels Accusations," *Washington Post,* March 22, 1985; Joel Brinkley, "Nicaraguan Ex-rebel Is Accused of Role in Salvador Death Squads," *New York Times,* March 22, 1985. Ambassador White, who helped convince Santivañez to come forward, found him credible. Santivañez was still far to the right ideologically, hated the leftist guerrillas, and said Archbishop Romero was a gullible man. Transcript of *The Houses Are Full of Smoke* film, 114; Kinzer, "Ex-aide in Salvador."

40. Brinkley, "Nicaraguan Ex-rebel." A *Washington Post* report on Santivañez's 1985 press conference pointed out that he had not mentioned Ricardo Lao in his previous, anonymous statements. Oberdorfer, "Wealthy Exiles Implicated."

41. Cynthia J. Arnson, *Crossroads: Congress, the President, and Central America, 1976–1993,* 2nd ed. (University Park: Pennsylvania State University Press, 1993), 125–28, 178–80. A 1982 law, strengthened in 1984, banned U.S. military assistance to Nicaraguan paramilitaries. The Reagan administration's actions to continue the flow of support to the Contras despite these "Boland amendments" played a central role in the later Iran-Contra scandal.

42. Testimony of Saravia, in "Report on the Death Squads." Saravia's diary includes a notation about a $40,000 payment to Nicaraguans, with Lao's name and phone number written below it.

43. Comisión de la Verdad, *De la locura,* 142. The phrasing in the Truth Commission report, however, seems to imply that the commission concluded that D'Aubuisson met Lao after Archbishop Romero's assassination.

44. All quotations in the remainder of this section are from the transcript of the film *The Houses Are Full of Smoke,* 108–11. During our investigation, Leonel Gómez played us a recording of Santivañez in 1984. On the recording, Santivañez said he had found sanctuary in Guatemala after the 1979 coup, and he described a safe house for extremists where operations into El Salvador were organized. It was there that Santivañez learned that something "big" was being planned. Military and civilian figures in Guatemala drew up a "death list" that included Romero. Although the plans were already in place, Santivañez said, Romero's strident March 23 homily accelerated the homicidal timeline. A small meeting took place in Guatemala right after the Sunday mass ended, and the participants decided to kill Romero the next day. The details on Gómez's tape were very similar to the interview Santivañez gave in *The Houses Are Full of Smoke.*

45. This was the first time I heard the allegation that the U.S. government might have had prior knowledge of the plot to kill Romero, but I was not convinced. I did not see a reason that Carranza had to tell the CIA ahead of time.

46. Oscar Romero, homily, January 6, 1980. See also Brockman, *Romero,* 217.

47. Diary entry, January 9, 1980, in *Mons. Oscar A. Romero.*

9. "YOU KNOW BETTER THAN TO ASK THAT"

1. Testimony of Karl, in *Doe v. Saravia*, August 27, 2004, 611.

2. Report by Cruz Argueta Hurtado to the Chief of the Investigations Unit of the Executive Unit of the Commission to Investigate Criminal Acts, May 16, 1987; Investigations Unit of the Executive Unit of the Commission to Investigate Criminal Acts, data sheet on Amado Antonio Garay, May 21, 1987, both in author's possession.

3. Cheek served as acting ambassador during Robert White's delayed Senate confirmation process. For details on the delay, see chapter 3 notes.

4. Diary entry, February 21, 1980, in *Mons. Oscar A. Romero*. Cheek recorded similar recollections of the meeting in a cable to Washington but also wrote that Romero "seemed to be making a special effort to impress upon us that he was not an enemy of the U.S." State Department document, "Discussion with Archbishop Romero and His Advisors," February 22, 1980.

5. Bonner, *Weakness and Deceit*, 179–80.

10. "A RABID ANTI-COMMUNIST"

1. Testimony of Cortina, in *Doe v. Saravia*, 390–91.

2. Comisión de la Verdad, *De la locura*, 49. In 2008, CJA filed a criminal case in Spain concerning the massacre of the six Jesuits, five of whom were Spanish, and their housekeeper and her daughter. CJA named as defendants fourteen former members of the Salvadoran military and El Salvador's president at the time, Alfredo Cristiani of the ARENA party. A Spanish judge issued formal charges and arrest warrants, initially leading to the detention of one defendant in the United States. In 2016, in a groundbreaking development, El Salvador's police arrested four of the defendants, but three were later released.

3. Joan Didion, *Salvador* (New York: Vintage, 1983), 55–56.

4. Óscar Romero, homily, February 24, 1980. Romero also criticized the forces of the Left for "proletariat terrorist violence."

5. Unless otherwise indicated, all quotations in this section are from the ARENA witness's testimony as a confidential source to the Truth Commission, in "Report on the Death Squads."

6. Antonio "Toño" Cornejo Arango served as general manager of Finca San Luis, where he, D'Aubuisson, Saravia, and others were arrested in 1980. Cornejo helped D'Aubuisson found ARENA. Years later, he faced prosecution in El Salvador in connection with a kidnapping ring. He fled, and the charges were eventually dropped. Americas Watch, "El Salvador: Impunity Prevails in Human Rights Cases," *News from Americas Watch*, September 1990, 3–4.

7. Regarding Sol and Lemus O'Byrne as colleagues, see Galeas, *Sol y acero*, chapter titled "La reforma agraria."

8. Testimony of Saravia, in "Report on the Death Squads."

9. In 1982, Amnesty International reported that Minister of Defense García publicly promised to investigate reports from a Mexican journalist that eighty-three young people and children had been beheaded by security agents in the Quality Meat processing plant. Amnesty International, *Amnesty International Report 1982* (London: Amnesty International Publications, 1982), 136. Journalist Raymond Bonner referred to the same incident, writing, "The heads had been so cleanly severed that there were reports that they were being murdered in a meat factory." Bonner, *Weakness and Deceit*, 330. Regarding Lemus O'Byrne's ownership of Quality Meat, see FBI, "Unknown Subjects."

10. State Department, "Reaction in Guatemala"; State Department, "D'Aubuisson Press Conference"; Frente Amplio Nacional, "El Frente Amplio Nacional ante la Escalada de Violencia," n.d.

11. State Department document, "Possible Leads on Rightist Terrorist Activities," December 11, 1980; FBI, "Furnishing of Funds"; Galeas, "La fundación de una bandera."

12. Geovani Galeas, "El día del golpe," *La Prensa Gráfica,* August 22, 2004.

13. *ERP* stands for People's Revolutionary Army (Ejército Revolucionario del Pueblo).

14. Later in 2004, *La Prensa Gráfica* mentioned the infiltration of ARENA by an ERP operative. D'Aubuisson and Negro Sagrera had concluded that there was a mole, code-named "Hare," inside ARENA but they never discovered the person's identity. The ERP's former intelligence chief told *La Prensa Gráfica* that an ERP spy had posed as a worker for D'Aubuisson's associates and occasionally D'Aubuisson himself. Geovani Galeas, "El camino de ARENA a la victoria," *La Prensa Gráfica,* October 10, 2004.

15. Mario Redaelli was on the list of people suspected of involvement in death squads that State Department officials gave to the FBI in 1983. FBI, "Furnishing of Funds." Redaelli, who grew up in the United States, admitted to *Albuquerque Journal* reporter Craig Pyes, "I have kidnapped." He appeared to have no regrets. "Why is the left always glorified when they do these things?" he said. "I'm not ashamed. It had to be done." Pyes, "Salvadoran Rightists," 34, 37.

16. This story is repeated in some variation elsewhere, including by Saravia. Testimony of Saravia, in "Report on the Death Squads."

11. "WE DON'T HAVE A CLUE WHAT THE HELL IS GOING ON"

1. Comisión de la Verdad, *De la locura,* 136; Americas Watch, *Decade of Terror,* 91; "Mons. Romero asesinado por terroristas de ETA," *El Diario de Hoy,* February 4, 1984.

2. Comisión de la Verdad, *De la locura,* 136; declaration of Adalberto Salazar Collier to the Salvadoran Attorney General's Office, August 14, 1985, in author's possession; Lawyers Committee for Human Rights, *Underwriting Injustice: AID*

and El Salvador's Judicial Reform Program (New York: Lawyers Committee for Human Rights, 1989), 22.

3. Declaration of Salazar Collier to Salvadoran Attorney General's Office.

4. Saravia Diary. See also James LeMoyne, "Picture of Death Squads Seen in Key Salvadoran Notebook," *New York Times,* December 2, 1987.

5. The day of our breakfast was the last time I saw Levinson. In 2007, he disappeared on a trip to the Iranian island of Kish. After years of mystery about Levinson's reason for traveling to Kish, news reports revealed he was on an unofficial mission for the CIA. He remains detained by unknown captors, making him the longest-held hostage in U.S. history. Lee Ferran, Brian Ross, and James Gordon, "Sunday Marks 7 Years in Captivity for Former FBI Agent Robert Levinson," *ABC News,* March 9, 2014, http://abcnews.go.com/Blotter/sunday-marks-years-captivity-fbi-agent-robert-levinson/story?id=22836769.

12. "GOD FORGIVE ME FOR WHAT I'M GOING TO DO"

1. Regarding the total attendance, see testimony of Cortina, in *Doe v. Saravia,* 404; and Greg Grandin, "Remembering Those Murdered at Oscar Romero's Funeral," *Nation,* March 25, 2015.

2. Testimony of Guerra, in *Doe v. Saravia,* 515–17. Estimates vary on how many people died at the funeral, but the number is likely between thirty and forty. Trial transcript in *Doe v. Saravia,* No. CIV-F-03–6249 OWW (E.D. Cal., September 3, 2004), 815; Grandin, "Remembering Those Murdered."

3. In conducting research for this book, I found declassified U.S. government documents showing that in February 1988 the State Department sought the help of the U.S. Marshals to get Garay out of Central America and into witness protection in the United States. According to a U.S. embassy cable, protection measures by the Salvadoran government were unsuccessful, and the U.S. Department of Justice granted Garay and his family entrance into the United States. State Department document, "Saravia Extradition Case: Witness Protection Request," February 11, 1988; State Department document, "Amado Antonio Garay Reyes," February 12, 1988. Former U.S. embassy official Richard Chidester told me it was common knowledge at the embassy that Garay was in witness protection. Chidester, interview with author.

4. All quotations in this section are from the testimony of Amado Antonio Garay, deposition transcript in *Doe v. Saravia,* No. CIV-F-03–6249 OWW (E.D. Cal., June 7, 2004).

5. Garay's 1987 testimony also named Nelson Morales. According to Garay, Nelson Morales and Nelson García slept in the same house as Garay the night of Archbishop Romero's murder. A State Department memo from November 1987 indicated that Morales was living illegally in the United States, but there is no indication the U.S. government ever found Morales. State Department, "Movement on Romero Case"; State Department, "GOES Meeting with State."

6. This may have been Sister María del Socorro Iraheta Flores, one of the nuns at Divina Providencia. She testified in 1985 that she had been outside the church immediately after the shooting and saw a man putting something into the car. Declaration of María del Socorro Iraheta Flores to the Fourth Criminal Court, December 18, 1985, in author's possession. The publication of her version of events caused a stir in El Salvador because she said the man looked like Roberto D'Aubuisson. "D'Aubuisson niega imputación crimen," *La Prensa Gráfica,* November 23, 1985. Her testimony later served as a justification for the Salvadoran Supreme Court to declare Garay's 1987 testimony invalid. The court concluded that none of Garay's testimony was credible because Garay said the shooter was inside the car whereas the nun saw the shooter outside the car. Salvadoran Supreme Court of Justice, judgment regarding Alvaro Saravia's habeas corpus petition.

13. "THERE MUST HAVE BEEN A THOUSAND ROMEROS"

1. Testimony of White, in *Doe v. Saravia,* 55–57.
2. Declaration of Alfredo Samayoa to Fourth Criminal Court; State Department, "Romero Assassination"; State Department document, "ARENA Incensed by Allegations against D'Aubuisson," November 27, 1987.

14. "OF A MAGNITUDE THAT IS HARDLY DESCRIBABLE"

1. Testimony of White, in *Doe v. Saravia,* 59–60.
2. Geovani Galeas, "La voz del 'Negro': Un testigo de excepción," *La Prensa Gráfica,* August 22, 2004.
3. Galeas, "El día del golpe."
4. All quotations from Nico van Aelstyn's opening statement and the audio of Romero's murder are from the trial transcript in *Doe v. Saravia,* August 24, 2004, 4–32.
5. All quotations from Garay and Judge Wanger in the following paragraphs are from the testimony of Amado Antonio Garay, trial transcript in *Doe v. Saravia,* No. CIV-F-03–6249 OWW (E.D. Cal., August 24, 2004), 89–121.
6. Testimony of Ramírez Amaya, in *Doe v. Saravia,* 229–30.
7. Testimony of Cortina, in *Doe v. Saravia,* 392–94.
8. All Acosta quotations are from the testimony of Francisco Acosta, trial transcript in *Doe v. Saravia,* No. CIV-F-03–6249 OWW (E.D. Cal., August 27, 2004), 487–90.
9. Testimony of Karl, in *Doe v. Saravia,* August 27, 2004, 573–75.
10. Testimony of Karl, in *Doe v. Saravia,* September 3, 2004, 704.
11. All quotations in the remainder of this chapter are from the trial transcript in *Doe v. Saravia,* September 3, 2004, 822–50.

1. Around the same time, an interesting but unsubstantiated article appeared in a Salvadoran newspaper. The story chronicled a businessman from a top coffee-exporting family who, in 1980, gave money that he believed was supporting a coup d'état in El Salvador. Later, talking to a friend about Archbishop Romero's assassination, the man posited that leftist subversives killed Romero. His friend, looking perplexed, said, "Listen, *chico,* you better than anyone should know that we killed Monseñor." Overcome by guilt after confirming this story with others, the man decided to confess to a Christian Democrat in the governing junta. He revealed a list of thirteen names that included organizers, contributors, and recipients of money as well as those who admitted to him that "we" killed Romero. The article concluded that those who paid for Romero's assassination were from the oligarchy. Ramón Wilfredo Jovel, "De cómo se consigue el financiamiento para deshacerse de un santo," *Diario Co Latino,* September 15, 2005.

2. All quotations in this section are from Gerardo Reyes, "Pide perdón el acusado del asesinato de Monseñor Romero," *El Nuevo Herald,* March 24, 2006; and Gerardo Reyes, "Monseñor Romero: La verdad se abre paso," *El Nuevo Herald,* March 26, 2006.

3. Neither Édgar Pérez Linares nor Héctor Regalado was the shooter, Saravia told us. Regalado, of course, had denied being the assassin multiple times, including to the Truth Commission and the Catholic Church. A 1983 CIA cable included Pérez Linares in a National Police death squad that allegedly carried out Romero's assassination and reported that he was an intermediary between the death squad and Roberto D'Aubuisson. CIA document, "Existence of a Rightist Death Squad within the Salvadoran National Police," March 19, 1983. Another associate of D'Aubuisson told a newspaper that Pérez Linares was the shooter. López Sibrián interview, republished in *Los Escuadrones.* A source for *Washington Post* journalist Douglas Farah said that Pérez Linares admitted to killing Romero. Farah also cited two Salvadoran officials who investigated Romero's death and indicated that a police sketch of the shooter based on the description by the getaway driver, Amado Garay, showed a strong resemblance to Pérez Linares and no one else. Farah, "Death Squad Began." According to our records, when Garay reviewed a photo lineup, he originally chose Pérez Linares as one of three possible matches but later discarded the picture because Pérez Linares's nose was flat. Report by Castillo Medrano to the Chief of the Executive Unit. Pérez Linares fled El Salvador after being implicated in a kidnap-for-profit ring, but he was arrested and killed. Farah, "Death Squad Began."

EPILOGUE

1. "Capitán Álvaro Rafael Saravia dice," *Diario Co Latino.*

2. Carlos Dada, interview with author, 2014; Óscar Monzón de León, "Carlos Dada: 'Así cazamos a los asesinos de monseñor Romero,'" April 12, 2010, https://

lavanguardiaelsalvador.wordpress.com/2010/04/12/carlos-dada%E2%80%9Casi-cazamos-a-los-asesinos-de-monsenor-romero%E2%80%9D."

3. All quotations related to Saravia's disclosures are from Dada, "Así matamos," except where indicated.

4. See Kinzer, "Ex-aide in Salvador"; and Arnson, *Crossroads*, 95.

5. Similar to his Truth Commission testimony and discussions with Almudena Bernabeu and me, Saravia told Dada about seeing the shooter on different occasions: "He would go to [Roberto] Daglio's offices and spend time there. And (Jorge) 'El Chivo' Velado was already an older man by then and he would go around with him."

6. Saravia mentioned Montenegro in previous accounts—to the Truth Commission in 1993 and to Almudena Bernabeu and me in 2006—but Dada was the first person to get Montenegro's own account that he was an eyewitness to the operation.

7. Xenia González, "Abucheos contra d'Aubuisson al salir de beatificación," *El Mundo*, May 24, 2015.

8. Archbishop Vincenzo Paglia, allocution, May 23, 2015, quoted in Carlos X. Colorado, "Allocution of Abp. Paglia," *Super Martyrio* (blog), May 29, 2015, http://polycarpi.blogspot.ca/2015/05/allocution-of-abp-paglia.html.

9. Óscar Romero, homily, March 24, 1980.

AFTERWORD

1. Benjamín Cuéllar is a former director of the Human Rights Institute at the Central American University (IDHUCA), investigator, and columnist.

2. Óscar Romero, homily, February 18, 1979.

3. Ibid.

4. Ignacio Ellacuría, *La lucha por la justicia: Selección de textos de Ignacio Ella-curía (1969–1989),* ed. Juan Antonio Senent (Bilbao: Instituto de Derechos Humanos, Universidad de Deusto, 2012), 454.

5. "Dada Hirezi: 'Monseñor Romero hacía lo que él creía y lo hacía con sanidad de espíritu,'" *El Faro,* March 24, 2014, www.elfaro.net/es/201403/noticias/15111/Dada-Hirezi-'Monseñor-Romero-hacía-lo-que-él-creía-y-lo-hacía-con-sanidad-de-espíritu'.htm?st-full_text=all&tpl=11.

6. Ibid.

7. L. Francis Bouchey et al., "Documento de Santa Fe I: Segunda parte; La sub-versión interna," translated at El Proyecto Desaparecidos, www.desaparecidos.org/nuncamas/web/document/docstfe1_02.htm.

8. Secretaría Técnica de la Presidencia de la República, *Medición multidimen-sional de la pobreza* (San Salvador: Gobierno de El Salvador, 2015), 15, www.secretariatecnica.gob.sv/medicion-multidimensional-de-la-pobreza-el-salvador.

9. Ibid.

10. Observatorio de los Derechos de la Niñez y Adolescencia, "2015: Un año con mucha violencia contra la niñez y adolescencia," December 2015, http://

observatoriodelosderechosdelaninezylaadolescencia.org/boletinas/Informativo_ 4_2015.pdf.

11. Instituto Universitario de Opinión Pública, "Evaluación de la situación del país a finales del año 2015," n.d., www.uca.edu.sv/iudop/wp-content/uploads /PPT-Evaluación-de-año-2015.pdf.

12. Ricardo Flores, "El peligro de tener 17 años en El Salvador," *La Prensa Gráfica,* February 8, 2016, www.laprensagrafica.com/2016/02/08/el-peligro-de-tener-17.

13. Ibid.

SELECTED BIBLIOGRAPHY

ARTICLES

Americas Watch. "El Salvador: Impunity Prevails in Human Rights Cases." *News from Americas Watch,* September 1990.

Anderson, Jack. "Guatemalan Tinderbox." *Washington Post,* February 22, 1981.

Associated Press. "AP Was There: Salvadoran Archbishop Assassinated in 1980." February 3, 2015.

———. "Ex-Salvador Ambassador, Critic of US Foreign Policy, Dies." January 19, 2015.

———. "Salvadoran Officer Linked to Deaths." May 19, 1983.

———. "Salvadoran Rebuts Charge of Death-Squad Link." February 7, 1984.

Ávalos, Jessica. "Fallo pone fin a litigio con Enel Tribunal sobresee a ocho acusados en caso CEL-Enel." *La Prensa Gráfica,* July 4, 2015.

Becklund, Laurie. "Illicit Money Figure Linked to D'Aubuisson." *Los Angeles Times,* February 19, 1985.

———. "Salvador Death Squads: Deadly Other War." *Los Angeles Times,* December 18, 1983.

Blum, Carolyn Patty. "The Settlement of *American Baptist Churches v. Thornburgh:* Landmark Victory for Central American Asylum-Seekers." *International Journal of Refugee Law* 3, no. 2 (1991): 347–56.

Bonner, Raymond. "The Diplomat and the Killer." *Atlantic,* February 11, 2016. www.theatlantic.com/international/archive/2016/02/el-salvador-churchwomen-murders/460320.

Brenner, Eliot. "Washington News." United Press International, February 6, 1984.

Brinkley, Joel. "Nicaraguan Ex-rebel Is Accused of Role in Salvador Death Squads." *New York Times,* March 22, 1985.

Buncombe, Andrew. "Pope Francis Recognises El Salvador's Slain Archbishop Oscar Romero as Martyr and Opens the Way for Beatification." *Independent,* February 4, 2015.

Chardy, Alfonso, and Elisabeth Donovan. "Torture Suspects Find Haven in U.S." *Miami Herald,* August 1, 2001.

Cooper, Linda, and James Hodge, "Archbishop Oscar Romero, El Salvador's Most Trusted News Source." *National Catholic Reporter,* March 21, 2015. http:// ncronline.org/news/global/archbishop-oscar-romero-el-salvadors-most-trusted-news-source.

Craddock, Blair. "Local Link to Assassination." *Modesto Bee,* September 18, 2003.

Dada, Carlos. "Así matamos a monseñor Romero." *El Faro,* March 22, 2010. www .elfaro.net/es/201003/noticias/1403.

Darling, Juanita. "Book Reveals Identities of El Salvador's Richest Families." *Los Angeles Times,* August 21, 1998.

Diario Co Latino. "Capitán Álvaro Rafael Saravia dice: 'D'Aubuisson cayó en una trampa.'" November 6, 2006.

Diario el Mundo. "Violenta huida de White de la residencia a la embajada de EUA." May 12, 1980.

Diario Latino. "El gobierno acusa al doctor Antonio Regalado de haber asesinado Monseñor Arnulfo Romero." February 7, 1989.

———. "Saravia fue detenido en Miami." November 25, 1987.

Dickey, Christopher. "The Truth about the Death Squads." *New Republic,* December 26, 1983.

EFE. "FBI investiga asesinato de Mons. Oscar Romero." March 28, 1980.

El Diario de Hoy. "Historia de *El Diario de Hoy:* 69 años haciendo historia." N.d. http://archivo.elsalvador.com/conozcanos/nota2.asp.

———. "Mons. Romero asesinado por terroristas de ETA." February 4, 1984.

———. "Nuestro fundador: Napoleón Viera Altamirano." N.d. http://archivo .elsalvador.com/conozcanos/nota1.asp.

———. "Tramitan extradición de acusado en caso Romero." November 25, 1987.

Elías Valencia, Francisco, Gabriela Castellón, and David Pérez. "El francotirador que disparó contra Monseñor Romero fue un ex Guardia Nacional." *Diario Co Latino,* September 10, 2011.

El Mundo. "D'Aubuisson entrega recurso a corte hoy." November 25, 1987.

Escalante Arce, Luis. "Salvadoran Reacts to Ambassador White's Accusation." Publication and date unknown, in author's possession.

Facts on File World News Digest. "Ex-envoy Charges D'Aubuisson Coverup." February 10, 1984.

Farah, Douglas. "Death Squad Began as Scout Troop." *Washington Post,* August 29, 1988.

Ferran, Lee, Brian Ross, and James Gordon. "Sunday Marks 7 Years in Captivity for Former FBI Agent Robert Levinson." *ABC News,* March 9, 2014. http://abcnews .go.com/Blotter/sunday-marks-years-captivity-fbi-agent-robert-levinson /story?id=22836769.

Ford, William P. "Film Preserves Haig's Words on Murders." *New York Times,* April 12, 1993.

Frente Amplio Nacional. "El Frente Amplio Nacional ante la escalada de violencia."
Publication and date unknown, in author's possession.

Galeas, Geovani. "El camino de ARENA a la victoria." *La Prensa Gráfica,* October 10, 2004.

———. "El día del golpe." *La Prensa Gráfica,* August 22, 2004.

———. "El exilio del ingeniero González." *La Prensa Gráfica,* August 29, 2004.

———. "Escuadrones, la leyenda negra." *La Prensa Gráfica,* October 3, 2004.

———. "La fundación de una bandera." *La Prensa Gráfica,* September 5, 2004.

———. "La voz del 'Negro': Un testigo de excepción." *La Prensa Gráfica,* August 22, 2004.

González, Xenia. "Abucheos contra d'Aubuisson al salir de beatificación." *El Mundo,* May 24, 2015.

Grande, Rutilio. "Violencia y situación social." *Estudios Centroamericanos* 262 (1970): 369–75.

Grandin, Greg. "Remembering Those Murdered at Oscar Romero's Funeral." *Nation,* March 25, 2015.

Grégori, Ruth. "Respetamos el fallo y las disposiciones que se han tomado." *El Faro,* September 6–12, 2004. http://archivo.elfaro.net/secciones/noticias/20040906/noticias5_20040906.asp.

Gruson, Lindsey. "U.S. Warns Salvador on Rights Cases." *New York Times,* January 7, 1989.

Hoeffel, Paul Heath. "The Eclipse of the Oligarchs." *New York Times,* September 6, 1981.

Hornblower, Margot. "The Exiles." *Washington Post,* March 22, 1981.

Jovel, Ramón Wilfredo. "De cómo se consigue el financiamiento para deshacerse de un santo." *Diario Co Latino,* September 15, 2005.

Kaiser, Robert G. "White Paper on El Salvador Is Faulty." *Washington Post,* June 9, 1981.

Kinzer, Stephen. "Ex-aide in Salvador Accuses Colleagues on Death Squad." *New York Times,* March 3, 1984.

La Prensa Gráfica. "D'Aubuisson acusa a López N. en caso muerte Mons. Romero." November 26, 1987.

———. "D'Aubuisson niega imputación crimen." November 23, 1985.

LeMoyne, James. "Picture of Death Squads Seen in Key Salvadoran Notebook." *New York Times,* December 2, 1987.

Lemus, Efren. "La farsa de la investigación del asesinato de monseñor Romero." *El Faro,* May 23, 2015. www.elfaro.net/es/201505/noticias/16994/La-farsa-de-la-investigación-del-asesinato-de-monseñor-Romero.htm.

Lewis, Anthony. "Abroad at Home; Showing His Colors." *New York Times,* March 29, 1981.

Maclean, John. "Salvadoran Death Plot Bared." *Chicago Tribune,* February 3, 1984.

Martínez, Carlos. "La hora más oscura de Arena." *El Faro,* December 6, 2009. www.elfaro.net/es/200912/noticias/643/La-hora-m%C3%A1s-oscura-de-Arena.htm.

McCartney, Robert J. "Salvadoran Police Chief Denies Link to CIA, Tells of Death Squad Probe." *Washington Post,* March 23, 1984.

Menchú Tum, Rigoberta. "Justice Comes for the Archbishop." *New York Times,* August 31, 2004.

Monzón de León, Óscar. "Carlos Dada: 'Así cazamos a los asesinos de monseñor Romero.'" April 12, 2010. https://lavanguardiaelsalvador.wordpress .com/2010/04/12/carlos-dada%E2%80%9Casi-cazamos-a-los-asesinos-de-monsenor-romero%E2%80%9D.

Moreno, Ismael. "End of ARENA and Future of the FMLN." *Revista Envio,* November 1987.

Nairn, Allan. "Behind the Death Squads." *Progressive,* May 1984.

New York Times. "Salvador Envoy Ousted in Death Squad Report." April 1, 1984.

Oberdorfer, Don. "Wealthy Exiles Implicated in Salvadoran Bishop's Death; Ex-intelligence Chief Levels Accusations." *Washington Post,* March 22, 1985.

Pyes, Craig. "Salvadoran Rightists: The Deadly Patriots." *Albuquerque Journal,* December 1983.

———. "Who Killed Archbishop Romero?" *Nation,* October 13, 1984.

Pyes, Craig, and Laurie Becklund. "Inside Dope in El Salvador." *New Republic,* April 15, 1985.

Reyes, Gerardo. "Monseñor Romero: La verdad se abre paso." *El Nuevo Herald,* March 26, 2006.

———. "Pide perdón el acusado del asesinato de Monseñor Romero." *El Nuevo Herald,* March 24, 2006.

Rice, Andrew. "The Long Interrogation." *New York Times,* June 4, 2006.

Rosales Martel, Metzi, and Christian Guevara Guadrón. "¿Quién es Álvaro Saravia?" *La Prensa Gráfica,* March 20, 2005.

Sancton, Thomas A., Bernard Diederich, and Roberto Suro. "The Land of the Smoking Gun." *Time,* August 18, 1980.

Severo, Richard. "Roberto d'Aubuisson, 48, Far-Rightist in Salvador." *New York Times,* February 21, 1992.

Taubman, Philip. "Salvadoran Was Paid for Accusations." *New York Times,* March 21, 1984.

———. "Top Salvador Police Official Said to Be a C.I.A. Informant." *New York Times,* March 22, 1984.

Universidad Centroamericana José Simeón Cañas. "La derogación de la ley de privatización de ANTEL." *Seminario Proceso,* no. 761 (June 11, 1997). www.uca.edu .sv/publica/proceso/proc761.html.

Valencia, Daniel, and Carlos Martínez. "Plática con Orlando de Sola: 'No soy escuadronero, ni un mercantilista aprovechado.'" *El Faro,* July 10, 2009. http://archivo.elfaro.net/Secciones/platicas/20090710/Platicas1_20090710 .asp.

Valencia, Roberto. "Beto Cuéllar, el abogado." *El Faro,* March 30, 2015. www.elfaro .net/es/201503/noticias/16761/Beto-Cuéllar-el-abogado.htm.

Weiss, Nicholas P. "Somebody Else's Problem: How the United States and Canada Violate International Law and Fail to Ensure the Prosecution of War Criminals." *Case Western Reserve Journal of International Law* 45 (2012): 579–609.

BOOKS AND REPORTS

Americas Watch. *El Salvador's Decade of Terror: Human Rights since the Assassination of Archbishop Romero*. New Haven, CT: Yale University Press, 1991.

Amnesty International. *Amnesty International Report 1982*. London: Amnesty International Publications, 1982.

Anderson, Thomas P. *Matanza: El Salvador's Communist Revolt of 1932*. Lincoln: University of Nebraska Press, 1971.

Arnson, Cynthia J. *Crossroads: Congress, the President, and Central America, 1976–1993*. 2nd ed. University Park: Pennsylvania State University Press, 1993.

Bonner, Raymond. *Weakness and Deceit: U.S. Policy and El Salvador*. New York: Times Books, 1984.

Brockman, James R. *Romero: A Life*. Maryknoll, NY: Orbis Books, 2005.

Cardenal, Rodolfo. *Rutilio Grande, mártir de la evangelización rural en El Salvador*. San Salvador: UCA Editores, 1978.

Castillo, Celerino, III, and Dave Harmon. *Powderburns: Cocaine, Contras and the Drug War*. Oakville, ON: Mosaic, 1994.

Combs, Jerald A. *The History of American Foreign Policy*. Vol. 2, *From 1895*. 3rd ed. Armonk, NY: M. E. Sharpe, 2008.

Comisión de la Verdad para El Salvador. *De la locura a la esperanza: La guerra de 12 años en El Salvador*. San Salvador: Naciones Unidas, 1993.

Didion, Joan. *Salvador*. New York: Vintage, 1983.

Freire, Paulo. *Pedagogy of the Oppressed*. Trans. Myra Bergman Ramos. New York: Continuum Press, 2006.

Galeas, Marvin. *Sol y acero: La vida de don Guillermo Sol Bang*. San Salvador: Editorial Cinco, 2011.

Gutiérrez, Gustavo. *A Theology of Liberation: History, Politics, and Salvation*. Maryknoll, NY: Orbis Books, 2004.

Inter-American Commission on Human Rights. *Report on the Situation of Human Rights in El Salvador*. November 17, 1978. www.cidh.org/countryrep /ElSalvador78eng/TOC.htm.

Kelly, Thomas M. *When the Gospel Grows Feet: Rutilio Grande, SJ, and the Church of El Salvador: An Ecclesiology in Context*. Collegeville, MN: Liturgical Press, 2013.

La Feber, Walter. *Inevitable Revolutions: The United States in Central America*. 2nd ed. New York: W. W. Norton, 1993.

Lawyers Committee for Human Rights. *El Salvador: Human Rights Dismissed*. New York: Lawyers Committee for Human Rights, 1990.

————. *Underwriting Injustice: AID and El Salvador's Judicial Reform Program.* New York: Lawyers Committee for Human Rights, 1989.

LeoGrande, William M. *Our Own Backyard: The United States in Central America, 1977–1992.* Chapel Hill: University of North Carolina Press, 1998.

Lernoux, Penny. *Cry of the People.* New York: Doubleday, 1980.

López Vigil, María. *Memories in Mosaic.* Washington, D.C.: EPICA, 2000.

Los escuadrones de la muerte en El Salvador. San Salvador: Editorial Jaraguá, 1994.

McClintock, Michael. *The American Connection: State Terror and Popular Resistance in El Salvador.* London: Zed Books, 1987.

Mons. Óscar A. Romero: Su diario. San Salvador: Imprenta Criterio, 2000.

Montgomery, Tommie Sue. *Revolution in El Salvador: Origins and Evolution.* Boulder, CO: Westview Press, 1982.

Morozzo della Rocca, Roberto. *Oscar Romero: Prophet of Hope.* London: Darton, Longman and Todd, 2015.

————. *Primero Dios: Vida de Monseñor Romero.* Buenos Aires: Edhasa, 2010.

Paige, Jeffery M. *Coffee and Power: Revolution and the Rise of Democracy in Central America.* Cambridge, MA: Harvard University Press, 1998.

Pinto, Jorge. *El grito del más pequeño.* Mexico: Editorial Comete, 1985.

Popkin, Margaret. *Peace without Justice: Obstacles to Building the Rule of Law in El Salvador.* University Park: Pennsylvania State University Press, 2000.

Stanley, William. *The Protection Racket State: Elite Politics, Military Extortion, and Civil War in El Salvador.* Philadelphia: Temple University Press, 1996.

Stephens, Beth J., Judith Chomsky, Jennifer Green, Paul Hoffman, and Michael Ratner. *International Human Rights Litigation in U.S. Courts.* 2nd rev. ed. Leiden, Netherlands: Martinus Nijhoff, 2008.

Whitfield, Teresa. *Paying the Price: Ignacio Ellacuría and the Murdered Jesuits of El Salvador.* Philadelphia: Temple University Press, 1994.

Wood, Elisabeth Jean. *Insurgent Collective Action and Civil War in El Salvador.* Cambridge: Cambridge University Press, 2003.

LEGAL DOCUMENTS AND TESTIMONY

"Certification of Extraditability and Order of Commitment." *In re: Extradition of Alvaro Rafael Saravia,* No. 87–3598-CIV-EXTRADITION-JOHNSON (S.D. Fla., September 27, 1988).

Declaration of Adalberto Salazar Collier to the Salvadoran Attorney General's Office. August 14, 1985. In author's possession.

Declaration of Amado Antonio Garay to the Fourth Criminal Court. November 20, 1987. In author's possession.

Declaration of Amado Antonio Garay to the Investigations Unit of the Executive Unit of the Commission to Investigate Criminal Acts. November 19, 1987. In author's possession.

Declaration of Francisco René Molina Quiroa to the Investigations Unit of the Executive Unit of the Commission to Investigate Criminal Acts. August 26, 1988. In author's possession.

Declaration of Julio Alfredo Samayoa to the Fourth Criminal Court. February 21, 1989. In author's possession.

Declaration of María del Socorro Iraheta Flores to the Fourth Criminal Court. December 18, 1985. In author's possession.

Declaration of María Ines Rosales Martínez de Nieto to the Investigations Unit of the Executive Unit of the Commission to Investigate Criminal Acts. August 23, 1988. In author's possession.

Declaration of Roberto Antonio Martínez Monterrosa to the Investigations Unit of the Executive Unit of the Commission to Investigate Criminal Acts. April 6, 1987. In author's possession.

Declaration of Roberto Girón Flores to the Fourth Criminal Court. February 10, 1989. In author's possession.

Ford v. Garcia, 289 F.3d 1283 (11th Cir. 2002).

Immigration and Naturalization Service. "Warrant of Arrest for Alien: Alvaro Rafael Saravia-Marino." October 22, 2004. In author's possession.

Inter-American Commission on Human Rights. *Monsignor Oscar Arnulfo Romero and Galdámez v. El Salvador,* Case 11.481, Report No. 37/00, OEA/Ser.L/V /II.106 Doc. 3. April 13, 2000. http://cidh.org/annualrep/99eng/Merits /ElSalvador11.481.htm.

Investigations Unit of the Executive Unit of the Commission to Investigate Criminal Acts. Data sheet on Amado Antonio Garay. May 21, 1987. In author's possession.

Judge Alberto Zamora Pérez. *Acta* memorializing activity with Amado Antonio Garay. November 21, 1987. In author's possession.

Kiobel v. Royal Dutch Petroleum Co., 569 U.S. 12, 133 S. Ct. 1659 (2013).

Letter from Julio Alfredo Samayoa to the Chief of the Executive Unit of the Commission to Investigate Criminal Acts. February 20, 1989. In author's possession.

Muyshondt v. White, No. 84–863 (D.D.C. 1985).

Police report by José Ramón Campos Figueroa to the Chief of the Police Investigations Unit. March 14, 1986. In author's possession.

Police report by Major José Francisco Samayoa to Major Miguel Antonio Méndez. May 12, 1980. In author's possession.

Report by Cruz Argueta Hurtado to the Chief of the Investigations Unit of the Executive Unit of the Commission to Investigate Criminal Acts. May 16, 1987. In author's possession.

Report by Cruz Argueta Hurtado to the Chief of the Investigations Unit of the Executive Unit of the Commission to Investigate Criminal Acts. June 3, 1987. In author's possession.

Report by Velarmides Castillo Medrano to the Chief of the Executive Unit of the Commission to Investigate Criminal Acts. February 2, 1988. In author's possession.

Salvadoran Supreme Court of Justice, Constitutional Chamber. Judgment regarding Álvaro Saravia's habeas corpus petition. December 19, 1988. In author's possession.

Saravia Diary daily planner. Trial exhibit in *Doe v. Saravia,* No. CIV-F-03–6249 OWW (E.D. Cal. 2004).

Saravia y Ciudad Real vrs. Juzgado Cuarto de lo Penal de San Salvador (Sala de lo Constitucional de la Corte Suprema de Justicia, October 4, 1994) (No. 5-S-94).

Testimony of Álvaro Saravia to the Truth Commission. "Report on the Death Squads in the Files of the El Salvador Truth Commission." N.d. In author's possession.

Testimony of Amado Antonio Garay. Deposition transcript in *Doe v. Saravia,* No. CIV-F-03–6249 OWW (E.D. Cal., June 7, 2004).

Testimony of Amado Antonio Garay. Trial transcript in *Doe v. Saravia,* No. CIV-F-03–6249 OWW (E.D. Cal., August 24, 2004).

Testimony of Atilio Ramírez Amaya. Trial transcript in *Doe v. Saravia,* No. CIV-F-03–6249 OWW (E.D. Cal., August 25, 2004).

Testimony of confidential sources to the Truth Commission. "Report on the Death Squads in the Files of the El Salvador Truth Commission." N.d. In author's possession.

Testimony of Francisco Acosta. Trial transcript in *Doe v. Saravia,* No. CIV-F-03–6249 OWW (E.D. Cal., August 27, 2004).

Testimony of Jon Cortina. Trial transcript in *Doe v. Saravia,* No. CIV-F-03–6249 OWW (E.D. Cal., August 26, 2004).

Testimony of Nicolás Carranza. Trial transcript in *Chavez v. Carranza,* No. 03–2932-Ml/P (W.D. Tenn., November 10, 2005).

Testimony of Robert White. Deposition transcript in *Doe v. Saravia,* No. CIV-F-03–6249 OWW (E.D. Cal., July 22, 2004).

Testimony of Robert White. Trial transcript in *Chavez v. Carranza,* No. 03–2932-Ml/P (W.D. Tenn., November 1, 2005).

Testimony of Robert White. Trial transcript in *Ford v. Garcia,* No. 99–8359-CIV-HURLEY (S.D. Fla., October 12, 2000).

Testimony of Robert White. U.S. Congress, House of Representatives, Committee on Foreign Affairs, *The Situation in El Salvador: Hearing before the Subcommittees on Human Rights and International Organizations and on Western Hemisphere Affairs,* 98th Congress, February 6, 1984.

Testimony of Robert White. U.S. Congress, Senate Committee on Foreign Relations, *The Situation in El Salvador: Hearing before the Committee on Foreign Relations,* 97th Congress, April 9, 1981.

Testimony of Terry Karl. Trial transcript in *Chavez v. Carranza,* No. 03–2932-Ml/P (W.D. Tenn., November 7, 2005).

Testimony of Terry Karl. Trial transcript in *Doe v. Saravia,* No. CIV-F-03–6249 OWW (E.D. Cal., August 25, 2004; August 26, 2004; August 27, 2004; September 3, 2004).

Testimony of Walter Guerra. Trial transcript in *Doe v. Saravia,* No. CIV-F-03–6249
OWW (E.D. Cal., August 27, 2004).

Testimony of William Wipfler. Trial transcript in *Doe v. Saravia,* No. CIV-F-03–
6249 OWW (E.D. Cal., August 24, 2004).

Trial transcript in *Doe v. Saravia,* No. CIV-F-03–6249 OWW (E.D. Cal., August
24, 2004; August 25, 2004; August 26, 2004; August 27, 2004; September 3,
2004).

U.S. v. Belfast, 611 F.3d 783 (11th Cir. 2010).

INDEX

Italic page references indicate photographs.

Camino Real hotel, 84

campesinos (peasants): in the civil war, 167; empowerment of, 39–40, 43, 188n34; indoctrinated against Communism, 30; and Jesuits, 39; meaning of to Romero, 166–67; military massacre of, xiii–xiv, 26–27; murdered by the National Guard, 44; plantation occupied by, 49–50; revolt by, 26–27; socioeconomic inequality of, 25

campos pagados (paid advertisements), ix–x, 48

Carranza, Nicolás, 91–92, 93, 152–53, 199n28, 199n33

Carter, Jimmy, xv, 53, 171

Carter administration: and the Christian Democrats, 35–36, 52–53; human rights policies of, 65; military aid provided by, 102, 171

Catholic Church: hierarchy in, 39–40, 42, 51; as perceived threat to stability, 49; persecution against, xv, 46; "politicizing" of, 44–45; theology of, xiv–xv, 39–44, 132, 189n62

CCR (Constitutional Rights, Center for), 19

Central Intelligence Agency (CIA), U.S.: awareness of Saravia's presence, 145–46; and Carranza, 91–92, 93, 199n33; funding of hard-line officers by, xvii, 91–92; on murder suspects, 6

Chávez, Esther, 132

Chidester, Richard, 82–83

Christian Democrats: and the Carter administration, 35–36, 52–53; in the civilian-military junta, 35–36; as Communists, 49; denounced by Romero, 52–53; investigation of Romero's murder by, 77–78, 194n17; in legislative elections of 1982, 67–68; and the Reagan administration, 88

Christian Federation of Salvadoran Campesinos (FECCAS), 188n34

churchwomen, rape and murder of, 10, 65, 66, 183–84n17

civilian intelligence networks, 29

civilian-military government, 6–8, 32–33, 34–37, 51–54

civil law in El Salvador, 2

civil lawsuits, 18–21, 59–60, 131–32, 150, 183–84n17

civil war: *campesinos* in, 167; end of, 83–84, 172–74; guerrillas in, 65–67; historical origins of, 25–28; onset of, 171; Romero's murder in, 130, 145–46; U.S. aid during, 87–88

CJA (Center for Justice and Accountability), xvi, 18–21, 94–96

Clarke, Maura, 10, 65, 66

clergy. *See* priests

closing argument, 146–48

coconspirators, search for, 97–103, 120–29

coffee barons, 26. *See also* oligarchs/ oligarchy

coffee production and export, 25–27, 166

Cohen, Russell, 60, 87, 114–15, 120–23

Cold War policy, U.S., 29–30

communal lands, 25

Communism/Communists: alleged U.S. support for, 36; fear of, 27–28, 29–30; forced confessions by, 144–45; guerrillas allegedly funded by, 66–67; military government fighting, xiii–xiv; moderates perceived as, 35; priests perceived as, 48; propaganda by, 171; and right-wing terrorism, 37; targeted by military hard-liners, xiv; in U.S. foreign policy, xvii. *See also* anti-Communist ideology

"Communist Interference in El Salvador" (U.S. white paper), 66–67

Communist Party of El Salvador, 26–27

concientización (consciousness raising), 43

Congress, U.S., 67, 87–89, 102

Conservative Religious Front, 43–44

constant interviewing, 28

Constitutional Rights, Center for (CCR), 19

Contras, Nicaraguan, 92

Coordinadora Revolucionaria de Masas, 170–71

Cornejo Arango, Antonio ("Toño"), 107–8, 110–11

Cortina, Jon, 104, 132, 142–43

counterinsurgency doctrine, 30

crime rates in 2014, 174

crime scene, *xx*, 3, 74, 141, 142–43

Cristiani, Alfredo, 201n2
Cuéllar, Roberto, 50
Cummings, Eldon, 9

Dada, Carlos, 163–66
Dada, Héctor, 170
Daglio, Roberto ("Bobby"), 76–77, 89–90, 195n5
D'Aubuisson, Roberto: anti-Communist ideology of, 31–32, 35; in anti-Communist strategizing, 186n56; and ARENA financiers, 110–11; arrest and release of, 8, 64; Catholic Church as enemy of, 49; in death squad leadership and activities, xvi, 33–34, 61, 143, 144–45, 157–58; on Death Squad TV, 143, 144–45; denounced by Romero, 52; in elections of 1982, 67–68; in elections of 1984, 88; financing of, 86, 91, 158; Garay driving for, 126–27; immunity of, 80, 85; *La Prensa Gráfica* series on, 135–36; Maximiliano Hernández Martínez Brigade led by, 107–8; and O'Byrne, 165; in the Pedro Lobo hoax, 114–15; photograph of, *xxii;* and the Reagan Administration, 12, 91–92; in Romero's murder, 9–10, 14, 17, 28–29, 83, 93, 116, 198n7; in Saravia's extradition, 78–79; on U.S. aid to Christian Democrats, 36; in the White Warriors Union, 48
"death list," 200n44
death squad financiers: culpability of, 165; FBI list of, 191n6, 198n9; and Guatemalan exiles, 91, 110–11; "Miami Six," 61–63, 76–77, 88–89, 191n6; oligarchs as, 61, 105, 158; and Saravia, 76, 117–18, 163; in the Saravia Diary, 63, 69, 191n10; search for, 85–87, 89–90, 96, 98, 105–6, 116–17, 121–22
death squads: in the anti-Communist strategy, 33–34; ARENA members in, 86, 107–8; attorney general murdered by, 5, 53; D'Aubuisson leading, xvi, 33–34, 157–58; defined, xvi; and El Playón, 33–34; and expatriates, 61–63, 88–89; Grande murdered by, 38–39; in the legislative assembly, 68; members of, 186–87n70; military officers in, 87–88;

91, 107–8; National Guard in, 31; and Nicaraguan Contras, 92; police in, 205n3; priests murdered by, 47–48; on Romero, 139–40; threats by, 51, 143–45; U.S. complicity with, xvii, 135; in U.S. foreign policy, 87–89
Death Squad TV, 143–45
default hearing, 131–32
demonstrators, massacre of, 51
deportation: of clergy, 45; of Saravia, 78, 81–82, 113–14; of war criminals from the U.S., 20, 183–84n17, 199n28
de Sola, Orlando, 63
Divina Providencia Church, *xx, 3,* 74
DOJ (Justice, Department of, U.S.), 19–20, 203n3
Donovan, Jean, 10, 65, 66
Dr. Death. *See* Regalado, Héctor
Duarte, Napoleón, 88

Eastern Regional Agricultural Front (FARO), 48
Ecclesial Base Communities, 43
economic inequalities. *See* socioeconomic inequalities
Eichmann, Adolf, prosecution of, 18
ejido system, 25
elections: 1982, 67–68; 1984, 88, 91–92, 114–15; Garay's testimony in, 194n17; hard-liners' fear of, 34; Leftists and guerrillas in, 193n40; post-civil war, 173–74; rigged, xiii
El Faro, 163–66
Ellacuría, Ignacio, 169, 170
Ellison, Gordon, 133
El Mozote massacre, 67
El Nuevo Herald, 153–54
El Playón, 34
Escalante, Luis, 89
Espinoza, Paulino, 98
evidence: Finca San Luis documents as, 7–8; lack of at crime scene, 3; provided by UN Truth Commission, xvi, 132; requests by police for, 3–4; in the verdict, 149

FAN. *See* Broad National Front (FAN)
FARO. *See* Eastern Regional Agricultural Front (FARO)

46–48, 51–52; guerrillas in, 54; military aid in, 53; and U.S. foreign policy, 65–67

Reyes, Gerardo, 153–54

Roht-Arriaza, Naomi, 132

Romagoza, Juan, 21

Romero, Óscar: appointed archbishop, 42–43, 45–46; beatification of, xiii, xvii, 162, 167, 175; and the Catholic Church, 47–48; on Christian Democrats, 52–53; education and career of, 40–41; evolution of, xv; friendship of with Grande, 42–43; intervention by, 144; legacy of, 147, 167–68; letter to Carter by, 171; motivation of, 147, 189n62; on the need for activism, 169–70; photographs of, *xix, xxi;* and "politicizing" of the church, 44–45; repression confronted by, 46–48, 51–52; theology of, 132, 189n62; value of, 150; written testaments to, 112–13, 145–46, 147. *See also* assassination of Romero; homilies

Sagrera, Fernando ("El Negro"), 78, 80, 83, 136, 158, 164–65

Salaverría, Alfonso, 63, 69, 191n7

Salaverría, Julio, 89

Salvadoran Bishops Conference, 51

Sánchez, Augustín, 56

Sandoval Alarcón, Mario, 64

San Salvador visit, 69–74

"Santa Fe I Document" (Reagan administration), 171–72

Santivañez, Roberto, 91–93, 100n38, 116, 200n44

Saravia, Álvaro: amnesty for, 161; and ARENA, 108; asylum requested by, 82, 118; and D'Aubuisson, 33; deportation charges against, 78, 81–82, 113–14; and DHS, 113–14; escape to Miami of, 76; extradition of, 77–79, 80–81; in Garay's testimony, 13–15, 77, 125–26, 128–29, 139; home of, in Modesto, CA, 22–23; impact of the verdict on, 151–59; insider details provided by, 77–78, 82–84; in Killer's testimony, 10–11; in the media, 162–63; photograph of, *xxii;* search for, 59–61, 75–76, 101–2, 113–18, 121; trial of,

131–34, 136–42, 148–50; and the Truth Commission, 84, 85–86

Saravia Diary: as evidence, 6–9, 10–12, 17; financiers listed in, 6–9, 63, 69, 191n10; Salaverría in, 191n7

Second Vatican Council. *See* Vatican II

shooter in Romero's murder: and ARENA, 197; compensation of, 82, 86, 165; in Garay's testimony, 13–14, 127–28; identifications of, 154, 197n4; Regalado misidentified as, 71–72, 205n3; in the Saravia Diary, 8; Saravia misidentified as, 156–57

Simán, Ricardo, 63, 191n10

Sobrino, Jon, 112

social movements, xiv–xv, 171

socioeconomic inequalities, xiv–xv, 24–25, 26, 41–42

Socorro Jurídico, 50

Sol, Guillermo ("Billy"), 70–71, 89–90, 108, 110, 186n56

solidarity mass, xv, 47

Sol Meza, Ricardo, 69

Soto, Eliseo, 5

Soviet Union, 29, 66–67, 172

Special Forces, U.S., 30

Special Investigations Unit (SIU), 133

spiritual development and material development, 42

State Department, U.S., 12, 145–46

statute of limitations, 149

Supreme Court of El Salvador, 79–81, 84, 161

terrorism: in hemispheric security, 171–72; and leftist guerrillas, 31; right-wing, 11, 37

testaments to Romero, 112–13, 145–46, 147

theology, xiv–xv, 39–44, 132, 189n62

threats: by death squads, 33, 51, 143–45; against priests and Romero, 48, 51, 65; in repression, xv; to stability, 35–36, 49; during the trial, 141–42

torture: of criminal defendants, 79; García and Carranza liable for, 152–53, 199n28; of priests by the National Guard, 44; prosecution for, 17–21, 183n12; in repression, xv, 45